# THE ESSENTIAL BIBLE COMPANION

**Also Available:**

*The Bible in 90 Days*™ curriculum

# THE ESSENTIAL BIBLE COMPANION

## KEY INSIGHTS FOR READING GOD'S WORD

JOHN H. WALTON, MARK L. STRAUSS,
& TED COOPER JR.

ZONDERVAN®

GRAND RAPIDS, MICHIGAN 49530 USA

ZONDERVAN.COM/
AUTHORTRACKER

We want to hear from you. Please send your comments about this book to us in care of zreview@zondervan.com. Thank you.

ZONDERVAN

*The Essential Bible Companion*

Requests for information should be addressed to:

Zondervan, *Grand Rapids, Michigan 49530*

Library of Congress Cataloging-in-Publication Data

Walton, John H., 1952–
The essential Bible companion / John H. Walton and Mark L. Strauss.—1st ed.
p. cm.
ISBN-10: 0-310-26662-9
ISBN-13: 978-0-310-26662-4 (softcover)
1. Bible—Introductions. I. Strauss, Mark L. II. Title.
BS475.3.W35 2005
220.6'1—dc22 2005010113

The authors kindly acknowledge the work of Melissa Moore in the creation of the glossaries and Liz Klassen for help in the editing.

*Interior design: Tracey Walker*
*Maps: International Mapping*

*Printed in China*

12 13 14 15 16 17 /CTC/ 25 24 23 22 21 20 19 18 17 16 15 14 13 12

# Contents

# Preface

Familiarity with the Bible has been largely lost to the church. For the most part, we believe that this is true because people don't have time to read it, and when they do, they simply don't know what to do with it. Many people desire to know God's Word, but feel that they are groping blindly as they seek to figure out how to make Scripture relevant to their lives. Often the Old Testament is presented as if it were a haphazard collection of moralistic lessons or endless lists of names and dates. The New Testament may seem more directly applicable to Christians today, but still much of it seems alien. What are we to make of references to phylacteries and tassels (Matt. 23:5)? And what of commands to greet one another with a "kiss of love" (1 Peter 5:14), or which forbid women from wearing pearls or braided hair (1 Tim. 2:9)? And what about all those strange and puzzling images in the book of Revelation? We want to obey the Bible, but don't know quite how it applies. We read and study the Bible, but our effort often leaves us empty and yet mystified about how its power works in our lives.

For many, their experience with the Bible is similar to the piñata game. A target is "out there," but they are blindfolded and have been turned around so many times that they are entirely disoriented and don't know where to aim. They flail wildly at the air and become frustrated with an exercise that offers so little return for their effort. In this book we want to remove the blindfold, and point you, the reader, in the right direction.

Our goal is to go beyond basic Bible content to help you know its meaning and just what you are supposed to do with it. We hope that this approach will remedy the all-too-frequent caricature of the Old Testament as little more than endless trivia, irrelevant history, and obscure prophecies only alleviated by some comforting psalms and models for living from the heroes and heroines of the faith; and that the New Testament narratives, letters, and prophecies are neither simple moral codes (which can all be applied directly to your situation) nor dry and dusty history. They are rather *our history,* the story of how God revealed himself in the person of Jesus Christ to men and women of faith—our spiritual ancestors, and how these followers of Jesus launched the greatest movement in human history. You will be impressed with the way that the Bible uniquely reveals the God of the universe. That *is* the purpose of the Bible. These 66 books do not contain simply human ideas and experiences of God.

They contain God's revelation of himself. When you read its pages, you encounter God himself.

In *The Essential Bible Companion*, you will gain not only an appreciation for the central importance of this sacred text, but in doing so will come to appreciate the literature, theology, and history for the contribution they make and the role that they play in the greater story of God's plan for reconciling his creation to himself, restoring his presence in his creation, and forging a relationship with his people.

# Overview

## What Is the Bible All About?

The Bible is all about connecting with God. Three key words will help us to get the big picture: Presence, Revelation, and Relationship. Everything God does in the Bible shows us that he deeply desires to be in relationship with us. That is why he created us. When we love someone, as God loves us, we want to be with that person. But being in the presence of a loved one is only one part of what is essential to a relationship. The other main ingredient is that we desire to know the other person as fully as we can. This is where the concept of revelation comes in. Being together with a loved one provides the opportunity to get to know one another, so that the relationship can grow.

Across the pages of the Bible God is building relationship with his people as he reveals himself to us. Seven stages of God's presence show us this process through the Old and New Testaments. A brief look at them will help us to have a framework that we can use as we read through the Bible.

### The Garden of Eden

When God created us he made this world to be like a temple. A temple in the ancient world was where God lived. So we would say that he built this world as a place to live—not because he needed a place to live, but because his plan was to create people to live with him here. The work of the Spirit of God in Genesis 1:2 shows his presence even in the initial stages of creation, until Eden was established as the first place of God's presence. Adam and Eve were put in Eden to be with God and in relationship with him. Unfortunately, the path of disobedience led to the rupture of the relationship and the loss of access to God's presence. Genesis 4:26 reports that people began to call on the name of God—an indication that they were invoking his presence—because they realized what they had lost. The builders of the Tower of Babel were attempting to recover God's presence by providing a stairway for him to descend and be worshiped. But this human initiative was based on distorted ideas of God, and therefore it failed.

### The Covenant

God's initiative to reestablish his presence and relationship came through the covenant that he made with Abraham (Gen. 12). Through

Abraham and his family all the nations of the world were to be blessed, because through them he would reveal himself (so that people could know him) and make relationship possible again.

## The Burning Bush and Mount Sinai

At the burning bush God's presence blazed as he revealed his name to Moses and told of how he would make himself known to Israel and the world. Through the plagues and the deliverance of the Israelites from Egypt, the theme is constantly repeated: "You will know that I am the Lord Your God." His presence will result in revelation (you will *know*) and relationship (*your* God). His presence is with them in the form of the pillar of cloud and fire as he leads them through the wilderness to Mount Sinai. Then his presence becomes manifest on Mount Sinai and the law is given, revealing his holiness to Israel and establishing the guidelines for them to be in relationship with him.

## The Tabernacle and Temple

The reason God revealed his holiness and guidelines for behavior was so that he could live in the midst of his people. This fourth stage involved God actually establishing a new outpost on earth. He gave Israel the design of a portable sanctuary called the tabernacle. It was to be a place to house his presence—a way that he could be with his people. After it was built, Exodus 40:34 reports that "the glory of the LORD filled the tabernacle." In the time of David and Solomon the portable sanctuary was replaced by a building, the temple. Throughout the rest of the Old Testament God continued to reveal himself to the Israelites through their history and through the prophets. This is the revelation preserved in our Bibles. Yet Israel's disobedience continued to hinder the relationship. God's presence continued to be evident in the temple, but it was also reflected in the work of the Spirit of the Lord that empowered people with his presence to do his work (including leaders—such as judges and kings—and spokesmen, the prophets).

## The Incarnation

The prophet Isaiah had spoken of a child called Immanuel—"God with us"—one who would represent God's presence among his people. Who could have imagined then that God would actually take on flesh in the person of his son, Jesus Christ, to be with his people? This fifth stage of God's presence is explained in John 1:14: "The Word became flesh and made his dwelling among us. We have seen his glory, the glory of the One and Only, who came from the Father, full of grace and truth." The word for "dwelling" is related to the word used for the tabernacle and temple from stage four. In the new age of salvation, Jesus replaces the Jerusalem temple (John 2:20–21), providing access to God's presence (Heb. 10:19–21). His sacrificial death supersedes the sacrifices made in the Old Testament temple, achieves full and complete forgiveness of sins, and establishes a new covenant between God and his people (Heb. 9:11–15). Jesus not only represented the next stage of God's *presence*, he also represented the climax of God's *revelation* (Heb. 1:1–2; John 1:18) and was God's provision for the full restoration of *relationship* (2 Cor. 5:17–19). Through Christ we can know God more fully and be reconciled to God through what Jesus did for us on the cross.

## Pentecost

Jesus assured his disciples that when he left, he would send another sign of God's presence, the Holy Spirit (John 14:15–27). This began on the day of Pentecost as the disciples were gathered in the upper room and the Spirit came rushing upon them. Here God's presence was established permanently on earth in the hearts of his people who had become the living temple of God (1 Cor. 3:16; 6:19; 1 Peter 2:5–6). Christians have been restored to *relationship* with God through Christ and enjoy his *presence* among us through the Holy Spirit which is in us. We are his ambassadors as he continues to *reveal* himself to the world through his people (2 Cor. 5:19–21).

## New Creation

Yet one stage remains, as the book of Revelation speaks of the return of Christ and the creation of the new heavens and the new earth. Revelation 21:3 says, "And I heard a loud voice from the throne saying, 'Now the dwelling of God is with men, and he will live with them. They will be his people, and God himself will be with them and be their God.'" God will have completed his plan of *revelation*, his *presence* will be established as it was in the beginning, and his people will be in *relationship* with him, enjoying his presence throughout eternity.

This is what the Bible is all about. God has revealed himself to us so that we might know him, be in relationship with him, and enjoy his presence. He created us for this, and the Bible tells us the story and the way. May God bless you as you read it.

# OLD TESTAMENT

# Genesis

## Key Concepts

- The covenant is God's program of revelation.
- The focus of creation is the establishment and maintenance of order and operation.
- The stories in the Bible are stories about God.

←*Model of a ziggurat tower from the Baghdad Museum. The Tower of Babel likely would have looked similar.*



## Key Terms

***Fall***–The result of the disobedience of Adam and Eve that brought sin into the world and alienated God from humankind.
***Flood***–God's judgment on the world due to the lawlessness and violence of humanity. Only Noah, a righteous man, and his family were spared.
***Tower of Babel***–Building project that offended God and prompted him to confuse the language.
***Patriarchs***–The founding ancestors of the nation of Israel: Abraham, Isaac, and Jacob.
***Birthright***–The material inheritance given to children on the death of their father. It usually went to sons, with the firstborn receiving twice what the other sons received.
***Yahweh***–The personal name for God.
***Covenant***–God's agreement with Abraham and his descendants by which he would bring blessing to the world.

## Key Teachings about God

- God established and maintains order in the cosmos.
- God overcomes obstacles to carry out his purposes.
- God reveals himself to his people.
- God's grace exceeds all logic.

## People to Know

| | |
|---|---|
| Adam and Eve | Rebekah |
| Cain and Abel | Esau |
| Noah | Jacob |
| Abraham | Laban |
| Sarah | Leah |
| Melchizedek | Rachel |
| Ishmael | Judah |
| Isaac | Joseph |

## Timeline

2500 BC — 2400 — 2300 — 2200 — 2100 — 2000 — 1900 — 1800

- Creation (?)
- Fall (?)
- Flood (?)
- Babel (?)
- Abram born 2166
- Abram moves to Canaan 2091
- Ishmael born 2080
- Isaac born 2066
- Jacob, Esau born 2006
- Abraham dies 1991
- Joseph born 1915
- Joseph sold into Egypt 1898
- Isaac dies 1886
- Jacob and family settle in Egypt 1876
- Jacob dies 1859
- Joseph dies 1805

## Purpose

The purpose of this first book of the Bible is to begin the story of God and his continuing relationship with his creation, including his disappointments and the actions he takes to overcome obstacles. God shows his mastery as he creates order in the cosmos and as he brings order to his relationship with people through the covenant. Though God created everything just right, sin alienated people from God so that they no longer had an accurate idea of what he is like. This is why God made a covenant with a chosen people, Abraham and his family, a relationship that gave God a means for giving people an accurate picture of what he is like. Genesis tells how, despite many obstacles, the covenant was established.

Genesis 1–11 traces the blessing recorded in Genesis 1:28–30. The genealogies show people being fruitful and multiplying. At the same time these chapters depict the advance of sin, first in the disobedience of Adam and Eve, then in Cain's murder of his brother Abel, and finally in the escalation of violence and corruption that results in the flood. After the flood, the people not only continue their movement away from God but make a vain attempt to reestablish his presence by building a stairway for him to come down from heaven and be worshiped on earth (the Tower of Babel).

↑ *The Beni Hasan tomb paintings date to the period of Abraham and depict Semitic travelers to the land of Egypt.*

Now in addition to the problem of bringing people back to God (Eden problem), there is the problem of restoring the lost knowledge of what God is like (Babel problem). Human initiative, first by Adam and Eve, then by the builders of Babel, has had devastating results. God's covenant with Abraham represents God's initiative to provide a means by which God can reveal himself to the world through Abraham and his family and how the entire world could be blessed through them. The covenant blessings that serve as benefits to Abraham and his family are extensions of the original blessings in Genesis 1. The patriarchal narratives in Genesis 12–50 trace the advance of the covenant and its blessings and, at the same time, show the many obstacles. As these obstacles are overcome, one by one, God demonstrates his mastery.

**KEY VERSES:**

***Gen. 1:28:*** *"Be fruitful and increase in number."*

***Gen. 12:3:*** *"All peoples on earth will be blessed through you [Abraham]."*

***Gen. 50:20:*** *"You intended to harm me, but God intended it for good to accomplish . . . the saving of many lives."*

← *THE LAND OF THE BIBLE*

# Exodus

## Key Concepts

- The law is part of God's revelation of himself; giving it is an act of grace.
- God's presence comes on his terms and in his time.
- Deliverance is God's business.
- "Then you will know that I am the LORD your God."

*←Replica of the ark of the covenant.*



## Key Terms

***Exodus***–When God delivers the people of Israel from slavery in Egypt and brings them to the land he promised them.
***Plagues***–Ten acts of judgment against Egypt to persuade the Egyptians to let the Israelites leave.
***Passover***–The commemoration of the tenth plague when God punished the Egyptians with death of their firstborn sons but spared the Israelites.
***Decalogue***–Another name for the Ten Commandments—the central laws that God gave to Moses on stone tablets.
***Election***–God's choice of individuals or groups to serve as his people in relationship with him.
***I AM***–The name God gives himself at the burning bush. It is from the same verb ("to be") as the name "Yahweh" and identifies God not only as the one who *is* but also as the one who "causes to be."
***Burning Bush***–The place where God revealed himself to Moses, identified himself, and explained his plan and Moses's role in it.
***Pharaoh***–The title of the supreme ruler of Egypt. No name is given in Exodus, so we do not know which pharaoh let the Israelites leave.
***Tabernacle***–The portable tent sanctuary constructed by Israel according to God's instructions.
***Ark of the Covenant***–A chest made of wood overlaid with gold that contained important signs of God's favor, including the stone tablets of the covenant. It was the most sacred object of Israel, as it represented the footstool of the invisible throne of the invisible God. The cherubim adorning the cover were guardians of the throne of God.
***Holy of Holies***–The central area of the sanctuary where the ark was kept and where God's presence dwelt. The only access was by the high priest once a year.

## Timeline

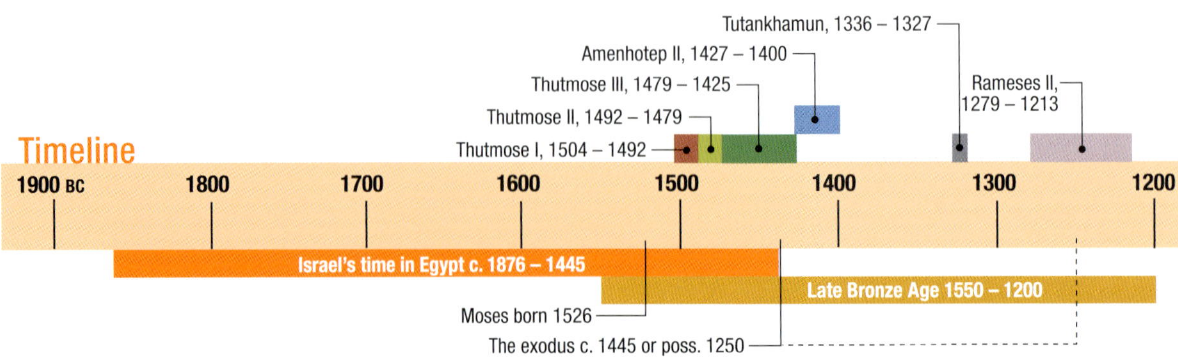

↑ *The Israelites passed through the Sinai Mountains on their way to the Promised Land.*

## Purpose

When Exodus opens, the Israelites are near the end of their time in Egypt. They had spent more than four centuries in Egypt and had become slaves in a foreign land. God is nowhere in evidence. Their covenant with God appears to be in disarray. They no longer enjoy the benefits of having connections in high places as when they first arrived, and with no land of their own, their survival is in jeopardy. When Pharaoh orders their baby boys to be cast into the Nile River, one mother creatively does so using a basket of reeds to protect her son. Pharaoh's daughter finds him afloat, names him Moses, and raises him as her own.

We are not told the extent to which Moses was aware of the plight of his people as he was growing up. But when he saw an Egyptian beating one of the Israelite slaves, he killed the Egyptian. Fleeing for his life, he took refuge in the wilderness among the people of Midian, where he met a tribal chieftain (Jethro), met the woman who would become his wife (Jethro's daughter Zipporah), and met his God. Seeing a bush ablaze but not consumed, Moses went to investigate and received the commission God had been preparing him to take up all his life—as the deliverer of Israel.

The purpose of Exodus is to explain how God revealed his presence and his power to his chosen people through the plagues and in their deliverance from Egypt. Just as in Genesis God overcame obstacles in establishing Abraham's family as his chosen people, in Exodus he overcomes obstacles that prevented him from dwelling in the midst of his people.

God guided and protected the Israelites through the wilderness and provided for them. At Sinai he told them how they needed to live so that his presence could dwell among them. Through the law, they learned how they were to honor and imitate his holiness. He told them how to build the tabernacle and how the priesthood was to prepare so that God could take up residence with them. God had chosen the Israelites to be his people and he intended to reveal himself to them and to the world by living in their midst.

**KEY VERSES:**

***Ex. 3:14:*** *"I AM WHO I AM."*

***Ex. 14:31:*** *"The Israelites saw the great power the LORD displayed."*

***Ex. 19:5–6:*** *"If you obey me fully and keep my covenant, then out of all the nations you will be my treasured possession."*

***Ex. 40:34–35:*** *"The glory of the LORD filled the tabernacle."*

### People to Know

Moses
Aaron
Miriam
Jethro
Zipporah

## Key Teachings about God

- **God demonstrates his power for his people and the world to see.**
- **God desires to live among his people.**
- **God delivers his people, and his ability to do so is without limit.**
- **God expects obedience from his people.**
- **God does not leave his people to guess what he expects of them.**
- **God chooses certain individuals and groups for special work.**

↓ *FROM EGYPT TO MOUNT SINAI*

# Leviticus

© Dr. James C. Martin

## Key Concepts

- **Ritual impurity is not the same as sin, but either can restrict access to God's presence.**
- **Holiness distinguishes God from people and distinguishes God's people from other people.**
- **Sacred space must be defined and preserved (the job of priests).**
- **Sacrifice is a mechanism to allow people to pray to God, thank God, preserve sacred space for God, and be in relationship with God.**

←*Reconstruction of the Sinai tabernacle located in Israel's northern Sinai.*

## Key Terms

***Holiness***–The sum total of godly traits.
***Sacrifice***–Giving something of value to God (usually an animal or grain during Bible times). Some involved a blood rite intended to eliminate the effects of sin.
***Sacred Space***–An area established by God's presence, which had strict rules of behavior and access. If sanctity was not preserved, the benefit of God's presence could be lost. Several zones of increasing sanctity surrounded the Holy of Holies.
***Feasts***–Days given special meaning because of God's work among his people. These were considered sacred times and were highly regulated.
***Sabbath***–The seventh day set aside each week to acknowledge God's control and provision by relinquishing for the day one's own attempts to control and provide for oneself.

## Key Teachings about God

- **God is holy.**
- **God expects his people to be holy.**
- **God desires to live among his people but has high standards that must be maintained.**
- **God is serious about holiness.**

## People to Know

Moses
Aaron
Nadab
Abihu

## Purpose

Leviticus contains information given to the Israelites while they were camped in the wilderness by Mount Sinai: instructions regarding management of sacred space (the tabernacle), sacred status (as God's people), and sacred time (in the festivals). These were considered important for maintaining holiness for God's presence, which was at the center of their lives. Sacred times must be identified, maintained by the priests, and observed. Sacred space must be guarded and its holiness preserved. The status of priests and people must be regulated by specific guidelines so they don't desecrate God's presence. God is holy, and Israel is expected to be holy so his presence can remain in their midst.

Sacrifice is treated in terms of the materials and procedures that will render it acceptable. These sacrifices constitute gifts to God or serve to purify the sacred things from the contamination of sin and uncleanness. It was more important for sacrifices to remove the effects of sin from God's presence than it was to remove sin from the people.

Priests are given their role. Though priests were responsible for teaching the people and making decisions as leaders, their primary role concerned performance of duties in the sanctuary. Instead of thinking of them as clergy, similar to pastors, consider them to be the ritual experts of Israel. Their job was to do whatever was necessary to preserve the sanctity of God's tabernacle. This meant guarding access to sacred space, maintaining the pure status of the people, and overseeing observances connected to sacred times—the festivals of Israel.

↑ *Full-scale replica of the Sinai tabernacle and altar.*

Holiness is the most important theme in Leviticus. God's holiness is not a separate attribute but the result of the sum total of all of his attributes—including but not limited to his sovereignty, omniscience, love, and righteousness. Holiness is a term that implies comparison. God is holy in relation to the people he created.

When God asks his people to be holy as he is holy, he means we are to maintain distinctions between ourselves and the world around us by imitating God himself. The distance between ourselves and the world will be defined by the attributes of God that we are able to imitate. As we become more godlike in attributes such as love, grace, faithfulness, and mercy, we are becoming holy by distinguishing ourselves from the fallen world.

**KEY VERSES:**

***Lev. 10:3:** "I will show myself holy."*

***Lev. 11:45:** "Be holy, because I am holy."*

***Lev. 18:5:** "Keep my decrees and laws."*

## Jewish Calendar

| | | | |
|---|---|---|---|
| **Nisan** | March-April | Barley harvest | 14—Passover<br>21—Firstfruits |
| **Iyyar** | April-May | General harvest | |
| **Sivan** | May-June | Wheat harvest<br>Vine tending | 6—Pentecost |
| **Tammuz** | June-July | First grapes | |
| **Ab** | July-August | Grapes, figs, olives | 9—Destruction of Temple |
| **Elul** | August-September | Vintage | |
| **Tishri** | September-October | Ploughing | 1—New Year<br>10—Day of Atonement<br>15-21—Feast of Tabernacles |
| **Marchesvan** | October-November | Grain planting | |
| **Kislev** | November-December | | 25—Dedication |
| **Tebet** | December-January | Spring growth | |
| **Shebat** | January-February | Winter figs | |
| **Adar** | February-March | Pulling flax<br>Almonds bloom | 13-14—Purim |
| **Adar Sheni** | Intercalary Month | | |

# Numbers

←The wilderness of Zin.



## Key Concepts

- **Some generations fail and lose benefits and privileges, but God faithfully offers new opportunities for faithfulness.**
- **Submission to God and trust in his plan and provision are essential to God's people.**

## Key Terms

***Twelve Tribes***–The Israelites are organized socially and politically by tribes descended from the sons of Jacob.
***Nazirite***–A person who engages in a designated period of dedication to God.
***Levites***–The clan responsible for priestly duties and for the care of the tabernacle.
***Wilderness***–Desolate regions, not necessarily desert. In Numbers the wilderness is usually rocky rather than sandy.
***Promised Land***–The land of Canaan to which God brought Abraham. Conquered under Joshua, it becomes the kingdom of Israel under David and Solomon. The gift of the land is one of the covenant promises God made to Abraham.
***Holy War***–In the ancient world all warfare was understood as being commanded by deity, fought by deity, and serving deity's purposes. The important distinction in the wars of Israel that eventually gain them the land is that all the spoils belong to God and do not go to enrich the people.

## Key Teachings about God

- **God is patient but does not take disobedience lightly.**
- **God is faithful to his promises.**
- **God provides for his people.**

## People to Know

| | |
|---|---|
| Moses | Korah |
| Miriam | Dathan |
| Aaron | Abiram |
| Joshua | Balak |
| Caleb | Sihon |
| Phinehas | Og |
| Balaam | |

## Timeline of Wilderness Years

1445 BC — 0 — Exodus; Arrival at Mount Sinai
1 — Completion of tabernacle
2 — Departure from Sinai
3...
41st year — Death of Moses?
1404 — Israel enters Canaan

## Purpose

Numbers gives an account of Israel's 40 years in the wilderness. The book's purpose is to contrast God's covenant faithfulness to Israel's faithlessness and rebellion. God keeps his promise to make them a numerous people (shown by the census) and to bring them to the Promised Land. But from the beginning, the people grumble, rebel against God's leadership, and refuse to enter the land. They not only wander in the wilderness, they wander into false worship. The people test God at every level even while God is providing their needs.

Numbers gives an account of the transition from the generation that left Egypt to the one that enters the Promised Land 40 years later. Chapters 1–10 concern the presence of the Lord as it pertains to traveling arrangements, as the people leave Sinai with the law and their new portable sanctuary. Though God delivers the first generation and provides for them, they are unwilling to trust him to bring them into the land. Chapters 11–21 detail God's provision for their needs and the constant complaints of the people. As a result, all but two of those who experienced the Exodus are doomed to die in the wilderness without seeing the Promised Land. God bestows his blessing on the new generation as he prepares them for entrance into the land. There is an extended contrast as the leadership transitions from the first generation to the second and a census is taken for both. The section on Balaam marks the transition, with God giving blessing instead of the deserved curse, and shows the zeal of the new generation.

The covenant theme of Genesis is continued as God reveals himself and fulfills promises despite obstacles. The Exodus theme of God's presence is continued as is the Leviticus theme of holiness.

↑ *Israelites passed along this road, also known as the King's Highway, on their way through Moab.*

**KEY VERSES**

***Num. 6:24–26:*** *"The LORD bless you and keep you; the LORD make his face shine upon you and be gracious to you; the LORD turn his face toward you and give you peace."*

***Num. 14:18–19:*** *"The LORD is slow to anger, abounding in love and forgiving sin."*

***Num. 23:19:*** *"God is not a man, that he should lie."*

***Num. 24:17:*** *"A star will come out of Jacob; a scepter will rise out of Israel."*

***Num. 32:23:*** *"Be sure that your sin will find you out."*

↓ *ISRAEL'S CONQUEST OF THE TRANSJORDAN*

↓ *This silver amulet is one of the earliest biblical inscriptions discovered to date and contains the "Priestly Benediction" of Numbers 6:24–26.*

# Deuteronomy

© Dr. James C. Martin

## Key Concepts

- One God, one people, one sanctuary, and one law.
- God's law impacts every area of life, and all law is rooted in the Ten Commandments.
- Obedience is only the beginning of what is expected of God's people—he wants his people to be in relationship with him.
- God's people are to love him.

←*Mount Nebo at sunset. Moses looked over the Promised Land from Mount Nebo.*

## Key Terms

***Covenant***–The covenant here is laid out in a form similar to how international treaty relations were structured in the ancient world. Thus the covenant formalizes the relationship between God and his people. Through this formalized agreement, God continues to reveal himself to his people.

***Law***–Sometimes called the Torah, the law refers to God's guidelines for his people to stay in relationship with him, to preserve his presence among them, and to imitate his holiness.

## Key Teachings about God

- God is faithful and expects his people to be faithful.
- God is one.
- God is concerned with justice.
- God blesses those who are faithful and punishes those who disobey.

## People to Know

Moses Joshua

## Timeline

| 1420 BC | 1410 | 1400 | 1390 |
|---|---|---|---|

Israelites travel to Plains of Moab
Moses dies 1406
Joshua becomes leader
Israelites enter Canaan

**KEY VERSES:**

***Deut. 4:29:*** *"If . . . you seek the LORD . . . you will find him."*

***Deut. 6:4–8:*** *"Love the LORD your God with all your heart . . . soul . . . strength."*

***Deut. 18:15:*** *"The LORD your God will raise up for you a prophet."*

***Deut. 34:10–12:*** *"Since then, no prophet has risen in Israel like Moses, whom the LORD knew face to face."*

## Purpose

Deuteronomy is comprised of a series of speeches by Moses at the end of his life. The people have traveled eastward from Kadesh, around the southern end of the Dead Sea, and have arrived on the Plains of Moab just east of the Jordan River. They are ready to cross over and inherit the land that God had promised so long ago. But Moses will not be going in with them, so he offers these speeches as his parting words to them before he dies.

The purpose of Deuteronomy is to summarize and renew the covenant in preparation for Israel entering the land, organizing laws in a way that the spirit behind the Ten Commandments will be understood. Obeying the law is only one of the ways that the people are expected to keep the covenant. The key themes can be summarized as: "One God, one people, one sanctuary, and one law." All of these need to be honored by God's covenant people, who are reminded of God's faithfulness and called upon to respond not only with obedience but with love. The blessings and curses found in chapters 28–29 show how serious a matter the covenant was. The careful reader will find connections to the curses in the books of the prophets as they condemn the people for unfaithfulness.

The book can be considered the charter document of Israel in her identity as God's covenant people, containing Israel's mission statement, values, and by-laws. It takes the form of treaties used in the ancient world to define the relationship between two parties. It identifies the parties, details recent history that brought them to this moment, and outlines responsibilities they must fulfill to maintain the relationship. This last element is represented in the middle section of Deuteronomy, which contains many laws, beginning with a repetition of the Ten Commandments (ch. 5). A recitation of laws in chapters 6–26 discuss the nuances and broader ramifications for each of the Ten Commandments.

↓→ *Code of Hammurabi, king of Babylon (1792–1750 BC). The book of Deuteronomy is a similarly structured document.*



↓ *ISRAEL PREPARED TO ENTER THE PROMISED LAND FROM THE PLAINS OF MOAB.*

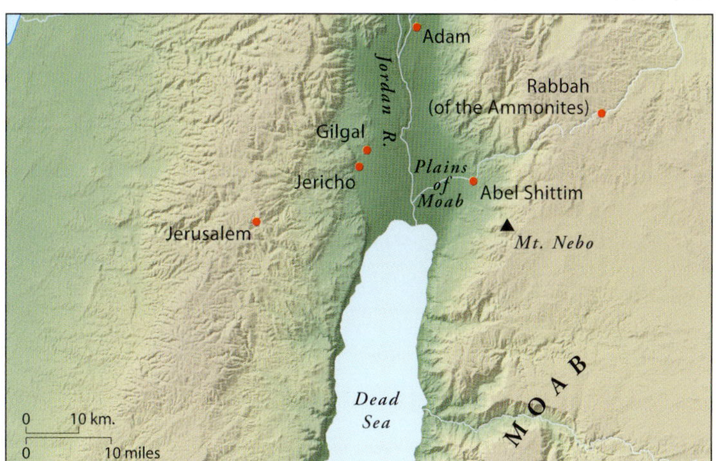

# Joshua

© Dr. James C. Martin

## Key Concepts

- God, not their own strength, gives Israel the land. Victory belongs to the Lord.
- Destruction of the Canaanites and Amorites is punishment for their sin.

← *Joshua marched around the city of Jericho.*

## Key Terms

***Land of Milk and Honey***–A phrase used to describe the natural resources of the Promised Land. Note that this does not indicate that Canaan is fertile farm country or rich in minerals, but is good for herding (milk) and for fruit (honey of the date palm).
***Conquest***–The wars through which God gives the Israelites possession of the land.
***Devoted to the Lord***–Sometimes referred to as the "ban," this refers to the instruction that the Israelites are to destroy the city including all residents—no captives, no plunder—except that precious metals belong to the sanctuary.
***Circumcision***–The sign of a family's membership in the covenant.

## Key Teachings about God

- God kept his promise, giving the land he had promised to Abraham many centuries earlier.
- God is the one who brings victory; there is no foe that can withstand him.
- God expects obedience.

## People to Know

Joshua
Achan
Rahab

## Timeline

1410 BC | 1400 | 1390 | 1380 | 1370 | 1360 | 1300

1406 Israelites enter Canaan
Conquests of Jericho, Ai, Bethel (?)
Joshua aids Gibeon (?)
Southern campaign (?)
Northern campaign (?)
Dividing of the land (?)
Joshua dies

## Purpose

Joshua portrays God as sovereign in world events, active on behalf of his people Israel, and faithful to the promises of the covenant. It affirms the theology that God brought victory and gave Israel the land promised to Abraham. At the beginning, the people of Israel are poised on the border of the Promised Land. The early narratives show little interest in political, military, or personal issues. They focus instead on God's role in overthrowing the cities of Canaan. It is clear that the destruction of the people was not simply to make room for the Israelites. The Canaanites and other inhabitants are portrayed as having brought the judgment of God upon themselves. The response of Rahab is important in Joshua 2 in that it shows that even one under the judgment of God who responds in faith will be spared.

The purpose of Joshua is summarized in 21:43–45, where it tells how God kept his covenant promise to give the land to Israel. The book recounts God's bringing Israel into the land (chs. 1–5), giving the Israelites victory over the inhabitants of the land (chs. 6–12), and distributing the land among the clans for settlement (chs. 13–22). This is how land takes on a sacred identity—its possession is seen as the covenant gift of God, though ultimately it still remains God's land.

The book concludes with a renewal of the covenant (chs. 23–24) as the people publicly and formally acknowledge that God has fulfilled his promises and that they are indebted to him, obliged by covenant to be faithful. The book highlights God's side of the covenant. It shows that God is serious about punishing those deserving of judgment. This is true whether the offenders are Canaanites or Israelites who violate God's commands (ch. 7).

↑ *According to Deuteronomy 28–31, Joshua and the Israelites were instructed to remember God's covenant by proclaiming God's blessings from Mount Gerizim (left ridge) and potential curses from Mount Ebal (right ridge). They obeyed this command, as recorded in Joshua 8.*

**KEY VERSES:**

***Josh. 1:2–9:*** *"Get ready to cross the Jordan River. . . . I will never leave you nor forsake you. . . . Be strong and courageous. . . . Do not let this Book of the Law depart from your mouth; meditate on it day and night."*

***Josh. 2:11:*** *"The LORD your God is God in heaven above and on the earth below."*

***Josh. 6:20:*** *"When the trumpets sounded . . . the wall collapsed."*

***Josh. 21:43–45:*** *"Not one of all the LORD's good promises . . . failed."*

***Josh. 24:14–15:*** *"As for me and my household, we will serve the LORD."*

↓ *THE ISRAELITE CAMPAIGNS IN THE PROMISED LAND*

# Judges

© Dr. James C. Martin

## Key Concepts

- **Leadership was lacking in the time of the judges, which worked to the disadvantage of the people.**
- **Israel worshiped other gods alongside Yahweh and thus failed to keep the covenant.**

← *Deborah and Barak met at Mount Tabor to battle against the Canaanites from Hazor.*

## Key Terms

***Judge***–A leader who brings justice for the people of Israel. This generally means a political or military leader who brings justice by defeating foreign oppressors.

***Spirit of the Lord***–In the Old Testament this is the way people spoke of God's power or authority being manifested through an individual. Though they were not familiar with the idea of the Trinity, today we can identify much that is attributed by them to the Spirit of the Lord as the work of the Holy Spirit.

***Cycles of the Judges***–Judges 2:11–19 details the cycle of unfaithfulness, subjugation, supplication to God for help, and deliverance through a judge. Six such cycles are connected to the major Judges (Othniel, Ehud, Deborah, Gideon, Jephthah, Samson).

***Minor Judges***–Judges mentioned in the book that are not connected to cycles.

## Key Teachings about God

- **God is patient, just, and merciful.**
- **God is able to accomplish his plan even through flawed individuals.**
- **God held the Israelites accountable to his expectations of them.**

## People to Know

Othniel
Ehud
Deborah
Barak
Sisera
Jael
Gideon
Abimelech
Jephthah
Samson
Delilah

## Timeline

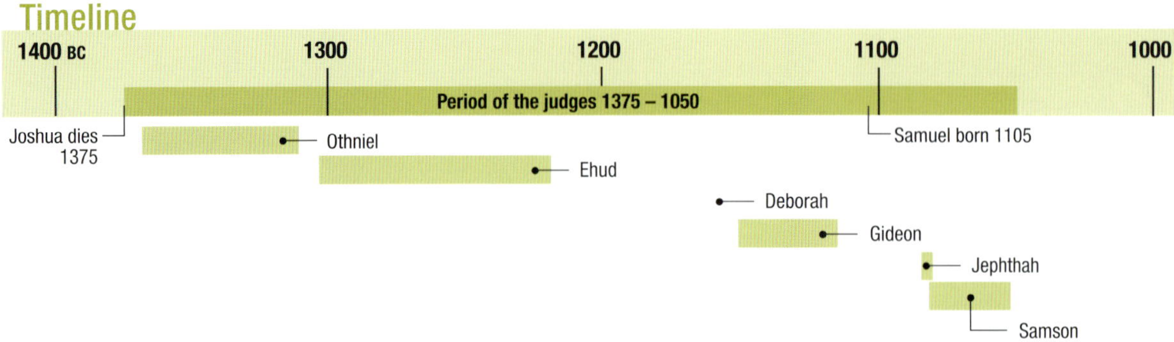

## Purpose

Even as the land is being delivered to Israel, signs of unfaithfulness begin to appear. God gave control of the land through Joshua's victories, but the tribes still had much work to do to secure the land and drive out the inhabitants. Instead of persisting in this task, the Israelites were content to settle alongside these peoples. As a result, they were increasingly under the political influence of the peoples around them and lured by unacceptable religious practices. Baal and other gods were adopted into Israelite worship along with Yahweh, thus compromising the ideals God had set forth in the law. This problem persisted over several centuries.

God continued his program of revelation by showing that he was as faithful to the covenant curses and penalties as he was to the covenant benefits and blessings. His grace did not negate his justice. As God judged her faithlessness, Israel found herself repeatedly subject to neighboring nations. Yet God periodically raised up deliverers. Through six cycles of events, each culminating in a military leader (judge), God demonstrated his power and mercy by delivering the Israelites even though his justice demanded that he bring punishment.

But even the deliverers became progressively less representative of God's ideals for leadership. Neither the leadership of the judges (chs. 3–16) nor the tribal leadership of priests and elders (chs. 17–21) succeeded in helping the people remain faithful. Instead, the leaders were sometimes as bad as the people. Both judges and tribes were hampered by the absence of a central authority. The book of Joshua shows God's faithfulness; the book of Judges shows the Israelites' failures.

←*Gideon chose his army at the spring, En Harod, located at the base of Mount Tabor.*



**KEY VERSES:**

***Judg. 2:11–19:** "The LORD raised up judges. . . . They [the people] refused to give up their evil practices and stubborn ways."*

***Judg. 10:10–16:** "We have sinned . . . please rescue us now."*

***Judg. 21:25:** "Israel had no king; everyone did as he saw fit."*

←*THE TRIBES OF ISRAEL*

# Ruth

© Direct Design

## Key Concepts

- **Faithfulness generates faithfulness.**
- **David's ancestry was populated by faithful people.**

← *Women from the village of Bet Sahour at the outskirts of Bethlehem harvest wheat by hand.*

## Key Terms

***Kinsman Redeemer***–In Israelite society, responsibility for the well-being of the members of the clan and protection of the clan's property lay with the clan. A kinsman redeemer would arrange for the freedom of those who had been reduced to the status of debt slave and would arrange to reclaim land belonging to the clan. It was a way of providing for those who had become disenfranchised or destitute.

***Levirate Marriage***–The propagation of the family line was very important, so if a man died before his wife could bear him a child, it was the duty of his brother to marry the widow and bear a child in the dead man's name.

## Key Teachings about God

- **God remained faithful to his people even when the times were characterized by unfaithfulness.**
- **God provides for those who are faithful.**

## People to Know

Naomi
Orpah
Ruth
Boaz

## Purpose

The story of Ruth is set in the time of the judges. The fact that it is several generations before David places it somewhere in the middle of that period, but exact chronology is immaterial. The importance of the book is that the main characters provide a poignant contrast to the Israelites in the book of Judges. Faithfulness survives. Ruth's purpose is to show how the faithfulness of one person to another can motivate the faithfulness of God. It is interesting that even as Israel suffered under the negative spiritual and political influence of other nations during this period, Ruth represents a positive influence from the Gentile nations. Her faithfulness to Naomi, her mother-in-law, stimulated Naomi's faith and impressed Boaz, a relative of Naomi and a prosperous farmer. God in turn responded favorably to Ruth's faithfulness. This is even more remarkable since she is a Gentile outsider who has no covenant and no law on which to base that faithfulness.

Sometimes we are quick to seize on the faith of Ruth, but the book offers little insight into her faith. It is enough that she is faithful to Naomi, however much or little she understands about Yahweh, the God of Israel's covenant. If her knowledge of Yahweh is slight, the point is made more forceful. Even a foreigner with little revelation of the true God is capable of faithfulness beyond all logic or expectation. Surely any Israelite of the judges period, regardless of how uninformed they might be, would have been capable of this level of faithfulness.

God's blessing on Ruth and Boaz brings blessing to all of Israel and to the world. Through them, all the nations of the earth are blessed. Ruth becomes another Abraham who left her land in an act of faith and got to see God provide an heir when all hope seemed lost. God preserved such families of faithfulness that were in the line of the future King David. Ruth provides an important faith link between Abraham and David and thus begins the transition from the period of the judges, where leadership was so painfully lacking, to the period of kingship.

↑ *Boaz met Ruth in the vicinity of the fields and threshing floors located on the east side of Bethlehem.*

**KEY VERSE:**

***Ruth 1:16–17: "Your people will be my people and your God my God."***

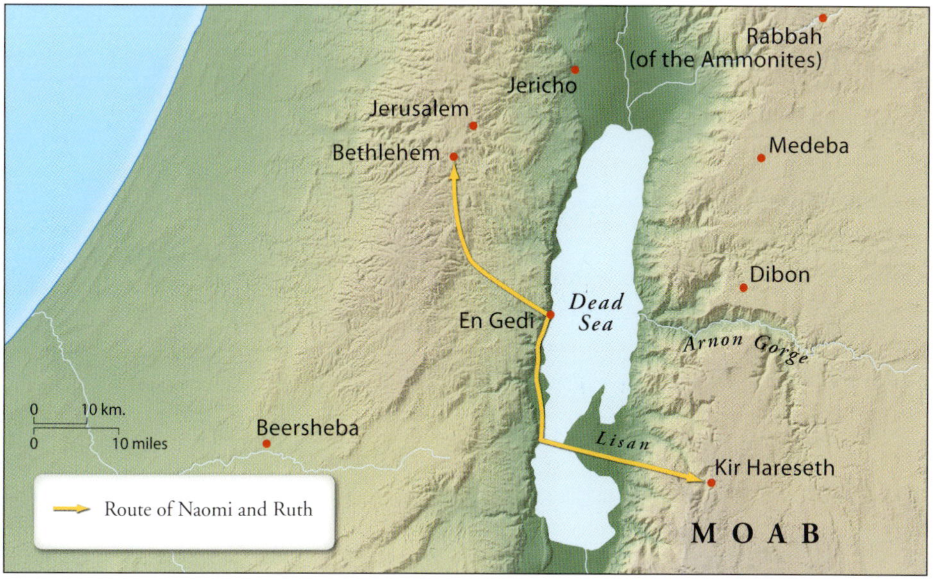


← *FROM BETHLEHEM TO MOAB AND BACK*

# 1–2 Samuel

## Key Concepts

- Samuel is established as a recognized and verified man of God.
- God established a kingship covenant with David and his descendants.
- The key to successful kingship is the recognition that Yahweh is the true king, therefore a king's reign must reflect Yahweh's values (represented in the law and the covenant).
- It is important to honor the presence of God (ark, temple).

← *The ark of the covenant came through the Sorek Valley located to the left of the oval-shaped site of ancient Beth Shemesh (bordering the western edge of the modern town of Beth Shemesh) on its return trip to the Judean Mountains.*



## Key Terms

***United Monarchy***–The period of Saul, David, and Solomon (just over a century long), when all twelve tribes were united under a single king.

***Kingship Covenant (Davidic Covenant)***–God continues to reveal himself to Israel and the world as king. To do so, he elects human kings (David and his line) to serve as the instruments of his kingship.

***Messiah ("Anointed One")***–Though this term will not achieve its full theological significance until the end of the Old Testament period, it refers to God's anointed king—specifically a king from David's line and eventually an ideal king from David's line.

## Key Teachings about God

- God provided a king for his people.
- God reigns.
- God's power and sovereignty are demonstrated through his king.
- God will punish even his chosen ones when they disobey.

## People to Know

Hannah
Eli
Samuel
Saul
David
Goliath
Jonathan
Michal
Joab
Abishai
Abner
Abigail
Nathan
Absalom
Bathsheba
Amnon
Ishbosheth

## Timeline

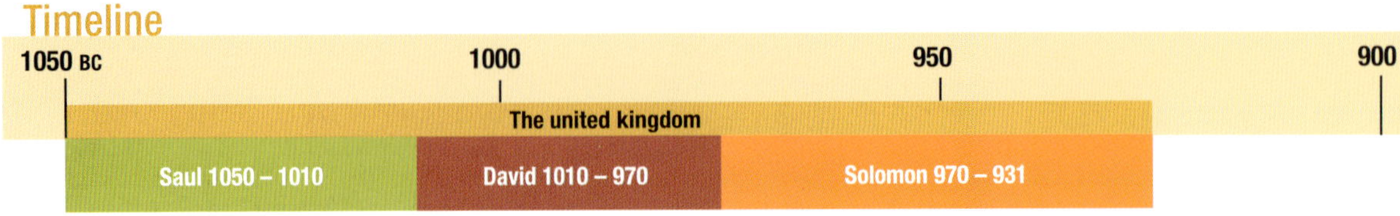

## Purpose

The purpose of the books of Samuel is to tell the story of the establishment of the covenant of kingship with David. After more than four centuries of failure (judges period), the people are frustrated with the lack of central leadership. They conclude that their troubles are political and therefore require a political solution, so they request a king to lead them in battle. They are blind to the fact that their political problems have a spiritual cause. Instead of a political solution (seeking a king), they should have opted for a spiritual solution: renewed faithfulness to Yahweh and the covenant. Yahweh has no objection to the institution of kingship (see Gen. 17:6). The problem is not the request itself but the reasoning behind the request.

The books establish the credentials of Samuel, who is to become the kingmaker, anointing Saul and then David. Saul is chosen by God following the criteria demanded by the people. In contrast, David is chosen according to God's criteria. The ideal king in the Old Testament is one who recognizes that Yahweh, the divine king, is the true king. That this is David's view is seen in the battle with the giant Goliath where he relies on God to bring victory against tremendous odds. He sees clearly that Yahweh is the one who fights the battles. With these ideals in mind, God establishes a covenant with David that extends a permanent place on the throne to him and his descendants. That covenant is the centerpiece of these books.

After a brief account of the largely unsuccessful rule of Saul, the last half of 1 Samuel demonstrates that David did not usurp Saul's throne by showing that Saul, not David, consistently initiates the conflict. The text illustrates that everyone, even the one who stands to lose the most, crown prince Jonathan, acknowledges that David would be king. David takes no action against Saul or his house to make himself king.

When David finally comes to the throne in 2 Samuel, it is clear that God, not his own political ambition, has brought him there. As the text details David's accession to the throne and his many successes (2 Sam. 1–9), it shows him as the one for whom God built an empire. As Yahweh establishes David's name, David establishes Yahweh's name by restoring the ark to its proper place. David then becomes the beneficiary of the covenant through which God promises him a dynastic line.

David later comes under condemnation when he fails to uphold the ideals of kingship. His adultery with Bathsheba and arrangement for the death of her husband, Uriah, show an abuse of power that is the polar opposite of God's kingship—a kingship he was supposed to reflect. God is in the process of revealing his sovereign rule through covenant kingship. David could be an instrument of that revelation or an obstacle, but God's kingship will be demonstrated regardless.

William L. Krewson/www.BiblePlaces.com

↑ *David used sling-stones like these when he fought Goliath.*

© Dr. James C. Martin, The British Museum

↑ *Assyrian slingers.*

↓ *THE UNITED KINGDOM OF ISRAEL*

**KEY VERSES:**

***1 Sam. 2:10:*** *"The Lord will judge the ends of the earth."*

***1 Sam. 8:7–8:*** *"It is not you they have rejected, but . . . me [God]."*

***1 Sam. 16:7:*** *"Man looks at the outward appearance, but the Lord looks at the heart."*

***2 Sam. 7:5–16:*** *"Your house and your kingdom will endure forever before me."*

# 1–2 Kings

© Dr. James C. Martin

## Key Concepts

- The two books of Kings, like the book of Judges, document covenant failure.
- The exiles are shown that the cause of the judgment was apostasy and idolatry.
- The kings were frequently warned by the prophets.
- Recurrent themes are the sins of Jeroboam (the golde calves) and the promises to David (covenant).

*← The large, square raised platform functioned as the "high place" at Dan where Jeroboam I instigated calf worship.*

## Key Terms

***Solomon's Temple***–David was not allowed to build a permanent temple to serve as the sanctuary of Yahweh, but a temple was completed and dedicated by his son Solomon.

***Divided Monarchy***–After Solomon's reign, the kingdom was divided into two parts. The south, Judah, was comprised of two tribes ruled by David's line with its capital in Jerusalem. The north, Israel, was ruled by a series of dynasties and eventually established its capital in Samaria.

***Exile***–Refers to when the Israelites are taken away from their land after being defeated by conquering armies. The north (Israel) was exiled by the Assyrians after the destruction of Samaria in 722. The south (Judah) was exiled by the Babylonians after the destruction of Jerusalem and the temple in 586. Technically, the exile refers to the time that the people of Judah are in Babylon (586–539).

***Pre-classical Prophets***–Prophets serving before the middle of the eighth century, who addressed mainly the king and whose oracles were not collected into books.

***Golden Calves***–During the divided monarchy, two golden calves were set up at shrines in Bethel (southern border) and Dan (northern border). They probably were intended to be substitutes for the ark. The ark was the footstool for Yahweh's throne. Bull calves were often thought of as pedestals on whose backs the deity stood.

## Key Teachings about God

- God is the source and giver of wisdom.
- God is pleased to live among his people.
- God's presence is conditional.
- God, in his grace, warns over and over again.
- Yahweh reigns.

## Timeline

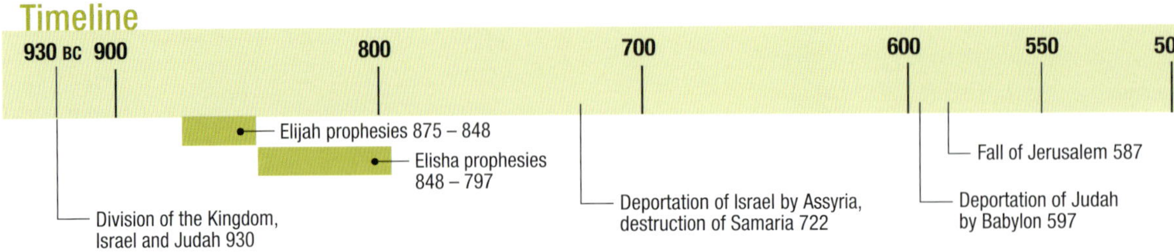

## Purpose

The purpose of the two books of Kings is to demonstrate that the kings of Israel and Judah failed to live up to the ideals of the kingship covenant made with David. God is therefore justified in exiling his people. Just as the judges period illustrates the failure of the people to live up to God's ideals, the monarchy period shows the failure of the kings. This failure is first evident in Solomon, after whose reign the kingdom is divided. Both resulting kingdoms are generally characterized by failure. God continues to reveal what he is like even through the kings' failures. Sometimes he does this through judgment. Other times he does this by raising up champions or better representatives of his kingship. When Ahab and Jezebel attempt to dethrone Yahweh as Israel's national God in favor of Baal, it is the prophet Elijah who becomes the champion of Yahweh's kingship. In many of the biblical accounts, Elijah's successor, Elisha, is seen as a surrogate king. Elisha brings justice for the people and victory over the armies of the enemy.

The books are written from the viewpoint of the exile and seek to offer an explanation of how Israel ended up so far off-course with regard to the covenant. The narrative seems like a blur of king following king, which is exactly the effect the author desired to create. One king blends into another as the pattern of failure emerges. The author was more interested in spiritual issues and the kings' relationship to God than in political events. The latter are reported only when they communicate something that God was doing. History is secondary to the theological purpose of tracking covenant failures. The books show how God tries to warn and guide the people. God's role in advising and influencing the kings is represented in the prophets. The continuing revelation of his instructions and warnings takes place through these men (and occasionally women) who serve as his spokesmen.

Yahweh's kingship is supreme, and the empires are under his command. When Israel falls to the Assyrians and Judah to the Babylonians nearly a century and a half later, the prophets and the text affirm that this did not happen because Yahweh was inattentive to his people, fickle in his loyalty, or outmatched by stronger gods. Instead it was testimony to his justice. Centuries of repeated faithlessness finally reaped the harvest of his judgment just as the covenant curses had warned. These curses had been reiterated in the dedication of the temple built by Solomon. When God's presence leaves the temple and abandons his people, the nation falls and goes into exile.

↑ *The ninth-century BC House of David stele discovered at Tel Dan describes how Hazael, king of Aram, "killed [Ahaz]iahu son of [Jehoram kin]g of the House of David."*



↓ *THE DIVIDED KINGDOM*

**KEY VERSES:**

***1 Kings 3:6–14:*** *"Give your servant a discerning heart to govern your people and to distinguish between right and wrong."*

***1 Kings 4:29–30:*** *"God gave Solomon wisdom and very great insight."*

***1 Kings 8:22–61:*** *"So that all the peoples of the earth may know that the LORD is God and that there is no other."*

***2 Kings 17:7–15:*** *"'Do not do as they do,' and they did the things the LORD had forbidden."*

### People to Know

| | | |
|---|---|---|
| Solomon | Ahab | Jeroboam II |
| Ahijah | Jezebel | Azariah (Uzziah) |
| Jeroboam | Asa | Hezekiah |
| Rehoboam | Jehoshaphat | Manasseh |
| Elijah | Jehu | Josiah |
| Elisha | Joash | Sennacherib |

# 1–2 Chronicles

## Key Concepts

- Seeks to understand the basis for continuity, transformation, and theological stability.
- Highlights retribution theology and role of the priests and Levites.
- Leads the post-exilic community to refocus from monarchy to theocracy.
- Recurrent themes: reform and repentance as means to God's blessing.

← *The ancient thirteen-acre Jebusite city conquered by David lies along the ridge due south of Jerusalem's Temple Mount.*



## Key Terms

***Theocracy***–The reign of God and the establishment of God's kingdom.
***Retribution***–The idea that God will bless his people with the covenant blessings when they are faithful, but will punish them with the covenant curses when they are unfaithful.
***Post-exilic Period***–Began when the people of Israel who had been living in exile in Babylon were given permission to return to their land in 538 BC.
***Reformer Kings***–Chronicles gives more attention to kings who instituted reform and tried to restore true worship. These included Asa, Jehoshaphat, Joash, Hezekiah, and Josiah.

## Key Teachings about God

- Sovereign rule as Creator (2 Chron. 20:6)
- Providential intervention as Sustainer (2 Chron. 20:12)
- Election of Israel (1 Chron. 16:13, 17)
- Faithfulness to his covenant promises (1 Chron. 17:18–24)
- Responsiveness to prayer (2 Chron. 6:40; 7:12)
- Justice (2 Chron. 19:7)
- Goodness (2 Chron. 30:18–20)
- Mercy (2 Chron. 30:9)

## People to Know

David
Solomon
Hiram
Queen of Sheba
Rehoboam
Shishak
Asa
Jehoshaphat
Joash
Jehoiada
Uzziah
Hezekiah
Manasseh
Josiah

## Timeline

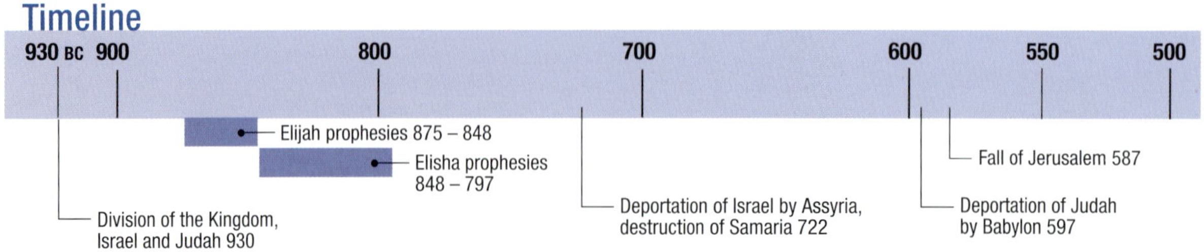

## Purpose

In contrast to the books of Kings, written *during* the exile, the books of Chronicles cover the same period but were written *after* the people returned from their exile. As a result, they are written from an entirely different perspective. The purpose of these two books is to show that throughout Israel's history, obedience led to blessing and disobedience led to trouble. The chronicler demonstrates that the most important defining quality of the kingdom is not political (dependent on a king's presence), but spiritual (dependent on God's presence). The priests and the temple are therefore most important. Serving God is more important than political and national status. Rather than focusing on failure the way the books of Kings did, the Chronicles focus the on hope in God's plan. Yet they focus on living out the kingdom in the present instead of simply looking to it in the future.

In the post-exilic period we find a transformed Israel. The people have finally gotten beyond their inclination to worship other gods, and we see the achievement of the monotheistic ideals represented in the law. They have a firm commitment to the centrality of worship and to maintaining the holiness of the temple—led in both by the Levites.

The lengthy genealogies at the beginning of 1 Chronicles trace the caretakers of the kingdom of God. Beginning with Adam and his descendants, the torch passes to the Israelites, then to the Davidic kings and Levites, and finally to the current community, the remnant of Israel. In this way the community sees itself in the long line of tradition that has stood for the kingdom of God as it is marked by his presence. As they understand their heritage and their identity, they can begin to shape their legacy: Kingship is of no avail if God is not present in their midst.

↑ *Facsimile of the inscription describing how "Hezekiah's Tunnel" was completed.*

**KEY VERSES:**

***1 Chron. 28:9:*** *"If you seek him, he will be found by you."*

***2 Chron. 7:14:*** *"If my people . . . will humble themselves and pray . . . and turn from their wicked ways, then will I hear . . . and will forgive their sin."*

↓ *ISRAEL UNDER ATTACK BY ASSYRIA AND BABYLON*

# Ezra and Nehemiah

## Key Concepts

- God had declared through the prophets, especially Jeremiah, that after he judged his people and gave them over to the Babylonians, he would bring them back seventy years later.
- Prayer is an important expression of trust.
- The law takes its proper place as the foundation of society.
- Even pagan kings are under God's control.

← *The Cyrus Cylinder (539 BC) reveals the restoration of the exiles to return to Judah.*



## Key Term

***Restoration***–The prophets had proclaimed that after a time in exile, the Israelites would return to their land, rebuild the temple, and be ruled by an ideal king from David's line. This would be a time of political and spiritual advance.

## Key Teachings about God

- God answers prayer.
- God is able to reform his people when they are responsive.
- God protects those who trust him.
- God works in the hearts of rulers to accomplish his plan.

## People to Know

| | |
|---|---|
| Cyrus | Artaxerxes |
| Ezra | Nehemiah |
| Jeshua | Sanballat |
| Zerubbabel | Tobiah |

**KEY VERSES:**

***Ezra 1:2–3:*** *"The LORD . . . has appointed me to build a temple . . . at Jerusalem."*

***Ezra 6:15:*** *"The temple was completed."*

***Neh. 6:15–16:*** *"The wall was completed . . . they realized that this work had been done with the help of our God."*

***Neh. 8:1–6:*** *"Ezra praised the LORD . . . and all the people . . . bowed down and worshiped the LORD."*

## Timeline

**600 BC** — **500** — **400**

- Fall of Jerusalem 587
- Fall of Babylon 539
- Zerubbabel's return and leadership 538 – 515
- Temple rebuilt 520 – 515
- Return of Ezra 458
- Return of Nehemiah 445

## Purpose

The exile serves theologically not only as God's punishment of Israel but also as his purging and purification of Israel. There may well have been those who decided that the fall of Jerusalem and the temple showed that Yahweh was weak, but the remnant who survived and owned up to their disobedience and unfaithfulness emerged a spiritually refined group. They learned reliance on God and curbed once and for all the inclination to turn to other gods. In the absence of kings, they learned to focus on God's presence as the primary feature of his kingdom.

The group that returns is ready to put the law in its proper place. They have come to recognize the law as the actual foundation of society that it was intended to be, rather than as some elusive theoretical ideal. In effect, the law becomes the characterizing feature of their society instead of a countercultural program that sought to transform society. Though they continue to yearn for a full restoration that includes their own Davidic king, they are able to turn attention to important spiritual issues. Worship becomes more focused, and the spiritual requirements of God's kingdom become more emphasized even as their hopes for the future begin to take shape. They come to a clearer sense of their identity as God's people and become more appreciative of the significance of the covenant. They embrace their heritage as initiated through Abraham and systematized in Deuteronomy.

The purpose of the books of Ezra and Nehemiah is to show the many ways that God is at work to restore the people of Israel to their land. God brings favor with the Persian rulers and helps the Israelites overcome the obstacles presented by their enemies as they rebuild the temple and the walls of Jerusalem and set up the law as the foundation of society.

Restoration is the key theme as these books trace the restoration of the temple (Ezra 1–6), the restoration of the community (Ezra 7–10), the restoration of Jerusalem (Neh. 1–7), and restoration of the covenant (Neh. 8–13).

© Dr. James C. Martin

↑ *Excavated remains of Jerusalem's "Broad Wall" showing Jerusalem's expansion west after the return of the exiles from Babylon.*

The books show intense interest in the role of the Persian kings. Most often this interest is directed toward demonstrating how God sovereignly worked through the kings to carry forward his plan of restoration. Most prominent in this is the decree of Cyrus (Ezra 1:2–4), the Persian king who permitted the Israelites to return to their land and financed the rebuilding of their temple.

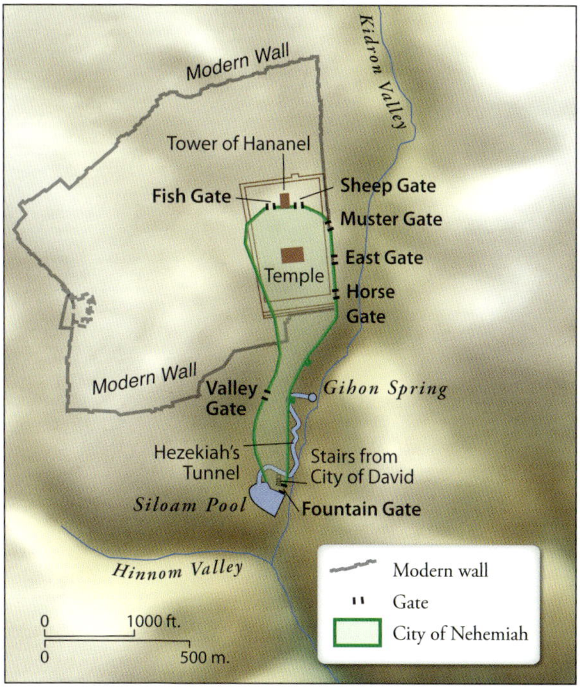


← *JERUSALEM DURING THE DAYS OF NEHEMIAH*

# Esther

© Dr. James C. Martin, Musée du Louvre

## Key Concepts

- **Chance and circumstance are fully within God's providence.**
- **Reversal and irony are evidence of God's hand in a book where he is never mentioned by name.**

← *Frieze of the Persian guard at the Susa palace—where Esther lived—dating to Xerxes' predecessor, Darius I (ca. 510 BC).*

## Key Terms

***Reversal***–When someone's fortune changes suddenly (in either direction).
***Irony***–When information the characters do not know is working against them.
***Purim***–The feast celebrating the deliverance of the Jews in the time of Esther.

## Key Teachings about God

- **God can deliver his people even if he chooses to work behind the scenes.**
- **God's means of deliverance are never exhausted.**
- **God's plans cannot be thwarted.**

## People to Know

Ahasueras (Xerxes)
Vashti
Mordecai
Haman
Esther

**KEY VERSES:**

***Est. 4:14:*** *"If you remain silent . . . deliverance . . . will arise from another place, . . .And who knows but that you have come to royal position for such a time as this?"*

***Est. 4:16:*** *"If I perish, I perish."*

***Est. 9:20–22:*** *"Mordecai recorded these events . . . as the time when the Jews got relief from their enemies . . . when their sorrow was turned into joy and their mourning into a day of celebration."*

## Timeline

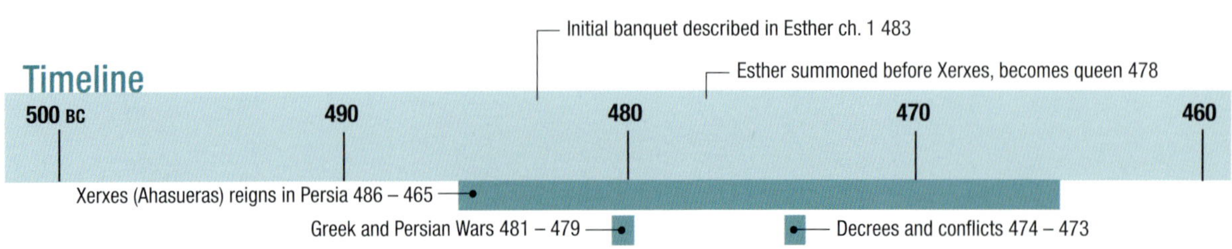

## Purpose

The purpose of the book of Esther is to show that God can accomplish his purposes just as easily through "coincidences" as he can through grand miracles of deliverance. Though he works behind the curtain to deliver his people, he is in control. Events that others see as chance or fate are seen as signs of God's sovereignty to believers. One of the most obvious ways that this purpose is demonstrated throughout the book is by the use of irony and reversal. The book thrives on hidden information:

- Haman hides the identity of the people he wishes to destroy when he procures the decree from the king.
- Esther hides her Jewish identity.
- The king hides the identity of the one he wishes to honor.
- Esther hides the reason for the banquets.
- Esther hides the identity of the people for whom she is seeking protection.
- Mordecai hides his relationship to Esther.

Irony and reversal are also seen in numerous details, for example:

- Haman thinks he is being honored by Esther when in reality he is being set up.
- Mordecai refuses to honor Haman; Haman is forced to honor Mordecai.
- Haman is hung on the gallows he had constructed for Mordecai.

The significance of the irony is that it demonstrates that there is always more going on than meets the eye and more in the works than any one individual understands or is aware of. God's control cannot be calculated, God's solution cannot be anticipated, and God's plan cannot be thwarted, because no one has all the information. God is still in the business of miracles, but more often than not, they are "miracles of circumstance," occurring behind the scenes in ways that could never be anticipated. Theologians today call this Providence. Even the absence of the name of God in the text of Esther serves to accentuate the fact that God's work is taking place behind the scenes—it is another piece of hidden information. Just as Esther hid her Jewishness, then worked behind the scenes for deliverance, so the book hid God's name, yet he worked behind the scenes for deliverance.

Finally, the book demonstrates that God is still in the business of protecting his people—even those who have not returned to the land.

↑ *Seventeenth–eighteenth century Hebrew scroll of Esther.*

↑ *Esther probably saw these capitals of the columns from the audience hall at Susa, originally built during the reign of Darius I but probably still in use during Xerxes' rule.*

← *THE PERSIAN EMPIRE*

# Job

© Dr. James C. Martin

## Key Concepts

- The fallen world does not operate by justice.
- There is such a thing as disinterested righteousness, and it is the ideal to be pursued.
- Believing that God is wise, we can trust him to be just.
- In situations of suffering, it is better to focus on the future (what *purpose* God has) rather than the past (what the *cause* of suffering is).

← *Just as Job's wealth was measured by the amount of his livestock and servants (Job 1:3), so is wealth measured by Bedouin today.*

## Key Terms

***Retribution Principle***–The belief that the righteous will prosper and the wicked will suffer. The converse was often believed, as expressed in Job, that those who are prospering must be righteous, and those who are suffering must be wicked.

***Adversary***–In the book of Job, the Hebrew word *satan* is a role, not a name, so it is best to translate it as "the adversary."

## Key Teachings about God

- God's attributes are not consistently manifested in nature.
- God delights in blessing the righteous.
- God is wise.
- God's justice is beyond our ability to assess.

## People to Know

Job
Eliphaz
Zophar
Bildad
Elihu

**KEY VERSES:**

***Job 1:8:*** *"Then the LORD said to Satan, 'Have you considered my servant Job?'"*

***Job 1:21:*** *"Naked I came from my mother's womb, and naked I will depart. The LORD gave and the LORD has taken away; may the name of the LORD be praised."*

***Job 2:10:*** *"Shall we accept good from God, and not trouble?"*

***Job 19:25–27:*** *"I know that my Redeemer lives . . . I . . . will see him with my own eyes."*

***Job 27:1–6:*** *"As surely as God lives, who has denied me justice . . . who has made me taste bitterness of soul . . . I will never admit you are in the right . . . I will maintain my righteousness and never let go of it."*

***Job 28:20–28:*** *"The fear of the Lord — that is wisdom, and to shun evil is understanding."*

***Job 38:4–11:*** *"Where were you when I laid the earth's foundation?"*

## Purpose

An important secret must be recognized to understand the book of Job. Job and his friends all believe that he is on trial, but the secret is that it is God's policies that are on trial. Satan claims that God's policy of bringing blessing on righteous people is flawed because they will then be motivated by prosperity rather than simply the desire to be righteous. When Job begins to experience suffering, he likewise concludes that God's policies are flawed if righteous people can be treated so harshly. So the question is established: How should God run the world with justice in mind and still promote true righteousness?

Job's friends think that Job must be wicked because of his suffering. Their advice reflects the standard conclusion that would be drawn in the ancient world: Deity has been offended by something and has brought punishment. They believe that whether or not Job can identify what his offense might have been, he should just take any action that will appease the anger of deity so he can get his blessings back. If Job does this, it would prove that Satan's accusation was right—Job doesn't really care about righteousness as long as he enjoys prosperity. Job refuses (Job 27:1–6).

Both Job and his friends believe that if God is just and truly runs the world, then the world must operate justly. The book builds the case, beginning in the interlude in Job 28, that the actual foundation of the operation of the world is wisdom. The justice of God's policies is what is under investigation. God does not try to defend his justice because no one is in a position to assess his justice. To assess God's justice in running the world, someone would have to have all the information about how the world is run. God's speeches make it plain that no one possesses such information (Job 40:8–14; 41:11). The conclusion of the matter and the point the book intends to make is that the world is too complex for us to be able to have all the information that we would need to affirm that God is just. We do have enough, however, to affirm that he is wise. If we believe he is wise, then we can believe he is just.

Job demonstrated that his righteousness was not simply a pursuit of blessing and prosperity. Consequently, Satan's accusation was shown to be false. God demonstrated that the operation of the cosmos was based on wisdom rather than on a simplistic sense of justice. Consequently, Job's charge of injustice was also shown to be false. God's policies were thus vindicated, and he showed his renewed commitment to doling out justice in his wisdom by again heaping blessings on Job.

God administers the world in wisdom, and from his sovereign wisdom, justice results.

↑ *Leprosy colony near Bethany in 1905.*

Courtesy of Preserving Bible Times, Inc.

# Psalms

© Dr. James C. Martin

## Key Concepts

- Many psalms are an expression of emotion, and God responds to us in our emotional highs and lows.
- Psalms is a book with purpose.
- Psalms 1–2 embody the message of the book.

← *Sheep graze in the Negev during early spring.*

## Key Terms

***Praise Psalm***–A psalm that expresses praise for who God is and what he has done. It typically does not include petitions.
***Lament Psalm***–A psalm that expresses a problem that the author would like God to address. It focuses on a petition and often includes a vow of praise in the expectation that God will answer.
***Wisdom Psalm***–A psalm addressed to people, rather than to God, that offers advice or thoughts about relating to God and understanding him.
***Royal Psalm***–A psalm that focuses on how God works through his anointed king.
***Imprecatory Psalm***–A psalm or section of a psalm in which the psalmist calls down specific curses on his enemy, indicating how his enemy would have to be treated for justice to be done.

## Key Teachings about God

- Yahweh reigns.
- God wants us to express trust in times of crisis.
- God is praiseworthy.
- God's law is a delight.
- God supports his king.
- God watches over the way of the righteous, but the way of the wicked will perish.

## People to Know

David
Solomon
Moses
Asaph
Heman
Ethan
Sons of Korah

## Purpose

The psalms were written over a thousand-year period across the whole range of Old Testament history. We find prayers to God by individuals as well as prayers designed for corporate use. Some arise out of historical or personal circumstances, while others address particular liturgical contexts.

Psalms, however, is not just a collection, it is a book. Though the psalms were often intended for prayer, we should not think of the book of Psalms being compiled as a hymnal or a book of model prayers. Not all psalms are prayers (for example, wisdom psalms are addressed to people, not to God). Even those that are prayers are not necessarily ones we can comfortably or appropriately pray (Pss. 59:10–11; 109:6–15; 137:8–9). It should also be noted that when Jesus offers his model prayer, he does not offer a psalm or point to Psalms. Though many of the psalms can be beneficially used as model prayers, either in private devotion or corporate worship, we would be mistaken to think that that is why they are in the Bible. They illustrate what Israelites prayed, but there is no biblical mandate for us to go and do likewise.

To understand the purpose of the book, we have to move beyond the reasons that motivated the composers to those that motivated the compilers, those who took 150 individual compositions and gathered them together. One suggestion is that in the book of Psalms, musical and poetic compositions have been brought together to offer an appreciation of the history of God's kingship as expressed in the Davidic covenant. This is similar to the story told in the narratives of Samuel and Kings, but there are many ways to tell a story. Some are told through narrative, others through song.

↑ *Hittite relief detailing a musical procession during the period of the Old Testament.*

The 150 psalms are arranged in five "books" that are marked in most English translations (1–41, 42–72, 73–89, 90–106, 107–150), each ending with a benediction. The theme of the book is introduced in Psalms 1–2, carried forward step by step in psalms joining the books together (41, 72, 89, 106, and 145), and then climaxed by a praise conclusion in Psalms 146–150.

Simply put, the message is, "God reigns." God is worthy of praise and is receptive to the petitions and laments of the righteous. The wise will trust in him. This is how God is revealed in the psalms. The psalms are Scripture because they portray God accurately. The reason why so many of the psalms are repeatable is because they give voice to this picture of God.

### KEY VERSES:

***Ps. 8:1:** "O LORD . . . how majestic is your name in all the earth!"*

***Ps. 19:1:** "The heavens declare the glory of God."*

***Ps. 23:1–6:** "The LORD is my shepherd, I shall not be in want."*

***Ps. 27:1:** "The LORD is my light and my salvation — whom shall I fear?"*

***Ps. 37:4:** "Delight yourself in the LORD and he will give you the desires of your heart."*

***Ps. 46:1:** "God is our refuge and strength, an ever-present help in trouble."*

***Ps. 51:10:** "Create in me a pure heart, O God, and renew a steadfast spirit within me."*

***Ps. 103:12:** "As far as the east is from the west, so far has he removed our transgressions from us."*

***Ps. 119:105:** "Your word is a lamp to my feet and a light for my path."*

***Ps. 139:14:** "I am fearfully and wonderfully made."*

# Proverbs

© Dr. James C. Martin

## Key Concepts

- Proverbs are general statements that affirm godly values and virtues.
- There are two ways, and the way of wisdom is to be chosen over the path to destruction.
- Wisdom is the foundation of a godly life.
- We show wisdom in the way we speak and the way we interact with others.

← *"Lazy hands make a man poor, but diligent hands bring wealth" (Proverbs 10:4). Industrious workers cutting alabaster into vessels.*

## Key Terms

***Wisdom***–That sense or insight which brings order to every aspect of life because one understands the proper place of God.

***Fool***–One who shows the lack of good judgment and an inability to live in consistent, integrated ways. The fool chooses to act in ways that suggest he does not believe God will act.

***Wife of Noble Character***–The description in Proverbs 31:10–31 is intended not to give an ideal profile of what every woman should be but a composite profile of what would constitute wise behavior in various female activities.

***Retribution Principle***–The belief that those who are righteous will prosper and those who are wicked suffer.

## Key Teachings about God

- God is wise and delights in the pursuit of wisdom, the imitation of him.
- God does not tolerate fools.
- God directs the path of those who trust him.
- God expects disciplined living.

## Person to Know

Solomon

**KEY VERSES:**

***Prov. 3:5–6:*** *"Trust in the Lord with all your heart and lean not on your own understanding; in all your ways acknowledge him, and he will make your paths straight."*

***Prov. 8:22–31:*** *"I [wisdom] was appointed . . . from the beginning, before the world began."*

***Prov. 9:10:*** *"The fear of the Lord is the beginning of wisdom."*

## Purpose

Wisdom literature does not operate like the commands of the law or the plot of narrative. It is not set forth as "Thus says the Lord" as in the prophets, nor is it even like the exhortations of the New Testament letters.

The first important point to establish is that a proverb by definition is a generalization. A generalization is considered useful when it is true most of the time and so reflects a value that can be affirmed. A generalization does not offer a guarantee or a promise. For instance, we consider the proverbial statement "Crime doesn't pay" to be true. The adage is a generalization, and we accept it as that.

Biblical proverbs work in much the same way. When Proverbs 22:6 states, "Train a child in the way he should go, and when he is old he will not turn from it," it is not making a promise or offering a guarantee. It is generally true that children will adopt in large measure the values they were raised with. As a proverb it advises the wise parent to raise a child well, and it offers a sense of confidence that the result will be a responsible adult ready to pass the value system on to the next generation.

Sometimes proverbs seem to present contradictory perspectives. Consider:

- He who hesitates is lost.
- Look before you leap.

Each is true in certain situations. The Old Testament has a similar example in Proverbs 26:4–5:

- v. 4: "Do not answer a fool according to his folly, or you will be like him yourself."
- v. 5: "Answer a fool according to his folly, or he will be wise in his own eyes."

Again, the wise person knows which advice to follow in each situation.

Dr. James C. Martin, The Cairo Museum

*← Schools for training select young people existed from early times. Proverbs such as those in this book likely would have been copied over and over.*

Proverbs not only teach wisdom but require a certain level of wisdom when applied. Wise words must be used wisely by wise people in order to result in wisdom. Proverbs says as much when it observes: "Like a lame man's legs that hang limp is a proverb in the mouth of a fool" (Prov. 26:7).

The purpose of Proverbs is to collect the wisdom of ancient Israel, offering insight into the wisdom that results from fear of the Lord. This wisdom functioned to shape character and develop virtue and was intended to promote a secure and functional family and society, both founded on fear of the Lord, which is to be at the center of their worldview.

*↓ JERUSALEM FROM DAVID TO SOLOMON*

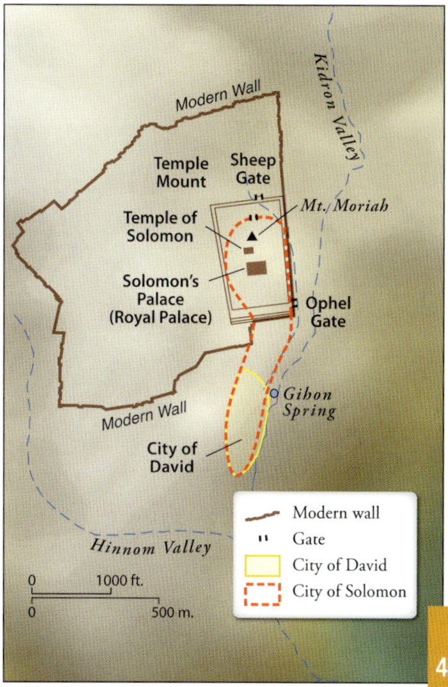

# Ecclesiastes

## Key Concepts

- We should not expect to find "meaning in life" or to experience self-fulfillment in life.
- The author is not talking about what should be pursued in a faith/covenant context but what should not be pursued from a worldly perspective.
- We are to enjoy life's good times as gifts from God's hand and accept adversity.

← *Shekels from Tyre. "Whoever loves money never has money enough" (Ecclesiastes 5:10).*



## Key Terms

***Meaningless***–Everything "under the sun" is described as meaningless. It is the opposite of self-fulfillment.
***Qoheleth***–The Hebrew title used for the one whose wisdom is represented in Ecclesiastes. The basic translation of the word suggests "one who gathers." It is uncertain what is being gathered (e.g., disciples, wisdom sayings, perspectives, experiences).
***Inclusio***–A literary device that uses a word or phrase to frame a discussion. In Ecclesiastes the inclusio is the phrase "Meaningless, meaningless, . . . everything is meaningless," which occurs in 1:2 and 12:8.
***"Under the sun"***–The author's way of referring to our temporal lives in this world—our experience in this life.

## Key Teachings about God

- God brings prosperity and adversity.
- God is in control of the "times" of life.

**KEY VERSES:**

***Eccl. 3:1–8:*** *"There is a time for everything . . . a time to be born and a time to die."*

***Eccl. 3:11:*** *"He has made everything beautiful in its time. He has also set eternity in the hearts of men."*

***Eccl. 7:14:*** *"When times are good, be happy; but when times are bad, consider: God has made the one as well as the other."*

***Eccl. 9:11:*** *"The race is not to the swift or the battle to the strong."*

## Purpose

Ecclesiastes is one of the most difficult books in the Bible to read and to understand. Its subject is the meaning of life. It investigates the validity of the common quest to find meaning in life "under the sun" or, as we would say, "in this life." The answer is that each path pursued (wisdom, wealth, pleasure, power, legacy) has several potential drawbacks:

- It proves an unworthy pursuit.
- It is unachievable (i.e., no matter how much of it you get, there is always more to get).
- In the end you die anyway, so what is the point?

The author therefore adopts the radical conclusion that there is no sense of self-fulfillment that can bring meaning to life, so the best choice is to stop pursuing self-fulfillment. The alternative he offers is the pursuit of a God-centered life. Even though pursuits under the sun may not be capable of providing self-fulfillment or giving meaning to life, much in life can be enjoyed when understood as the gift of God.

The book recognizes that there are many things in life that cannot be enjoyed and would not be called gifts. Ecclesiastes 3:1–8 lays out some of these as contrasts in our experiences that can often result in frustration. Whether our frustrations in life are great or small, the book establishes that we dare not entertain the idea that life without frustrations is possible. We must adjust our expectations accordingly. Both prosperity and adversity come from the hand of God (Eccl. 7:14). No one's life is problem free. Ecclesiastes teaches that, without being fatalistic, we ought to adjust our thinking to absorb or even embrace the difficult trials that life brings our way.

↑ *"A time to plant and a time to uproot" (Ecclesiastes 3:2). Farmers plowing up their field in 1905.*

Courtesy of Preserving Bible Times, Inc.

To summarize the message of Ecclesiastes: Find enjoyment in the gifts of God. It will not suffice to think that "normal" is when everything is going well in life. Both prosperity and adversity are normal and come from his hand; both can shape us in important ways. It is normal that we have times of difficulty because it is a broken world and, ultimately, death is the final result. Life is not under our control. If we lower our expectations, we can increase our contentment. There is no sure path to self-fulfillment. Since self-fulfillment cannot be obtained, it should not be pursued.

The fear of the Lord is the beginning of wisdom. Fear of the Lord and wisdom, not meaning in life through self-fulfillment, are worthy pursuits.

# Song of Songs

© Dr. James C. Martin

## Key Concepts

- **Love and sex are powerful forces in our lives.**
- **Wisdom will result in discipline and an understanding of appropriate timing in love.**

← *Solomon's beloved took care of the vineyards (Song of Songs 1:6). Grapevines in antiquity grew on the ground and required special attention to prevent the grapes from mildew.*

## Key Terms

***Love Poetry***–This type of literature exists throughout the ancient world. In Song of Songs, it is erotic, often subtly so, whereas in the larger ancient world it is at times more graphic, even bawdy. Love poetry was sometimes used in the context of fertility festivals and would generally evoke feelings of passion whatever one's sociological situation might be.

***Allegory***–Use of symbolism to suggest a deeper or hidden meaning. Allegorizing takes place in the mind of the interpreter without obvious intention on the part of the author to create an allegory. Jewish allegorists viewed the book as concerning Yahweh's relationship to Israel. Christian allegorists saw in it Christ's love for the church.

## Key Teaching about God

- **God is not mentioned, but we can infer that he created love and sexuality for our enjoyment, yet he expects us to be wise and disciplined.**

## Person to Know

Solomon

**KEY VERSES:**

***Song 2:7:*** *"Do not arouse or awaken love until it so desires."*

***Song 8:6–7:*** *"Love is as strong as death . . . it burns like a blazing fire . . . many waters cannot quench love."*

## Purpose

The most common interpretation of Song of Songs in both Jewish and Christian circles has been an allegorical one. In this approach the Song is really about God's love for his people Israel (Jewish interpretation) or Christ's love for the church (Christian interpretation). The obvious difficulty to this approach is that the conclusions are subjective—only imagination can provide the details.

Interpreters commonly construct a plot that runs beneath the poetry. Such constructions tend to create a moralizing story around the lives of Solomon and a woman he loves, sometimes bringing in a third-party shepherd boy whom the woman loves. Again the difficulty is that we are forced to read too much between the lines.

No moralistic story is necessary to provide the teaching of the book—it contains love songs with a number of observable and important themes. When Song of Songs talks about love, it emphasizes the necessity that love be kept under control despite the passion, the longing, and the anticipation. These characteristics must be controlled because they give love power over a person. That power can work in positive ways to overcome the obstacles of circumstance or in negative ways as it breaks through barriers of propriety. Love has this power whether applied to young unmarried sweethearts, those who are betrothed, newlyweds, or those married for decades. Its power is not only evident when the flames are burning but when the flames are dying. This power is addressed directly in Song of Songs 8:6–7: "Love is as strong as death, its jealousy unyielding as the grave. It burns like blazing fire, like a mighty flame. Many waters cannot quench love; rivers cannot wash it away. If one were to give all the wealth of his house for love, it would be utterly scorned."

The love songs preserved in this book illustrate different faces of love's power. A wise person must be aware of that power and recognize its faces and its dangers. So in that sense, this is a wisdom book. Love and sex wield incredible power, and the wise person will understand that and learn to harness and discipline that area of life.

*This terracotta plaque of an affectionate couple from Ur (2000–1700 BC) is a reminder of the Song of Songs, "Your love is more delightful than wine" (Song of Songs 1:2).*

# Isaiah

© Dr. James C. Martin, The British Museum

## Key Concepts

- Kings who trusted alliances brought on disaster, while kings who trusted God experienced deliverance.
- Prophecy is not simply prediction of the future, it is God's revelation of himself, his requirements, and his plan.
- It is important to have confidence in God's plan and trust him to carry it out.

← *Assyrians used impaling rods—a precursor of crucifixion later used by Persians, Greeks, and Romans.*

## Key Terms

***Branch***–A term describing the future ideal king from David's line (11:1).

***Remnant***–Used in various ways throughout the Old Testament. Sometimes refers to those who survive a catastrophic invasion, sometimes to those who are left in the land after many are deported, sometimes to those who are deported and in exile. Theologically Isaiah has in mind a faithful remnant who stayed true to the covenant and therefore are brought back from exile to begin the restoration.

***Servant of the Lord***–There are four sections in Isaiah 41–53 that talk about an individual in this way, with a variety of opinions on identifying him. Sometimes it seems that he is Cyrus, other times a corporate group in Israel. Some have seen the characteristics of Moses or, specifically, the prophet like Moses who is to come. Many (including New Testament authors) see the role as fulfilled in Jesus. In Isaiah, the role played by the Servant is similar to that played by the ideal Davidic king, so it is easy to conclude that the Servant is a royal figure.

## Key Teachings about God

- God is planning to raise up an ideal king from David's line and elevate Jerusalem through his reign of peace.
- God is trustworthy.
- God is more powerful than even the greatest empires and armies.
- Yahweh is God—there is no other.
- God has a plan and is capable of accomplishing that plan.
- God's solutions are often unexpected.
- God persists in warning his people even after they have stopped paying attention.

## Timeline

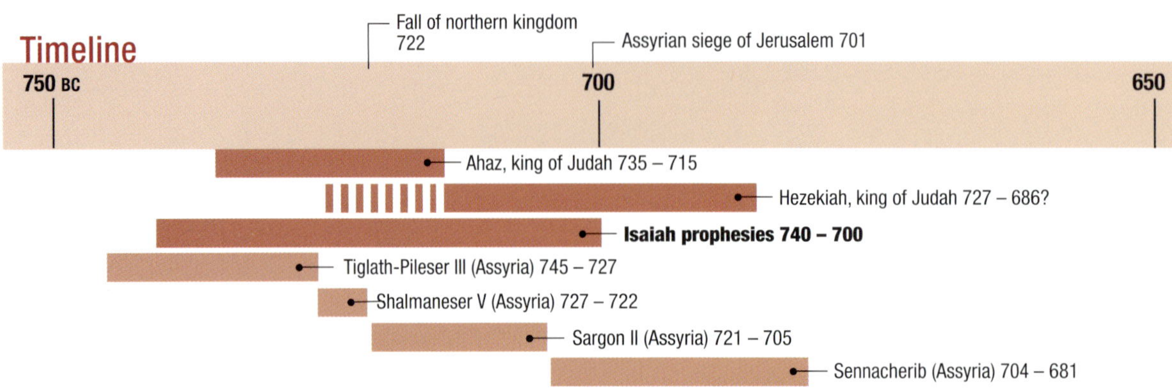

## Purpose

While early prophets dealt primarily with the king, in the eighth century BC the prophets turn much of their attention to the people and begin to call them to a renewed faithfulness to the covenant. As the monarchy period progresses, the covenant blessings are increasingly in jeopardy. The prophets, as defenders of the covenant, announce the covenant violations of the people and king and give warning that the covenant curses are about to be enacted. Their messages gradually begin to include indications that Samaria or Jerusalem will be destroyed and the people taken captive as enemies conquer and overrun the land.

In this way the Assyrian and Babylonian empires are seen as instruments under the control of Yahweh. If Israel trusts God, relying on him and being faithful to the covenant, he is able to deliver them from the fiercest and largest of enemies. This is demonstrated in the Assyrian siege of Jerusalem under Sennacherib when Hezekiah, advised by the prophet Isaiah, trusts Yahweh in the face of overwhelming disaster and sees his mighty deliverance. On the other hand, if they rely on their own strength and political alliances, or if they seek to achieve peace by compromising their faithfulness to Yahweh, they are swept away. In the ancient world, turning to other nations was the same as turning to the gods of those nations.

The purpose of the book of Isaiah demonstrates the trustworthiness of the Lord. The first king whom Isaiah serves, Ahaz, does not trust the Lord. He ignores Isaiah's advice and follows his own schemes. This leads to defeat and servitude at the hands of the Assyrians. Ahaz's son Hezekiah, in contrast, trusts the Lord and Jerusalem is delivered from Sennacherib and the Assyrians. In the second half of the book the exiles are also encouraged to trust the Lord to bring deliverance and to respond like Hezekiah, not like Ahaz.

A significant theme is the hope in a future ideal Davidic king. The book provides a template for Messianic expectation as it develops a profile of God's plan, including the exaltation of Jerusalem (ch. 2), the coming child who is to reign (ch. 9), peace and stability of the reign of the Davidic heir (ch. 11), and how the ideal Servant of the Lord will carry out God's mission (chs. 42–53).

### People to Know

| | |
|---|---|
| Isaiah | Sennacherib |
| Ahaz | Merodach-Baladan |
| Hezekiah | |

↑ *The Sennacherib inscription confirms biblical history as it provides details of how he attacked Jerusalem and had Hezekiah "like a bird in a cage."*

↓ *ASSYRIAN INVASIONS OF THE PROMISED LAND*

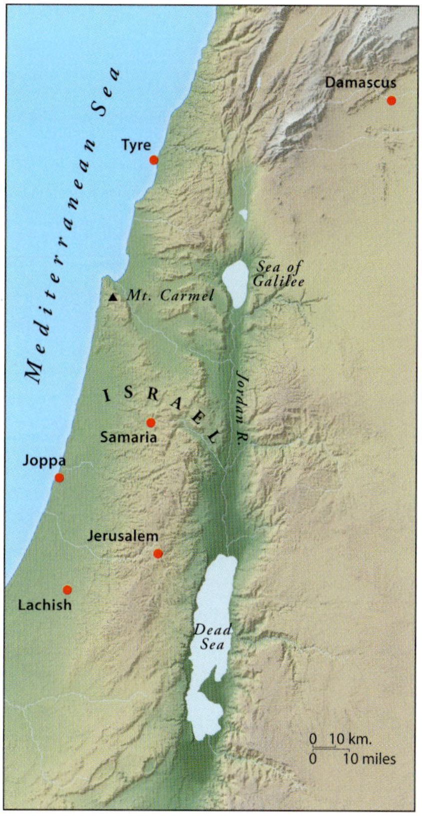


**KEY VERSES:**

***Isa. 1:16–20:*** *"Though your sins are like scarlet, they shall be as white as snow."*

***Isa. 6:1–8:*** *"Holy, holy, holy is the LORD Almighty; the whole earth is full of his glory."*

***Isa. 9:6–7:*** *"For to us a child is born, to us a son is given."*

***Isa. 40:1–5:*** *"A voice of one calling: 'In the desert prepare the way for the LORD.'"*

***Isa. 43:2:*** *"When you pass through the waters, I will be with you."*

***Isa. 53:1–6:*** *"We all, like sheep, have gone astray … and the LORD has laid on him the iniquity of us all."*

***Isa. 55:6–7:*** *"Seek the LORD while he may be found; call on him while he is near."*

***Isa. 65:17–19:*** *"Behold, I will create new heavens and a new earth."*

# Jeremiah

© Dr. James C. Martin

## Key Concepts

- The presence of the temple will not shield the people of Judah from God's judgment through the Babylonians.
- The covenant was broken and judgment (covenant curses) will come about.
- Restoration will not come for Israel until after judgment.
- The new covenant continues God's revelation of himself by providing forgiveness of sin.

← *Site of Lachish. Jeremiah's warning to king Zedekiah of Judah took place "while the army of the king of Babylon was fighting against Jerusalem and the other cities of Judah that were still holding out—Lachish and Azekah" (Jeremiah 34:7).*

## Key Terms

***Disaster from the North***–Jeremiah's way of referring to an invader who will bring widespread destruction. This designation is quite ambiguous because anyone coming from the east (Mesopotamian nations of Assyrian or Babylonia) would go northwest along the Euphrates River before turning and coming south into Israel.

***Oracles against the Nations***–All of the major prophets and a few of the minor prophets feature oracles of judgment against a number of nations, small and great. These were not generally proclaimed to these nations, but were declared to Israel to give the people a sense of hope and of God's sovereignty.

***New Covenant***–A new stage of God's agreement with his people whereby he will be revealed through the law in their hearts. This will enable improved knowledge of God and forgiveness of sins.

## Key Teachings about God

- God's ways and God's plans are not always easy to understand.
- God is not conflicted by vested interests; that is, he does not slavishly protect his temple, his chosen city (Jerusalem), or his chosen people.
- God has a new covenant planned for his people.

## Timeline

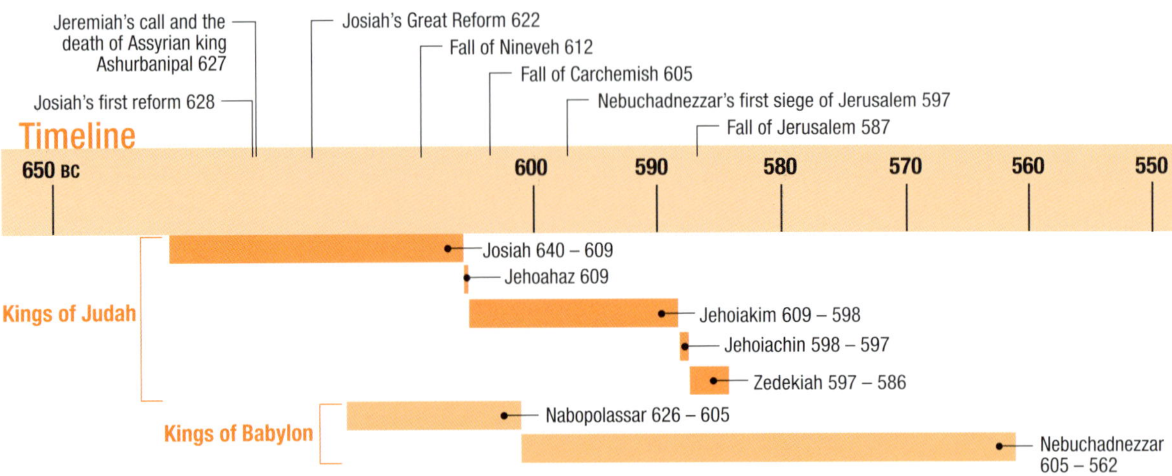

## Purpose

God calls Jeremiah to his prophetic ministry at a critical moment in the ancient world. The Assyrian Empire, which has dominated Israel and the rest of the Near East for almost 150 years, is on the verge of collapse. The Babylonian kingdom, the next major empire, is gaining power. At the same time, Josiah, the godly young king of Judah, has come of age and is beginning to institute sweeping spiritual reforms meant to drive the people back to covenant faithfulness. Jeremiah stands as the prophetic voice in this dramatic window of opportunity.

Jeremiah calls the people of Judah back to faithful dependence on the Lord. He warns them of impending exile at the hands of a foe "from the north" who he eventually identifies as the Babylonians. Jeremiah is given a mandate in 1:10: "Today I appoint you over nations and kingdoms to *uproot* and *tear down*, to *destroy* and *overthrow*, to *build* and to *plant*" (emphasis added). These six verbs define Jeremiah's role as champion of the covenant.

As champion of the covenant, Jeremiah addresses the covenant made with Abraham and with Moses as he warns the people about the imminent loss of land and decimation of the nation. These are among the curses laid out through Moses if the people are unfaithful to the covenant. Jeremiah is commonly known as the weeping prophet because of his dismay at the message of judgment that he is obligated to bring to his people, who are now poised precariously on the brink of destruction.

But his message does not stop there. He also addresses the Davidic covenant as he offers hope of a future ideal ruler from David's line. But perhaps his greatest contribution is found in his proclamation of the new covenant (31:31–33). As history unfolds, this prophecy becomes the basis of the covenant initiated by Christ with his church. Consequently, even though the book ends with an account of the destruction of Jerusalem, it gives reason for hope to be rekindled, even from the flames of destruction.

© Dr. James C. Martin, The British Museum

↑ *Examples of some of the twenty-one Lachish letters written during the Babylonian invasion of Judah that ultimately resulted in the destruction of the Jerusalem temple in 586 BC.*

### People to Know

| | |
|---|---|
| Jeremiah | Zedekiah |
| Baruch | Hananiah |
| Nebuchadnezzar | Ebed-Melech |
| Jehoiakim | |

**KEY VERSES:**

***Jer. 1:10:*** *"I appoint you over nations and kingdoms to uproot and tear down . . . to build and to plant."*

***Jer. 4:1–2:*** *"'Return to me,' declares the Lord . . . 'then the nations will be blessed.'"*

***Jer. 29:11:*** *"For I know the plans I have for you . . . plans to prosper you and not to harm you, plans to give you hope and a future."*

***Jer. 31:31–33:*** *"The time is coming . . . when I will make a new covenant . . . I will put my law in their minds and write it on their hearts."*

←*THE BABYLONIAN INVASION OF THE PROMISED LAND*

# Lamentations

© Dr. James C. Martin, The British Museum

## Key Concepts

- **Lament targets not only one's situation but one's spiritual condition.**
- **Any circumstance in life can provide an opportunity to know God better.**

← *The first deportation of Israelites occurred in 734 BC under the Assyrian ruler Tiglath-Pileser III (745–727 BC). The later exile of Jewish inhabitants of Judah took place under the Babylonian ruler Nebuchadnezzar around 586 BC.*

## Key Term

***Lamentations over Fallen Cities***–In the ancient world there are a number of examples of lamentations written concerning the fall of cities when they were abandoned by the patron deity.

## Key Teachings about God

- **God's wrath is terrible.**
- **God is righteous and will judge.**
- **God's faithfulness and compassion never fail.**
- **God is good to those who hope in him.**

**KEY VERSES:**

***Lam. 2:17:*** *"The Lord has done what he planned; he has fulfilled his word."*

***Lam. 3:22–25:*** *"Because of the Lord's great love we are not consumed, for his compassions never fail. They are new every morning; great is your faithfulness. . . .The Lord is good to those whose hope is in him, to the one who seeks him."*

***Lam. 5:15–22:*** *"The crown has fallen from our head. Woe to us, for we have sinned!"*

## Purpose

Lamentations is not connected to a particular prophet, though tradition sees it as composed by Jeremiah. It records a number of funeral songs for Jerusalem that express the sadness of the people of Judah over the tragedy of the city's destruction in 586 BC. The people weep from the feeling that God has abandoned them. The poems show the people's sense of guilt, confession, and repentance as they realize how deeply they have hurt God by their sin and unfaithfulness.

The laments express the full impact of the covenant curses and prophetic pronouncements of judgment as the horror of the people's loss is realized. The city was the place God had chosen for his temple to be built and his presence to be manifest. Its destruction represents not only the loss of homes and life but also the abandonment of the people by God. He withdrew his presence and his favor as he said he would if the people were unfaithful.

The highlight of the book is in chapter 3 where, in first-person form, the full grief of the poet is revealed. He gives voice to the despair of the corporate people and the personified city. But at the bottom of his grief he turns to the unfailing faithfulness of the Lord and his compassion toward his people. The call to repentance anticipates God's acts of deliverance and mercy for his people and judgment on the enemies who carried out the destruction. The book ends in a fervent prayer for restoration.

←Seal inscription: "Belonging to Gemaryahu ben Shaphan." Discovered in the ruins resulting from Babylon's destruction of Jerusalem during the time of Jeremiah, this burned seal inscription contains names mentioned in Jeremiah 29:3 and is a reminder of Jeremiah's lamentation of Jerusalem.

→A nineteenth-century painting with Hebrew inscription depicts Jeremiah among the sanctuary ruins as the Jews were deported to Babylon by King Nebuchadnezzar.

# Ezekiel

## Key Concepts

- The people of Israel will be reborn.
- God will return to again dwell among his people.
- There will be a new covenant between God and his people.
- Israel will know that Yahweh is God.

← *Human bones inside the tomb adjacent to the pyramids near Cairo are reminders of Ezekiel's prophecy of the gathering of dry bones (Ezekiel 37).*



## Key Terms

***Sign-acts***–A number of Ezekiel's oracles consisted of dramatic performances, some in pantomime, some using limited props, in order to act out the message.

***Valley of Dry Bones***–A vision of Ezekiel's that symbolizes a nation that is dead coming back to life.

***Watchman***–Ezekiel's role as a prophet is described as a watchman who looks for coming trouble and warns the people.

## Key Teachings about God

- God holds individual generations responsible for their sin.
- God does not need a place for his residence, and he revokes the privilege of his presence if his people are faithless.
- God is the sanctuary for his people.

**KEY VERSES:**

***Ezek. 12:15–16:*** *"They will know that I am the Lord."*

***Ezek. 18:25–32:*** *"Repent! Turn away from all your offenses . . . get a new heart and a new spirit."*

***Ezek. 36:22–23:*** *"It is not for your sake . . . but for the sake of my holy name."*

## Timeline

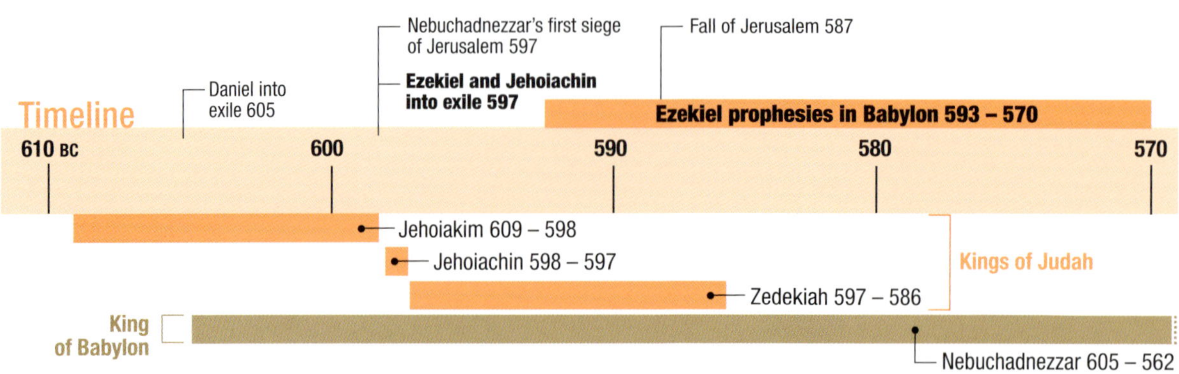

## Purpose

When Ezekiel began his ministry, Jeremiah had already been prophesying for almost 35 years. Jeremiah lived through the reforms of Josiah, experienced the disappointment of the king's death in battle, and then witnessed the collapse of Judah through the unfaithfulness of Josiah's sons—all from his "front-row seat" in Jerusalem. In contrast, Ezekiel was taken into exile in the first major deportation in 597 BC and was ministering among the exiles living on the outskirts of Babylon. During the early years of his ministry, the temple and the city of Jerusalem still stood, but many of the people were already experiencing the hardships and disappointments of exile.

Ezekiel tells the Israelites that destruction of the city of Jerusalem is coming because the Lord's presence is about to leave the temple, exposing the people to Babylonian invasion. In fact, the temple and city are destroyed halfway into the book. After that happens, Ezekiel turns his attention to the hope for the future, including declaring the formation of a new covenant, just as his contemporary Jeremiah had. He anticipates the time when the people will wake up and return to the Lord. In his vision of the valley of dry bones (ch. 37), Ezekiel sees a people reborn. But one of the most important themes in the book is to be found in the oft-repeated refrain, "Then you will know that I am the LORD." This refrain urges the people to gain a new appreciation of the attributes that constitute God's holiness. Whether they are experiencing judgment or trusting in future deliverance and hope, knowing God is the important end result.

In the distressing aftermath of the fall of Jerusalem and the destruction of the temple, Ezekiel tells of a future restoration, including a vision of a glorious new temple. All of this anticipates a time when God's presence will return to the temple (chs. 40–48) and the greatest heritage of the covenant will be restored: The name of the city will be Yahweh Shammah (meaning "the LORD is there").

↑ *The Ishtar Gate in Babylon.*



↓ *EZEKIEL IN BABYLON*

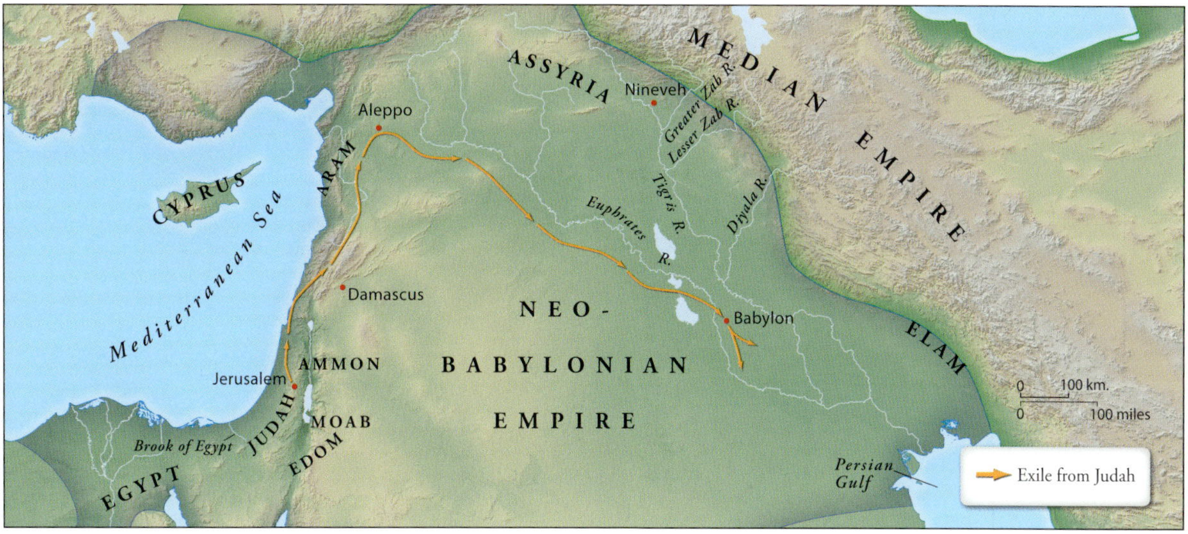

# Daniel

© Dr. James C. Martin

## Key Concepts

- Daniel uses his training to develop knowledge and skills that God in turn draws on to use Daniel in his service.
- Even the most powerful and successful kings the world has known acknowledge the sovereignty of Yahweh.

← *Excavated remains of Belshazzar's palace in Babylon, where the writing on the wall occurred (Daniel 5).*

## Key Terms

***Cosmic Tree***–In the ancient world they often imagined a tree at the center of the world that had its top branches in the heavens and its roots in the netherworld. It was the source of provision and protection for the creatures of the world. This probably is the tree in Nebuchadnezzar's dream in chapter 4.

***Four-Empire Scheme***–It was common to systematically arrange world history by thinking in terms of four successive empires.

***Seventy Sevens***–In chapter 9 it is likely that this designation refers to weeks of seven-year periods, thus seventy sevens would equal 490 years.

***Divination***–A process through which the king's advisers aid the king. Signs were sought or investigated as a means to understand what the gods were doing and to decide on a course of action. Part of divination was the interpretation of dreams.

## Key Teachings about God

- God is sovereign over the kingdoms of the world.
- God is able to deliver but offers no guarantees that he will do so in every instance.
- The future is in God's hands and under his sovereign control.

## People to Know

Daniel
Shadrach
Meshach
Abednego
Nebuchadnezzar
Belshazzar
Nabonidus
Darius the Mede
Antiochus Epiphanes
Gabriel
Michael

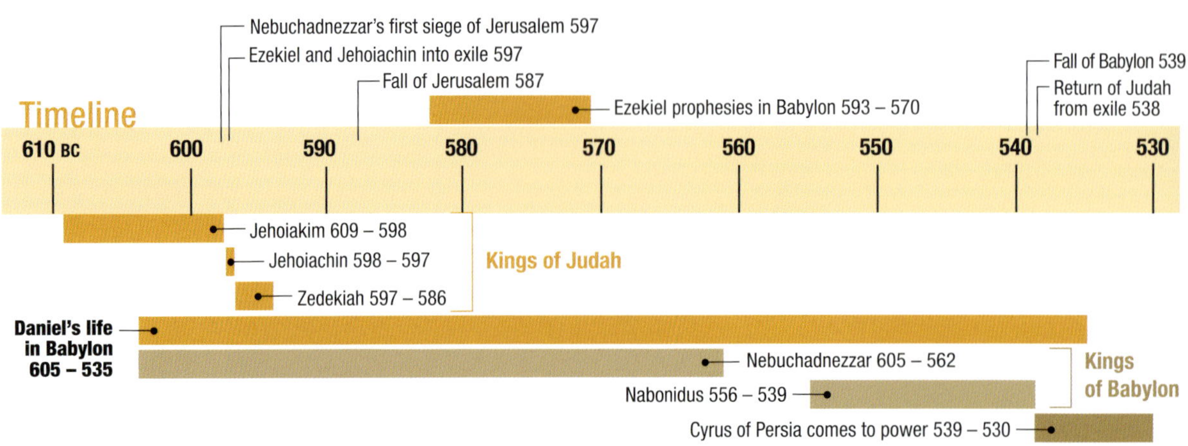

## Purpose

Daniel is set in the sixth century BC while Israel is in exile. Daniel and his friends have been taken into exile as young men who are to be educated as diplomats and scholars in the court of Babylon. Though their training immerses them in the Babylonian worldview, culture, literature, and religion, they remain faithful to God and stand as witnesses to, and sometimes illustrations of, his sovereignty over even the greatest empire the world had known.

People in the ancient world would have been inclined to think that Israel's defeat indicated the weakness of their God in relation to the great Babylonian Empire and its powerful gods. The purpose of the book of Daniel is to illustrate and proclaim the sovereignty of Israel's God. As Daniel and his friends trust the Lord, God shows himself able to protect and deliver them. At the same time, they have ample opportunity to declare God's sovereignty as he demonstrates his power over the kings and gods of Babylon. On a variety of occasions Nebuchadnezzar honors Daniel and his friends (2:46; 3:28), praises Israel's God (3:28; 4:34–37), and commands that God be honored (3:29). At the end of Daniel's career, Darius the Mede goes so far as to command reverence for Daniel's God throughout the empire. Daniel's visions likewise proclaim God's sovereignty over kings, nations, and empires. His prophecies tell the people of Israel that the kingdom they were waiting for would be longer in coming than expected. In the meantime, they are to live out their faith in the midst of an unbelieving world, trusting in God for deliverance and protection as Daniel and his friends had.

The central message is summarized in the decree of Darius after the lions' den incident when he declares of Yahweh: "He is the living God and he endures forever; his kingdom will not be destroyed, his dominion will never end. He rescues and he saves; he performs signs and wonders in the heavens and on the earth" (6:26–27).

↑ *This basalt stella represents Nabonidus (555–539 BC), the last ruler of the Neo-Babylonian empire during the time of Daniel.*



**KEY VERSES:**

***Dan. 1:20:** "In every matter of wisdom and understanding … he found them ten times better."*

***Dan. 2:20–23:** "Praise be to the name of God for ever and ever … he changes times and seasons; he sets up kings and deposes them."*

***Dan. 3:17–18:** "If we are thrown into the blazing furnace, the God we serve is able to save us from it.… But even if he does not … we will not serve your gods."*

***Dan. 4:34–35:** "I, Nebuchadnezzar, raised my eyes toward heaven, and my sanity was restored. Then I praised the Most High."*

***Dan. 6:26–27:** "He is the living God and he endures forever.… He has rescued Daniel from the power of the lions."*

↓ *THE BABYLONIAN AND MEDIAN KINGDOMS*

# Hosea and Amos

## Key Concepts

- Loving God and being compassionate and merciful to those around you are the values most desired by God.
- Israel is guilty of syncretism and injustice.
- The key theme of the prophets concerns whether the people will respond to God's warnings and instructions.

← *A farmer works in his orchard in the hill country of Judah outside of Tekoa, the hometown of the prophet Amos.*



## Key Terms

***Baal Worship***–"Baal" is the title of the Canaanite god Hadad, the storm god associated with fertility. Israel was predominantly an agrarian society that often turned to Baal in hope of procuring good harvests.

***Syncretism***–Mixing together of elements from different religions. Israel brought in Canaanite Baal worship alongside their worship of Yahweh. If they treated Yahweh as if he were like the gods of the other nations, that would also be syncretism.

## Key Teachings about God

- God is faithful even when his people are not.
- God disciplines his people, at times harshly, for their reclamation.
- God is the one responsible for providing.
- God desires to be in relationship with people.
- God's justice is tempered by his mercy, not eliminated by it.
- God expects his people to be proactive in working for social justice.

## Timeline

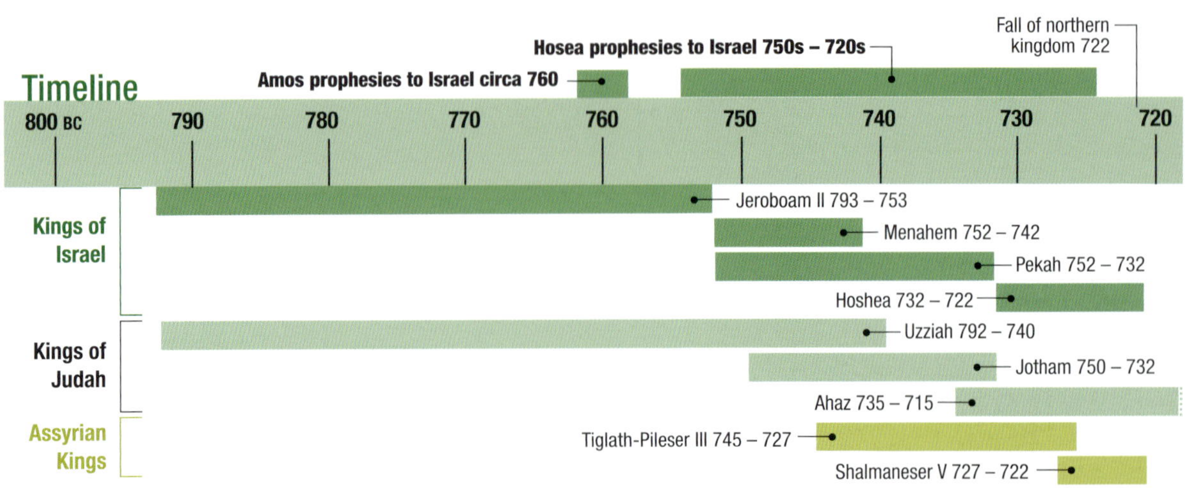

## Purpose

Amos and Hosea are the only two writing prophets in the Old Testament who focus on the northern kingdom of Israel. A generation earlier Elisha and, before him, Elijah, had likewise targeted the northern kingdom. Amos and Hosea are the earliest of the writing prophets and are the first of the classical prophets (see Micah for explanation). Both begin in the days of Jeroboam II (793–753 BC), but Amos prophesies for a very brief period, while Hosea may continue almost to the fall of the northern kingdom in 722 BC.

Jeroboam II brought a time of prosperity unparalleled since the glorious days of Solomon—both politically and economically. Amos and Hosea expose the fragile nature of this prosperity that will be shattered in the sudden change that will occur with the emergence of the Assyrian Empire (745 BC). The judgment of God on the nations—including Israel and Judah—is fast approaching.

Amos identifies the offenses of Israel in his fiery condemnation of the injustice of their society. Evidence appears in the moral and social collapse, political corruption, and religious apostasy. He urges the people to do what is right and to reform society.

Hosea is more concerned with the unfaithfulness of Israel to the Lord and to the covenant. The symbolism of Hosea's marriage to an unfaithful wife is used as a metaphor of God's covenant with unfaithful Israel. Despite the numerous proclamations of judgment, Hosea is filled with love language as the Lord yearns for a renewed relationship with his people. The book also offers significant glimpses of hope and restoration.

Sadly, there was no response from the people, and within a generation the northern kingdom collapsed under the weight of Assyrian imperialism. The "day of the Lord" that the people anticipated as one that would bring fulfillment of the covenant blessings brought instead the full weight of the covenant curses, as they were carried off into captivity and their land left in ruin.

*← The destruction of Israel by the Assyrians prophesied by Hosea and Amos is likely verified by these inlaid furniture ivories discovered in an Assyrian palace, most probably remnants of the spoils that the Assyrians took from places such as Ahab's palace at Samaria.*



### People to Know

- Hosea
- Gomer
- Amos
- Amaziah
- Jeroboam

**KEY VERSES:**

***Hos. 6:6:*** *"For I desire mercy, not sacrifice, and acknowledgment of God rather than burnt offerings."*

***Hos. 13:14:*** *"I will ransom them from the power of the grave; I will redeem them from death."*

***Amos 5:14–15:*** *"Hate evil, love good; maintain justice in the courts."*

***Amos 5:24:*** *"Let justice roll on like a river, righteousness like a never-failing stream!"*

***Amos 9:11–15:*** *"'The days are coming,' declares the Lord … 'I will plant Israel in their own land, never again to be uprooted.'"*

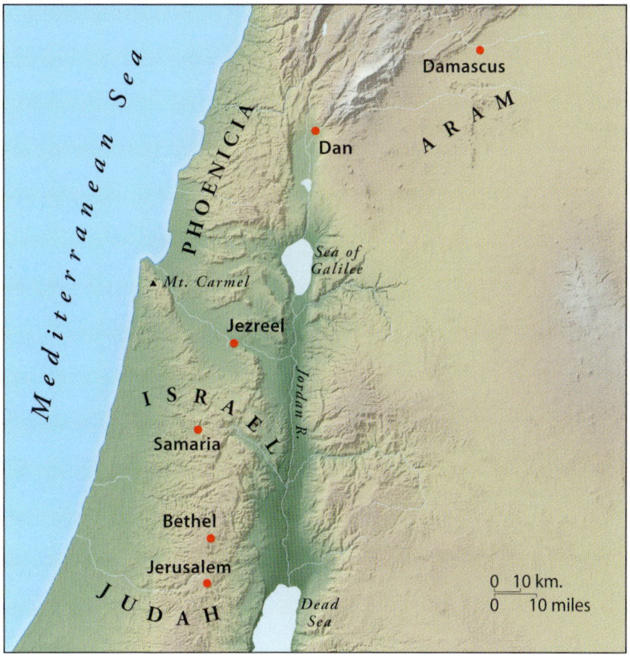


*← THE NORTHERN KINGDOM OF ISRAEL*

# Joel and Obadiah

© Dr. James C. Martin

## Key Concepts

- Natural disasters (like the locust plague in Joel) can serve as the judgment of God, but not all who suffer the consequences should therefore be judged guilty. Such disasters draw our attention to God and stimulate us to self-examination.
- The day of judgment is to be feared, and therefore should motivate us to change our ways.
- Prophecy is more important for what it reveals about God than for what it reveals about the future. Fulfillment is sure, but the message is primary.

← *The mountains of Edom. Joel proclaims destruction on Edom "because of the violence done to Judah, in whose land they shed innocent blood" (Joel 3:19).*

## Key Terms

***Prophecy***–God's proclamation of his plan, whether it refers to past, present, or future.

***Day of the Lord***–A time when the current state of affairs will be replaced with the Lord's intended order—a time of justice and covenant fulfillment. This will result both in judgment on those opposing God and in blessing for God's people. Though many nations experience a "day of the Lord" (for example, Babylon, when it was judged), there will be a final "day of the Lord" when a permanent world order of God's choosing will be established.

## Key Teachings about God

- God wants us to respond to him wholeheartedly.
- God is jealous for his people, meaning that he is energetically seeking their loyalty in a committed relationship.
- God holds the nations responsible for how they treat his people.
- God forgives the sin of his people.

**KEY VERSES:**

***Joel 1:15:*** *"For the day of the Lord is near; it will come like destruction from the Almighty."*

***Joel 2:13:*** *"Rend your heart and not your garments. Return to the Lord . . . for he is gracious and compassionate, slow to anger and abounding in love, and he relents from sending calamity."*

***Joel 2:28–32:*** *"I will pour out my Spirit on all people. . . . And everyone who calls on the name of the Lord will be saved."*

***Joel 3:16–17:*** *"The Lord will roar from Zion and . . . the earth and the sky will tremble. But the Lord will be a refuge for his people."*

***Obad. 15–17:*** *"The day of the Lord is near. . . . As you have done, it will be done to you."*

## Purpose

These two books are among the most difficult to place in time. Most of the prophetic books indicate the name of the king(s) who ruled during the prophet's time, but Joel only mentions the elders and Obadiah gives no indication. In Joel the temple is in operation, and Israel is already scattered (3:1–2). If there is a temple and no king, a date of about 500 BC might be in view. Obadiah's harsh message of destruction against Edom would also fit well there but could just as easily fit in several other periods. The dates of these books must remain an open question.

The occasion for Joel's prophecy is a locust plague. These were common enough in the ancient world and devastating to the economy, which was largely agricultural. In most of the prophetic books before the exile, the prophets proclaimed a coming judgment. Joel, like prophets after the exile, interprets a current crisis as the judgment of God. As the book proceeds, the prophet makes it clear that the plague is going to get worse before it gets better. He calls the people to repentance and they respond (an unusual situation for the prophets).

The last part of the book provides one of the most familiar discussions of the day of the Lord because Peter quotes sections in his sermon at Pentecost. The connection between the day of the Lord in Joel and Pentecost is the widespread outpouring of the Spirit and the opportunity for any to call on the name of the Lord and be saved.

Joel is one of the most positive prophetic books as it exemplifies the process of God's people responding to his prophet with repentance, followed by declarations of coming restoration for his people and judgment of their enemies.

© Dr. James C. Martin, The Israel Museum

↑ *Anthropomorphic vessels from the Edomite religious shrine at En Hazeva.*

Obadiah is an example of the last part—judgment of Israel's enemies. This shortest book in the Old Testament is an oracle of judgment against the Edomites for their treachery against Israel.

↓ *THE DIVIDED KINGDOM*

# Jonah

© Dr. James C. Martin

## Key Concepts

- Much of the significance of the book depends on understanding that the Ninevite response is superficial, yet God responds anyway.
- Jonah is put in Nineveh's shoes in order for the book to make its point about God's compassion being undeserved.
- Jonah is not a missionary, he is a prophet.
- Jonah's message is of judgment, not instruction or hope.

← *The site of ancient Gat Hepher, Jonah's hometown. Jesus grew up in Nazareth, only a few miles away.*

## Key Term

***Oracle***–A message given from God to a prophet for him to declare to a particular audience.

## Key Teachings about God

- God delights in giving second chances to those who take steps in the right direction.
- God's compassion is not earned.
- God is interested in response from people who encounter him.

**KEY VERSES:**

***Jonah 3:10:*** *"When God saw . . . how they turned from their evil ways, he had compassion and did not bring upon them the destruction he had threatened."*

***Jonah 4:10–11:*** *"You have been concerned about this vine, though you did not tend it or make it grow. . . . Should I not be concerned about that great city [Nineveh]?"*

## Timeline

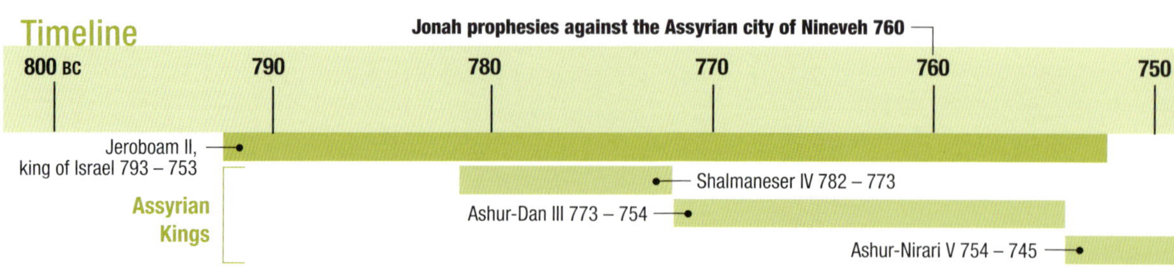

## Purpose

Jonah is quite different from the other prophetic books in that it contains mostly narrative, includes a psalm, and has only one short oracle (3:4). Since it is principally a narrative about a prophet rather than a collection of oracles, it is essential that we consider its purpose in light of the narrative form.

Jonah is a prophet from the mid-eighth century BC. God gives him an assignment to go to Nineveh, which he is reluctant to accept. He thinks he can avoid his commission by fleeing to Tarshish—in the opposite direction. Despite his one-way ticket to Tarshish, God brings him back by special carrier (a large fish) before he even reaches his destination. Oddly, no one in the book is less responsive to God's Word than Jonah. Both the sailors and the Ninevites acknowledge the power of God with far less information to go on than this Hebrew prophet.

Jonah offers theological justification for his reluctance in Jonah 4:2—he knew God would be compassionate and, in Jonah's opinion, the Ninevites were not deserving of compassion. The message of the book emerges when God puts Jonah in the position of having received compassion that he did not deserve (the benefit of the vine, 4:6). Since Jonah resented God's undeserved compassion on the Ninevites, God used a worm to take away the benefit of the vine to see whether Jonah would respond consistently ("Oh well, I didn't do anything to deserve that anyway."). Instead, Jonah is just as angry about losing his undeserved benefit as he was about the Ninevites getting theirs.

The book of Jonah teaches that compassion and grace are not given by God based on what we deserve but based on our responsive steps in the right direction. When people respond to God, he responds to them. This is an important message to include among the prophetic books where the prophets are continually giving oracles of judgment against Israel and Judah. What does God expect from them? Even small steps in the right direction will bring gracious and compassionate responses. It worked for wicked and uninformed Nineveh, why not for God's precious covenant people?

↑ *Late Roman sarcophagus with scenes from the life of Jonah.*

← *JONAH'S ROUNDABOUT TRIP TO NINEVEH*

# Micah

© Dr. James C. Martin

## Key Concepts

- Spiritual renewal begins with putting an end to one's unjust treatment of others. This is not all there is, but it is the essential first step.
- Oracles of the prophets generally fall into four categories: *indictment* (telling the people what they are doing wrong), *judgment* (indicating how God is going to punish their sin), *instruction* (identifying what response is appropriate), and *aftermath* (outlining the hope for deliverance and restoration after the judgment).

← *Micah's hometown of Moresheth-Gath.*

## Key Terms

***Messiah***–As in the prophetic books in general, when Micah speaks of the Messiah, he does not use the term. He refers to "one who breaks open" and the "king" in 2:13 and to the "ruler" in 5:2. "Messiah" does not become the major term for referring to the future ideal Davidic king until the end of the Old Testament period, though kings in the line of David generally are described by that term often in Psalms.

***Classical Prophets***–Prophets who address the people as a whole and begin to declare national judgment for sin. Earlier prophets ("pre-classical"), such as Samuel, Elisha, and Elijah, addressed primarily the king with messages of indictment, judgment, or deliverance.

## Key Teachings about God

- God is against those who plan evil.
- God is a righteous judge.
- God will rule in Jerusalem forever.
- God does not require us to fix all of society's problems, but expects us to right the wrongs in our own behavior toward those who are vulnerable or oppressed.
- God forgives.

## People to Know

Micah
Jotham
Ahaz
Hezekiah

## Timeline

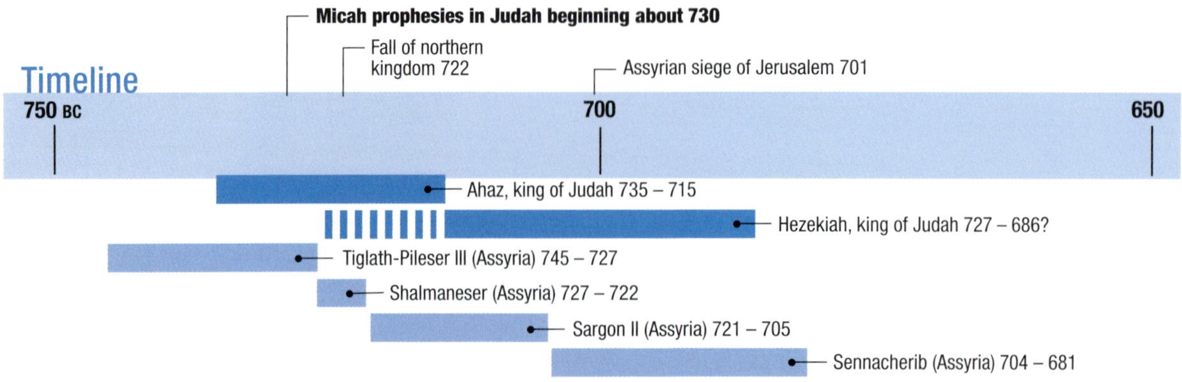

## Purpose

Micah was a contemporary of Isaiah, prophesying in the latter half of the eighth century BC. He is among the earliest of the classical prophets in the southern kingdom of Judah. Beginning with Amos and Hosea in the eighth century, prophets made their proclamations to the people instead of the king, and it was the people who would suffer the consequences. Because these oracles were gathered into books, the classical prophets are also known as the writing prophets.

Micah is one of the few prophets who actually stated his purpose: "But as for me, I am filled with power, with the Spirit of the LORD, and with justice and might, to declare to Jacob his transgression, to Israel his sin" (3:8). A large portion of the book is taken up with indictment and judgment. During his ministry, the northern kingdom of Israel falls to the Assyrians, and Jerusalem barely survives a major campaign by Sennacherib. This is a time of great fear and anxiety. Like his predecessor Amos, Micah denounces his audience for their injustice.

A number of sections offer hope and deliverance to a remnant of the people. These suggest the possibility of short-term deliverance from the Assyrians and speak of restoration in the indefinite future. Micah's most familiar prophecy concerns the birth of the future ruler in Bethlehem. The location he names is not simply arbitrary. Most rulers in the line of David would be expected to be born in Jerusalem. The choice of Bethlehem indicates a fresh beginning for the line of David since Bethlehem was his birthplace. Micah therefore announces the coming of a new David.

↑ *This tablet contains a record of the military campaigns of Tiglath-Pileser III during the reign of Ahaz, including those against the kings of Phoenicia, Israel, Ammon, Moab, and coastal cities along the Philistine plain.*

**KEY VERSES:**

***Mic. 3:8–12:* "Hear this . . . you rulers of . . . Israel . . . because of you, Zion will be plowed like a field, Jerusalem will become a heap of rubble."**

***Mic. 4:3–5:* "They will beat their swords into plowshares and their spears into pruning hooks. Nation will not take up sword against nation, nor will they train for war anymore."**

***Mic. 5:2:* "But you, Bethlehem . . . out of you will come . . . one who will be ruler over Israel."**

***Mic. 6:8:* "What does the LORD require of you? To act justly and to love mercy and walk humbly with your God."**

***Mic. 7:18:* "Who is a God like you, who pardons sin . . . You do not stay angry forever but delight to show mercy."**

↓ *THE SOUTHERN KINGDOM OF JUDAH*

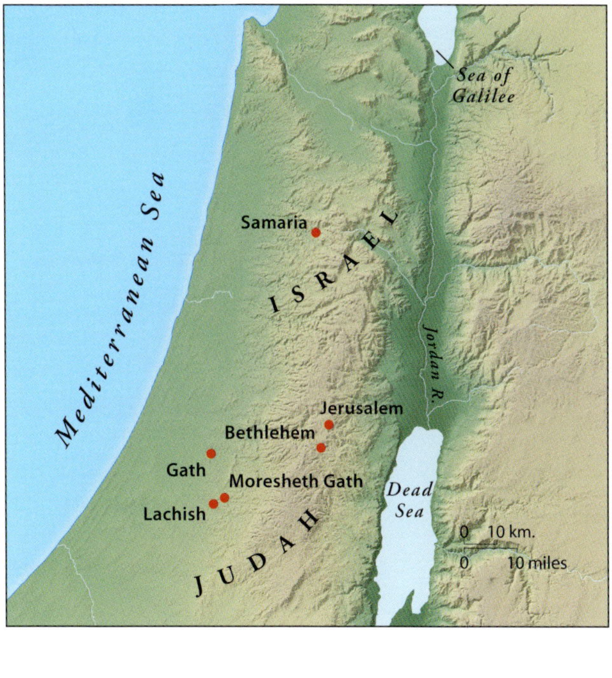

# Nahum, Habakkuk, and Zephaniah

© Dr. James C. Martin, Musée du Louvre

## Key Concepts

- The prophets arose in troubled times to declare the messages God gave them.
- The prophets at times were perplexed about what God was doing.
- Even in times of crisis and confusion, God expects his people to be faithful and trust him.
- With God, there is always reason for hope.

*← Nahum proclaimed the fall of Nineveh, which was fulfilled in 612 BC. The last great ruler of Assyria was Ashurbanipal (669–627 BC), seen here in his chariot.*

## Key Terms

***Theodicy***–Explaining God's justice in light of evil or suffering. In Habakkuk the theodicy focuses on how God works with nations. In Job it focuses on how God's justice works in individual lives.

***Apostasy***–Refusal to follow or obey a religious faith.

## Key Teachings about God

- God takes vengeance on behalf of his oppressed people; he will not let the wicked go unpunished.
- God is slow to anger, great in power.
- God is good and a refuge for his people.
- God cares for those who trust in him.
- God is mighty to save.

## People to Know

| | |
|---|---|
| Manasseh | Ashurbanipal |
| Josiah | Nabopolassar |
| Esarhaddon | Nebuchadnezzar |

## Timeline

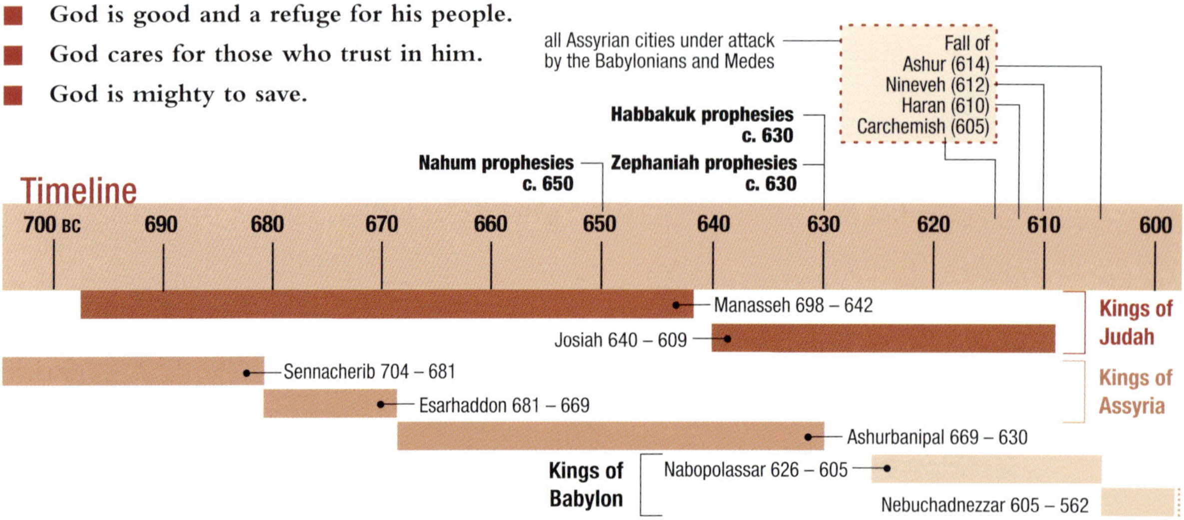

## Purpose

The prophetic ministries of Micah and Isaiah were followed by a dark period in Judah. Hezekiah is succeeded by his wicked son Manasseh, who reigns for 55 years. For most of his reign, he is a comfortable vassal to the Assyrians. The historical books of the Old Testament portray his apostasy as he sets up worship of Baal and Asherah in the temple. Toward the end of his reign, as the Assyrian Empire begins to reach its final stages and the Babylonian Empire prepares to arise, another round of prophets emerges.

Nahum's oracle of judgment on the Assyrian capital of Nineveh can logically be placed between 655 and 650 BC when Manasseh, toward the end of his reign, decided to rebel against the Assyrians. Nahum prophesies the fall of Nineveh (a century after their reprieve in the time of Jonah), which could have encouraged Manasseh to ally himself with the Babylonian revolt against Assyria in 652 BC. But the time for the fall of Nineveh had not yet come. The revolt failed and Manasseh was disciplined by the Assyrians. Nahum's prophecy was fulfilled a generation later in 612 BC.

Habakkuk focuses on a central issue—God's justice in dealing with nations. The book opens with a lament: Why does God tolerate injustice in his people? The Lord's answer is an oracle of judgment against Judah at the hands of the Babylonians. The astonishing fact that the invaders would be Babylonians rather than Assyrians suggests that the Babylonians are not yet an obvious threat, thus placing the book logically between 640 and 630 BC. God's answer perplexes Habakkuk as he cannot understand how God's justice can be satisfied by punishing Judah using a nation even more wicked. A second oracle indicates that the Babylonians too will be punished in due course. The book closes with a prayer of submission to God's plan.

The third prophet of this period, Zephaniah, calls for the kind of reform that Josiah enacted in 622 BC, therefore placing his prophecy a few years prior to that reform (see Jeremiah, his contemporary, for more information about this crucial decade).

Zephaniah proclaimed the coming of the day of the Lord, which would bring judgment on Judah. The day of the Lord is a time when the current state of affairs will be replaced with the Lord's intended order—a time of justice and covenant fulfillment. The prophets drive home the point that covenant fulfillment includes not only the covenant promises but also the threat of curses for unfaithfulness. In anticipation of the day of the Lord, Zephaniah instructs the people to seek the Lord. He projects a time of restoration when the nations will be judged.

↑ *This text chronicles the history of Babylon's capture of Jerusalem in 598 BC during the reign of Nebuchadnezzar.*



**KEY VERSES:**

***Nah. 1:7:*** *"The Lord is good, a refuge in times of trouble."*

***Hab. 2:4:*** *"The righteous will live by his faith."*

***Hab. 2:14:*** *"The earth will be filled with the knowledge of the glory of the Lord, as the waters cover the sea."*

***Hab. 2:20:*** *"The Lord is in his holy temple; let all the earth be silent before him."*

***Hab. 3:16–19:*** *"Though the fig tree does not bud and there are no grapes on the vines . . . I will rejoice in the Lord, I will be joyful in God my Savior . . . he makes my feet like the feet of a deer, he enables me to go on the heights."*

***Zeph. 3:11–17:*** *"You will not be put to shame. . . . The Lord your God is with you, he is mighty to save. He will take great delight in you, he will quiet you with his love, he will rejoice over you with singing."*

# Haggai and Zechariah

## Key Concepts

- **Spiritual restoration must precede social or political restoration.**
- **God's presence is the key to restoration, thus the importance of rebuilding the temple.**

← *Replica of an elaborate tabernacle/temple lampstand.*



## Key Terms

***Apocalyptic***–A type of prophetic literature that uses visions and symbolism in times of crisis to offer the people hope. Often there is an angelic guide. The text indicates the meaning of those symbols the reader is expected to know. The reader must focus on the prophecy's message rather than trying to interpret all the symbols and getting distracted.

***Visions***–The visions of the prophets are not themselves the message, they are only the occasion for the message. In Zech. 1:8–17, the message is not that there are going to be horsemen giving a report among the myrtle trees. The message is that God is still jealous for his people, angry at the nations that mistreated them, and the temple will be rebuilt. The vision simply provides an occasion for this message to be delivered to the prophet.

## Key Teachings about God

- **God expects to be our highest priority.**
- **God remains with his people even when they are under discipline or judgment.**
- **God desires to dwell among his people.**
- **God will deal with those who mistreat his people.**
- **God delivers his people.**
- **God is establishing his kingdom.**

## People to Know

Haggai
Zechariah
Zerubbabel
Jeshua
Darius

## Timeline

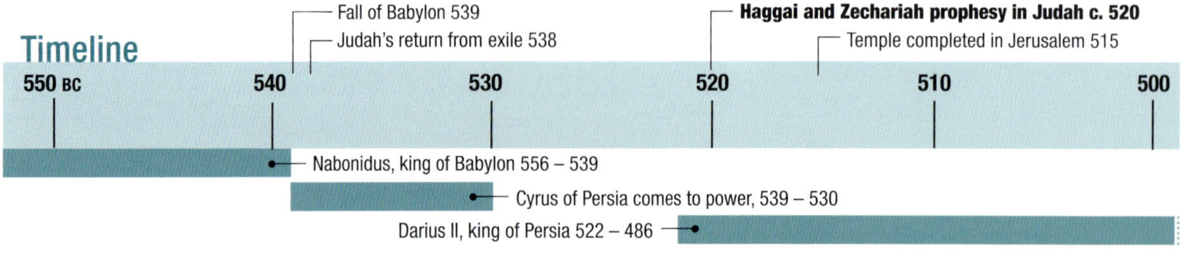

## Purpose

When Moses shattered the tablets of stone containing the terms of the covenant, he dramatized the way the covenant had been broken by construction of the golden calf. Nearly a millennium later, it was the temple and the city of Jerusalem that were shattered by the hand of God that dramatized the same thing. The covenant people were carried away from the land God had provided for them and into exile in Babylon. This is known as "the exile." After 70 years, as prophesied by Jeremiah, the covenant people returned, filled with expectation that the restoration and kingdom, of which the prophets had spoken, would at last be realized.

Just as earlier prophets had been raised up by God during times of crisis, into this critical juncture in history (establishment of the Persian Empire) stride the prophets Haggai and Zechariah. (Isaiah and Micah came as the Assyrian Empire emerged; Jeremiah and Zephaniah were on the scene at the crucial moments when the Babylonian Empire emerged.) Cyrus, the king of Persia, had already done the work of conquest, and the dominion of the Persians over the ancient world was already 20 years old. But in 522 BC, the sudden death of his son Cambyses and the scramble for control of the empire threatened to undo it all. Darius emerged and brought peace and renewed control, and the empire that would last until the time of Alexander the Great, nearly two centuries distant, was established.

As realization of Judah's continued submission to the Persians grew, these prophets stepped forward to proclaim the Lord's plan for his people. When Cyrus allowed the exiles to return to Jerusalem in 538 BC, they immediately began work on the temple. Various circumstances halted that work and now, 20 years later, only the altar is functioning. The prophets call on the people to realign their priorities and reignite their fervor for the house of the Lord.

Haggai accomplishes this through four prophetic sermons over the span of four months. He supports the work of the leaders of the community, Zerubbabel and Jeshua, as they undertake the completion of the temple project.

Zechariah's visions also undergird the construction project, supporting the leadership roles of Zerubbabel and Jeshua. But Zechariah makes it clear that building the temple is not all that is needed. The people also have to deal with the sin that led to the destruction of the temple and rebuild their covenant relationship with God. The latter part of the book offers more than any other Old Testament prophet (other than Isaiah) about the restoration of the people, the coming Messiah, and the establishment of the kingdom of God.

↑ *This clay tablet describes the extent of the empire of Darius the Great (521–486 BC). It was during the second year of his rule (520 BC) that Haggai received his messages from the Lord (Haggai 1:1).*



**KEY VERSES:**

***Hag. 1:7–8:*** *"Give careful thought to your ways."*

***Hag. 2:6–7:*** *"In a little while I will once more shake the heavens and the earth ... I will shake all nations."*

***Zech. 1:2–6:*** *"Return to me ... and I will return to you."*

***Zech. 1:14–17:*** *"I am very jealous for Jerusalem and Zion, ... I will return to Jerusalem with mercy."*

***Zech. 2:10–13:*** *"Shout and be glad.... For I am coming."*

***Zech. 9:9:*** *"Rejoice.... See, your king comes to you, ... riding on a donkey."*

***Zech. 14:9:*** *"On that day there will be one LORD, and his name the only name."*

↓ *CUTAWAY OF TEMPLE INTERIOR*

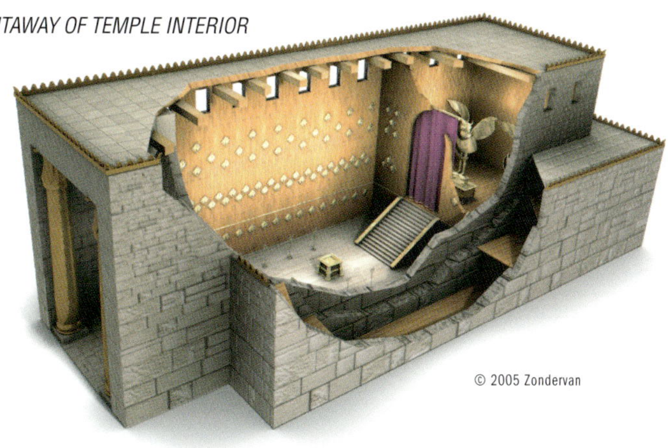

# Malachi

© Dr. James C. Martin

## Key Concepts

- God does not need the worship of his people, but he is worthy of highest honor and praise and is rightly offended when he is treated with disdain.
- The prophets cry out for God's people to respond to him and deal with their shortcomings.

*← Storehouse. After the return of the exiles there is a concerted effort to rebuild the temple in Jerusalem. The Lord speaks through the prophet Malachi to instruct the people to bring their tithes into the temple storehouse (Malachi 3:8).*

## Key Terms

***Disputation***–A literary device in which an author anticipates objections from an audience and refutes them.
***Book of the Twelve***–A term for the twelve minor prophets.

## Key Teachings about God

- God should not be shortchanged in what we give to him.
- God's name is respected worldwide and is to be honored.
- God does not change.
- God has a claim on a portion of our income.
- God makes note of those who honor him.
- God purges his people.

**KEY VERSES:**

***Mal. 1:11:** "My name will be great among the nations, from the rising to the setting of the sun."*

***Mal. 3:1–3:** "I will send my messenger, who will prepare the way before me.... He will be like a refiner's fire or a launderer's soap."*

***Mal. 3:6–7:** "I the Lord do not change.... Return to me, and I will return to you."*

***Mal. 4:1–5:** "Surely the day is coming; it will burn like a furnace."*

## Timeline

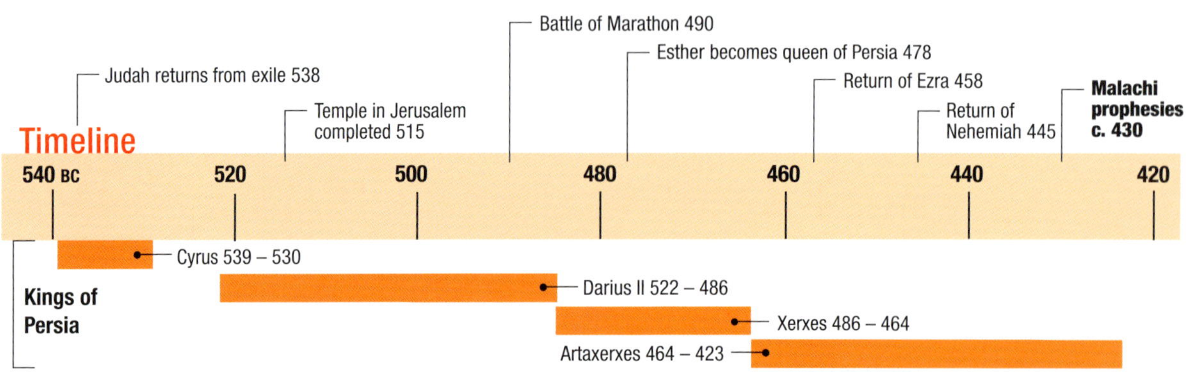

## Purpose

Malachi, addressing a fifth-century BC audience, is the last of the minor prophets. (The twelve smaller prophetic books, from Hosea to Malachi that were transmitted as a group, are sometimes called the Book of the Twelve.) In some ways Malachi serves as a conclusion to that group. Throughout the prophetic books we see the positive results of responding to the prophetic call and the negative results of failing to respond. In Malachi, the question of whether the people will respond is left hanging.

The book is structured in six disputations. The points are that God desires honesty, true worship, and faithfulness. These serve as the prophetic marching orders into the long silent period between the Old and New Testaments. The book ends with a warning that the Lord is coming to judge the wicked (4:1), a call to remember the covenant (4:4), and an indication that the greatest prophet, Elijah, will come before the day of the Lord (4:5–6).

The book of Malachi serves a prophetic bridge to John the Baptist and Jesus, who both used many of Malachi's themes in their preaching. The portrayal of the religious leaders at the time of Christ suggests that Israel had failed to respond to the basics of Malachi's message.

Sometimes it is difficult to see how the prophets are relevant to us today since their messages were directed toward Israel. However, when we break the prophetic message down to its basics, we see that the prophets indicted the people for unfaithfulness, oppression of the defenseless, misplaced reliance, confused priorities, and improper treatment and understanding of God. Though we may not commit these offenses in the same way, we are guilty of them nonetheless. In the judgment oracles we learn that God is serious about sin, especially the sin of his people—and he will act.

← *Incense altar. "'In every place incense and pure offerings will be brought to my name, because my name will be great among the nations,' says the LORD Almighty" (Malachi 1:11).*



When we read the prophets, we are not asking whether we are guilty of the same sins or subject to the same punishments or whether the specific promises of deliverance or messages of hope apply to us. Instead we learn about God—how our sin offends him, how his justice calls for punishment, how his compassion urges us to respond to him, and how his grace offers hope. The Bible is God's revelation of himself and we read it not to learn about the people but to learn about God so that we might know him and respond to him.

↓ *JERUSALEM*

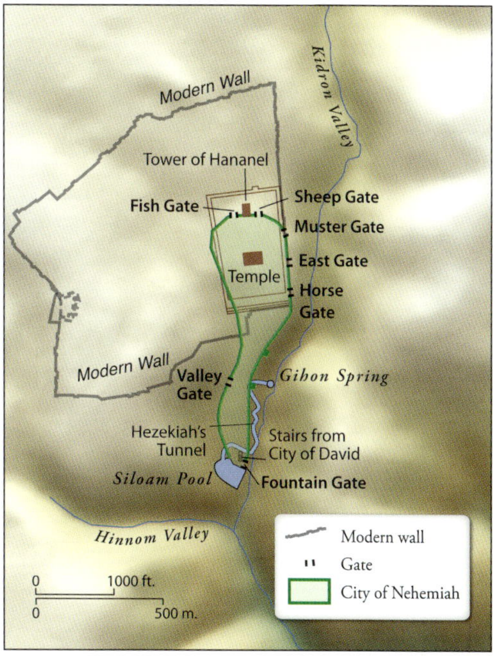

# How the Old Testament Relates to the New

At the end of the third Gospel, Luke tells us about an amazing little sermon Jesus preached to two of his disciples after the resurrection: "And beginning with Moses and all the Prophets, he explained to them what was said in all the Scriptures concerning himself" (Luke 24:27). Wouldn't it have been great to be a fly on the wall for that message! Jesus begins with Genesis and moves all the way through Malachi, showing how the whole Old Testament story reaches its culmination in him. This has profound implications for the way we read both the Old Testament and the New Testament. To truly understand the Bible, we have to recognize that all of God's plan as it unfolded in the Old Testament, all of his revelation as it progressed through the Old Testament, all of his intention for relationship that was nurtured through the Old Testament covenant came to a grand climax in Christ and was carried through its final steps by him. It is impossible to fully understand God's purpose of the Old Testament without reading the "rest of the story" in the New. In the same way, it is impossible to understand the New Testament story without the foundation laid in the Old. All of the central themes of the New Testament have their background and context in the Old.

## Creation, Fall, and Reconciliation: The Restoration of God's Reign

At its heart, the Bible is the story of humanity's fall and restoration. In the book of Genesis God creates a perfect world for Adam and Eve, yet they rebel against him and human nature, together with all of creation, becomes "fallen"—standing under the judgment of God (Gen. 1–3). The rest of the story is about God's plan for reconciliation, how he will bring humanity and all of creation back into a right relationship with himself.

When Jesus appeared on the scene, his central message was "the kingdom of God is near" (Mark 1:15). Although the exact phrase *kingdom of God* does not appear in the Old Testament, this theme permeates the whole biblical story. The kingdom of God means that God is the sovereign Lord of the universe, the creator and owner of all things. He started history and he will bring it to its conclusion. When Adam and Eve disobeyed God, they rejected his sovereign authority and chose to make themselves gods over their own lives. Since then, humanity has stood in rebellion against the kingdom of God, alienated from their creator and headed for destruction. Yet the Old Testament prophets predicted that one day God would reestablish his authority over all things. He would provide the means to redeem his people, forgive their sins, and bring them back into a right relationship with him. When Jesus announced that the kingdom of God was at hand, he was calling people to submit again to God's lordship and to once again follow his purpose and plan for the world.

## Old and New Covenants

The word *testament* means "covenant," and God's plan of redemption centers around a series of covenants, or binding agreements, which God makes with those willing to trust and serve him. When all humanity turns to wickedness after the fall in Eden, God destroys the world with a flood, delivering only Noah and his family and making a covenant with them (Gen. 9:1–17). Through the line of Noah's son Shem, God chooses a family to be his special people and to mediate his presence to the world. God makes a covenant with Shem's descendant, the patriarch Abraham, promising to create through him a great nation (Israel), to give him the land of Canaan as an inheritance, and to bless all nations through his descendants (Gen. 12, 15, 17). In response Abraham owes God obedience and faithfulness.

The covenant made to Abraham is expanded to David, Israel's greatest king, in the Davidic covenant. Through David's descendants, God promises to raise up a king who will reign in righteousness and justice, and will bring in an era of peace and restoration (2 Sam. 7; Isa. 9:1–7; 11:1–16). It is through this "anointed one" (or, "messiah") that God will reverse the results of the fall and restore creation. Finally, the prophet Jeremiah predicts that God will one day establish a "new covenant" with his people, greater than the covenants of old. It will bring about true knowledge of God, and full and complete forgiveness of sins (Jer. 31:31–34).

The New Testament presents Jesus as the fulfillment of the covenants made to Abraham and David (see Matt. 1:1). As promised to Abraham, through Jesus all nations on earth will be blessed (Gal. 3:8). In fulfillment of the Davidic covenant, he will reign forever on David's throne with justice and righteousness (Luke 1:32–33). He is the new Moses who leads God's people on a "new exodus" out of slavery to sin and death and into the freedom of eternal life and rest in the promised land—the presence of God. At his Last Supper, Jesus announces to his disciples that the new covenant is being established through his sacrificial death (Luke 22:19–20; 1 Cor. 11:23–26). The writer to the Hebrews confirms that through Jesus' death on the cross, the new covenant has been established (Heb. 8:7–13). Salvation from sin has been achieved.

## The Fulfillment of the Law

In the Old Testament Israel's means of maintaining covenant faithfulness was by obedience to the law, those commandments given by God to Moses at Mount Sinai. Yet Israel repeatedly violated God's law and suffered the consequences of judgment, oppression, and exile.

In the New Testament Jesus rebukes the Jewish religious leaders for superficially keeping the outward requirements of the law, yet ignoring its true spirit. They exalt their own human traditions above God's righteous commandments (Mark 7:6–8). Ultimately, Jesus presents himself as the fulfillment of the law, who brings the old age of promise to a close and establishes the new age of fulfillment (Matt. 5:17). Believers in the new age of salvation no longer serve under the written code of the Old Testament law, but rather have God's law written on their hearts through the internal guidance of the Holy Spirit (Jer. 31:33; Heb. 8:10; 10:16).

In the New Testament epistles Paul points out that while the law was holy, righteous, and good, it could never provide true forgiveness of sins, since no one could keep it perfectly (Rom. 3:20; 7:9–12). The law was rather put in charge over us while we were immature children, awaiting our true adoption as God's heirs (Gal. 3:23–4:7). Christ is the fulfillment and culmination of the law; salvation comes through faith alone in him (Rom. 10:4).

## Jesus Christ: God's Agent of Salvation

According to the New Testament writers, the person and work of Jesus is the climax of God's plan of salvation (Gal. 4:4–5; 1 Cor. 10:11). He is the Messiah (Greek: "Christ" = "Anointed One"), the promised king from David's line (Matt. 1:1; Luke 2:11; Rom. 1:3). He is the divine Son of God who came from heaven to bring glory to the Father and eternal life to all who believe (John 3:16–18). He is the "second Adam," whose faithful obedience to God reversed the effects of Adam's disobedience and brought restoration to a fallen world (Rom. 5:12–21; 1 Cor. 15:21–22). He is the final high priest, whose once-for-all sacrifice on the cross inaugurated the new covenant, paid an eternal debt of sin, and achieved salvation for those with persevering faith (Heb. 9:11–15). Ultimately, Jesus is God himself, the self-revelation of the Father and the creator and sustainer of all things (John 1:1–18; 8:58; 20:28: 1 Cor. 8:6; Col. 1:15; 2:9; Heb. 1:2–3).

## The Final Restoration

The Old Testament starts "In the beginning . . . ," with the creation of the present heaven and earth (Gen. 1:1). The New Testament ends with a new beginning—the creation of a new heaven and a new earth (Rev. 21:1; cf. Isa. 66:22). Again Jesus is the central figure of human history—God's agent of restoration. He is "the Alpha and the Omega, the First and the Last, the Beginning and the End" (Rev. 22:13; 1:17; 2:8; cf. Rev. 1:8; 21:6; Isa. 44:6; 48:12). He is the lamb who was slain to provide salvation for people from every tribe, language, people, and nation (Rev. 5:9–12). At the consummation of history he will return to judge the wicked, to deliver the righteous, and to right every wrong (Rev. 19–22). God's universal reign and presence with his people will again be established. As in the garden of Eden, God himself will dwell with his people: "They will be his people, and God himself will be with them and be their God. He will wipe every tear from their eyes. There will be no more death or mourning or crying or pain, for the old order of things has passed away" (Rev. 21:3–4). God's plan for reconciliation and relationship will be complete.

# NEW TESTAMENT

# Matthew

## Summary Overview

Matthew's gospel shows Jesus as the promised Messiah whose death brought salvation from sins. While some Jews rejected Jesus, claiming his death proved he was a fake, Matthew writes that Jesus is truly the Messiah, whose birth, life, and death on the cross fulfilled the promises of the Old Testament. His resurrection vindicated his claims and brought in a new era of salvation for all who believe in him.

← *The Mount of Beatitudes, traditional site of Jesus' Sermon on the Mount (Matthew 5–7).*

## Key Themes

Jesus is the ***fulfillment of the Jewish Scriptures***.
***Jesus the teacher***, a new Moses for the new age of salvation.
Jesus as ***son of David and Son of God***.
***Jesus as the new Israel***, bringing the message of God's salvation to the world.
Jesus as ***"Immanuel"*** (Isa. 7:14)—God's presence with us.
***The "kingdom of heaven"*** is Matthew's Jewish way of referring to God's reign.
***The Great Commission***. The command to spread the message of salvation and make disciples of all nations.

## The Four Gospels

The first four books of the New Testament—Matthew, Mark, Luke, and John—are called "gospels," meaning "good news." Each tells the story of Jesus from a unique perspective, emphasizing different aspects of who he is and what he came to accomplish.

The first three (Matthew, Mark, and Luke) are called the Synoptic Gospels. Synoptic means "viewed together," and these three share a similar structure and relate many of the same stories. The gospel of John is more theological, with a greater stress on the identity of Jesus and the spiritual significance of his life.

Strictly speaking, the authors of all four gospels are anonymous since they do not identify themselves in the text. Their authorship comes from the titles on early manuscripts ("according to Matthew," "according to Mark,") and early church traditions.

### Matthew—The Gospel of the Messiah

| Birth Narrative Chs. 1–2 | Sermon on the Mount Chs. 5–7 | Commissioning the Twelve Ch. 10 | Kingdom Parables Ch. 13 | Church Life and Discipline Ch. 18 | Woes & Olivet Discourse Chs. 23–25 | Passion, Resurrection, Great Commission Chs. 26–28 |
|---|---|---|---|---|---|---|

**Narrative Structured around Five Key Discourses**

## Purpose

Matthew writes to confirm to Christian believers that Jesus is indeed the Jewish Messiah and that through his life, death, and resurrection he has fulfilled the prophecies of the Hebrew Scriptures (the Old Testament). The church of Jesus Christ, made up of Jews and Gentiles, represents the true people of God in the new age of salvation.

Matthew structures his gospel around Jesus' five major discourses, or teaching sections—Sermon on the Mount (chs. 5–7), commissioning of the twelve disciples (ch. 10), parables of the kingdom of heaven (ch. 13), church life and discipline (ch. 18), and woes against the religious leaders and end-time teaching on the Mount of Olives (chs. 23–25). Each of these discourses ends with a similar formula: "When Jesus finished saying these things. . . ." Some have suggested that Matthew imitated the Pentateuch, the five books of Moses (Genesis–Deuteronomy), presenting Jesus as the new Moses.

↑ *The present Church of the Nativity in Bethlehem was built by the Emperor Justinian (c. AD 529) over the traditional site of Jesus' birthplace.*

Matthew's orderly narrative is the most Jewish of the four gospels. The place of writing is unknown, though scholars commonly suggest either Antioch in Syria or Palestine. The date is also uncertain, and suggestions range from the mid to late first century.

↓ *ISRAEL DURING THE NEW TESTAMENT PERIOD*

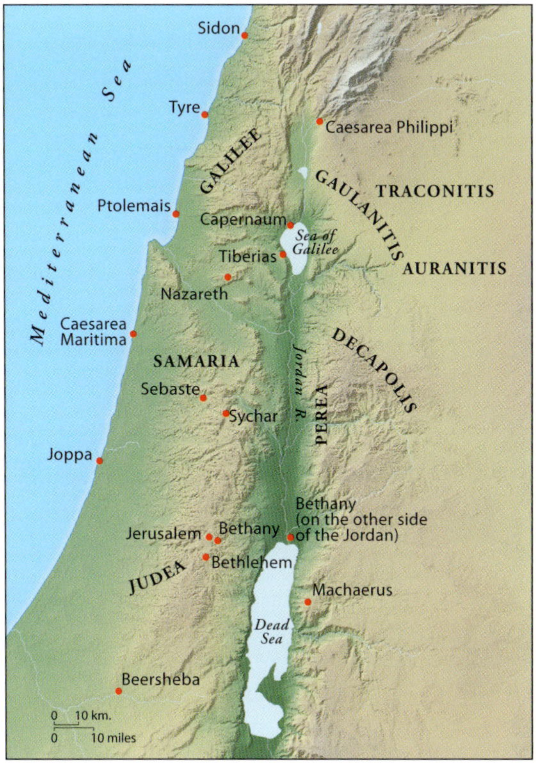


### Author

The apostle Matthew, also known as Levi, a tax collector.

### Recipients

Jewish and Gentile Christians when the church—originally composed entirely of Jews—was coming into conflict with the synagogue and was beginning to break away.

## Interesting Facts about Matthew

- **The gospel of Matthew is the most topical of the four gospels, often grouping material thematically rather than chronologically.**
- **Jesus chose the most unlikely people to be his disciples—common fishermen and despised tax collectors. Tax collectors were hated for their collusion with Roman authorities and their reputation for greed and extortion.**
- **Matthew's other name, Levi, may indicate he was from the tribe of Levi, making him especially hated because the Levites were supposed to be set apart for God's service.**

# Mark

## Summary Overview

Mark presents Jesus as the mighty Messiah and Son of God who exercises extraordinary authority to overcome the forces of Satan, sin, and disease. This powerful Messiah has not come to conquer the Roman legions, but to suffer and die as the Servant of the Lord and to pay the ransom for sins. The theme verse could be Mark 10:45: "For even the Son of Man did not come to be served, but to serve, and to give his life as a ransom for many."

← *Jesus spent much of his ministry in the regions surrounding the harp-shaped Sea of Galilee.*

## Key Themes

***The Gospel***. Mark introduces his work as "the beginning of the gospel"—the "good news" of salvation prophesied by Isaiah (1:1–3).

***The Kingdom of God***. The content of the gospel is the kingdom, or "reign," of God (1:14–15). While God is and has always been king of the universe, Jesus announces that God's end-time salvation—his sovereign reign—is arriving through Jesus' words and deeds.

***Jesus the Authoritative Christ and Son of God***. Jesus' authority in teaching and healing confirms that he is indeed the mighty Messiah. The climax of the gospel comes when the centurion at the foot of the cross recognizes through Jesus' suffering that he is indeed the "Son of God" (15:39).

***Jesus the Servant of the Lord***. Though the mighty Messiah and Son of God, Jesus' role at his first coming is not to conquer but to suffer and die as the righteous Servant of the Lord predicted by Isaiah the prophet (Isa. 53).

***A Call for Cross-bearing Discipleship***. True disciples of Jesus are not to seek honor and power but to take up their cross, following their Master through sacrifice and suffering (10:45).

## Author

John Mark, son of Mary of Jerusalem, cousin of Barnabas, missionary companion of the apostle Paul, and later companion to the apostle Peter.

## Recipients

A suffering church—perhaps in Rome during persecutions by Nero (about AD 64).

## Mark—The Gospel of the Servant-Messiah

| Preparation of the Messiah 1:1–13 | Galilean Ministry The Authority of the Messiah 1:1–8:30 | Peter's Confession & First Passion Prediction 8:27–38 | Journey of the Servant to Jerusalem 8:31–10:52 | Suffering, Death, and Resurrection of the Servant Chs. 11–16 |
|---|---|---|---|---|
| **Jesus the Mighty Messiah** | | **Jesus the Suffering Servant** | | |

## Purpose

Mark's action-packed gospel was written at a time when allegiance to Jesus could cost one everything: family, friends, possessions, and even life itself. In the context of growing opposition from the Roman government and from society in general, Mark calls God's people to follow the example of Jesus, who remained faithful to God no matter what the cost.

Whereas the gospels of Matthew and Luke begin with stories of Jesus' birth, Mark jumps right to the ministry of John the Baptist (1:1–8). Jesus' mission begins with his baptism and temptation (1:9–13), followed by a powerful preaching and healing ministry throughout Galilee (1:14–8:30). The Galilean ministry climaxes with Peter's confession that Jesus is the Christ, God's promised deliverer (8:27–29). From that point on, Jesus begins teaching his disciples that he must suffer and die in Jerusalem to pay the ransom price for sins. The rest of the gospel describes Jesus' journey to Jerusalem and his passion there as the suffering Servant of the Lord.

A pattern of "threes" runs through the gospel, starting with three boat scenes illustrating the disciples' incomprehension (4:35–41; 6:45–52; 8:14–21). There are three cycles on pride and servant leadership (8:31–38; 9:31–37; 10:32–45), three calls for readiness in the Olivet Discourse (13:33, 35, 37), Jesus three times finds his disciples sleeping in Gethsemane (14:37, 40, 41), and Peter denies Christ three times (14:68, 70, 71). Even the crucifixion has three three-hour intervals (15:25, 33, 34).

Mark wrote for at least three reasons: to provide the church with an authoritative written account of the gospel story, to confirm Jesus' identity as the suffering Messiah and Son of God, and to encourage believers to cross-bearing discipleship—to persevere through trials and suffering as Jesus did.

According to church tradition, Mark gathered the information about Jesus from Peter's preaching. He then wrote the gospel either while Peter was ministering in Rome or sometime later, after Peter's death (late AD 60s).

↑ *The modern octagonal Catholic church is built over fourth and fifth century Byzantine remains. The partial reconstruction of the white limestone synagogue sits on top of the basalt synagogue foundation of Capernaum, dating to the first century. At top is the Sea of Galilee.*

## Interesting Facts about Mark

- **For its length Mark relates more miracles of Jesus than the other gospels.**
- **Mark delights in a literary device known as "intercalation," where one story is interrupted by another and the two mutually interpret each other. See the examples in 5:21–43 and 11:12–25.**
- **The motif of amazement is common throughout Mark, as people marvel at Jesus' astonishing words and deeds.**
- **Most scholars think that Mark was the first gospel written and that Matthew and Luke used his gospel and other sources when they wrote.**
- **Some think Mark himself may appear in this gospel, that he is the young man who fled naked in the strange episode related in Mark 14:51–52. Unfortunately there is no evidence to prove or disprove this.**

↓ *THE SEA OF GALILEE*

# Luke

© Dr. James C. Martin

## Summary Overview

The gospel of Luke is the most universal of the four gospels, confirming that Jesus is the Savior of the whole world who draws people to himself from every race, culture, and social status. The message of salvation, which arose from within Israel, is now available to all. A theme verse could be Luke 19:10: "For the Son of Man came to seek and to save what was lost."

← *Jesus raised the widow's son at Nain located at the northern base of Mount Moreh, the same mountain where the Lord used Elisha to restore the Shunammite's son to life (Luke 7:11–17; 2 Kings 4:8–37).*

## Key Themes

***Historical Foundations***. The grounding of the gospel message in historical truths.
The ***universal scope*** of the gospel. It is for all people everywhere.
***Fulfillment of Prophecy***. All the Scriptures speak of the Christ (24:27).
***God's Purpose and Plan***. Jesus' death was no accident of history, but was God's purposeful action to accomplish salvation.
***Jesus*** as Prophet, Messiah, Savior, and Lord.
***The Holy Spirit*** as the sign of the new age of salvation.
***Joy and praise***, because the time of salvation has arrived.
***Outsiders***. Jesus' special concern for outsiders, especially the poor, sinners, and Samaritans.
***Women***. Special emphasis is placed on women.
***Jerusalem and Jesus***. The importance of Jerusalem and the temple and Jesus' journey there (9:51–19:28).

## Author

Luke, a physician and part-time missionary companion of the apostle Paul. Luke probably was a Gentile.

## Recipients

Theophilus, possibly Luke's patron who financially supported the writing of the books of Luke and Acts. Yet Luke clearly writes to a larger audience, probably mostly Gentile churches wrestling with their identity as the true people of God.

## Luke—The Gospel of the Savior for Lost People

| Birth of the Savior<br>Chs. 1–2 | Galilean MInistry:<br>The Authority of the Savior<br>3:1–9:50 | Journey of the Savior to Jerusalem:<br>Seeking and Saving the Lost<br>9:51–19:27 | Passion, Resurrection and<br>Ascension of the Savior<br>19:28–24:53 |
|---|---|---|---|

## Purpose

Luke assures believers of the historical foundation for their faith. The coming of Jesus and the growth of his church represents the culmination of God's purpose and plan for the salvation of the world.

Luke's gospel is one half of a two-volume work; the other half is the book of Acts. The two together are referred to as Luke–Acts. Luke's gospel tells the story of Jesus from his birth through his ascension to heaven after his resurrection. Acts picks up the story from there and tells how the good news about Jesus spread from its Jewish roots to the Gentile world. The overall theme of Luke–Acts is that God's great plan of salvation has come to fulfillment in the events of Jesus' life, death, resurrection, and ascension, and continues to unfold in the growth and expansion of the church.

Luke follows Mark's basic outline: Jesus' ministry in Galilee climaxes in Peter's confession, after which Jesus predicts he must go to Jerusalem to suffer and die. Yet Luke's structure is unique in that Jesus' journey to Jerusalem takes 10 chapters in Luke (only one in Mark). In this section Luke presents many of Jesus' most beloved parables and stories.

Many of the parables from Luke's travel narrative stress God's love for those on the margins of society: sinners, outcasts, and the poor. The lesson in the good Samaritan (10:25–37) is that a true neighbor is one who loves others, whatever their social status or ethnic background. In the persistent widow (18:1–8), God is a loving and caring judge who will reward the persistent prayer of his people. The Pharisee and the tax collector (18:9–14) deals with forgiveness, which is granted to those with a heart of true repentance, but not to the proud and self-righteous. In 12:13–21, the rich fool deals with the eternal consequences of greed and self-centeredness—not being rich toward God. The message of the prodigal son (15:11–32) is that all of heaven rejoices when lost sinners are found and return to the Father's arms. And the lesson of the great banquet (14:16–24) is that insiders, the spiritually elite, reject the invitation to God's salvation banquet while outsiders respond. Lazarus and the rich man (16:19–31) shows that attitudes and actions toward the less fortunate carry eternal consequences.

Courtesy of Preserving Bible Times, Inc.

↑ *The village of Nazareth in 1905. Jesus' rejection at Nazareth in Luke 4:14–30 foreshadows the rejection by his own people and the later mission to the Gentiles in Acts.*

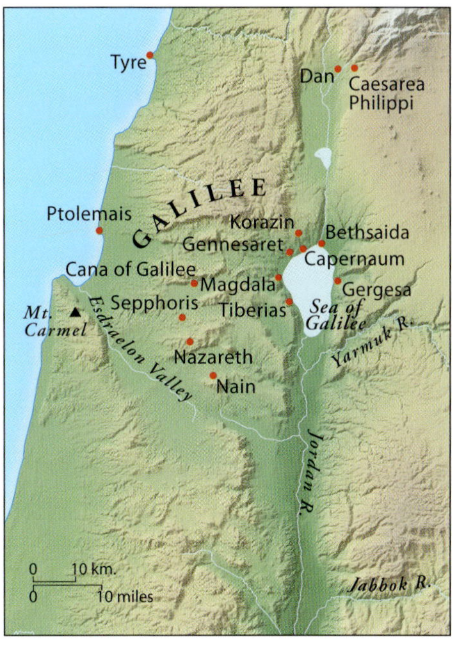


← *JESUS' EARLY MINISTRY TOOK PLACE MOSTLY IN GALILEE.*

### Interesting Facts about Luke

- **Luke wrote more of the New Testament than any other author (even Paul), when both the third gospel and its companion volume Acts are counted.**
- **Luke's writings contain some of the finest stylistic Greek in the New Testament. Only the book of Hebrews rivals it in literary quality.**
- **Luke probably was the only New Testament writer who was a Gentile.**

# John

## Summary Overview

John gives a portrait of Jesus as the divine Son who came to earth to reveal the Father and to bring eternal life to all who believe in him. The message of this gospel can be summed up in John 3:16: "For God so loved the world that he gave his one and only Son, that whoever believes in him shall not perish but have eternal life."

*Aerial view of Jerusalem.*



## Key Themes

***Jesus as the Son***. Emphasis on Jesus' identity as the divine Son who reveals the Father.
Strong ***dualistic perspective***. People are either "of God" or "of the world."
***Miracles***. Identified as "signs" revealing Jesus' identity.
***Spiritual Symbols and Metaphors***. New birth, living water, light, bread, shepherd, gate, and so on.
***Jesus' Self-revelation***. "I am . . ." statements.
***The Holy Spirit*** as counselor/advocate (*paraclete*) who will mediate Jesus' presence.

## Interesting Facts about John

- The prologue of John (1:1–18) contains the highest Christology (description of Jesus' identity) in the New Testament. It sets the stage for the rest of the gospel by presenting Jesus as the self-revelation of God.
- No other book in the New Testament so clearly and explicitly confirms the deity of Jesus Christ (1:1–3, 18; 8:58; 20:28, etc.).
- While emphasizing Jesus' deity, John also has a strong "submission" theme. In his humanity, Jesus wholly submits to the Father's will to accomplish his purpose.
- John's gospel provides the most systematic teaching in the New Testament on the role of the Holy Spirit as comforter, guide, and convicter of sin (chs. 14, 16).
- Most of the events and teaching in John are unique to this gospel. The feeding of the 5,000 (6:1–15) is the only miracle to appear in all four gospels.

## John—The Gospel of the Eternal Son of God

| Prologue<br>1:1–18 | Book of Signs<br>1:19–12:50 | Book of Glory<br>13:1–20:31 | Epilogue<br>21:1–25 |
|---|---|---|---|
| | **Signs of the Book of Signs**<br>1. Water into wine, 2:1–11<br>2. Official's son healed, 4:43–54<br>3. Healing at Bethesda Pool, 5:1–15<br>4. Feeding 5,000, 6:1–14<br>5. Walking on water, 6:16–21<br>6. Healing man born blind, 9:1–12<br>7. Lazarus raised, 11:1–43 | **Events of the Book of Glory**<br>1. Last Supper, ch. 13<br>2. Farewell Discourse, chs. 14–16<br>3. Prayer for the Disciples, ch. 17<br>4. Passion, Crucifixion, and Resurrection, Chs. 18–20 | |

←References to the "Jews" in John's gospel usually denote the corrupt Judean temple vanguard threatened by Jesus.



## Purpose

Have you ever closely examined a blade of grass or the petal from a flower? Their features are so simple, yet so profound. The gospel of John is just such a paradox. It is written in simple Greek with a basic vocabulary. Jesus describes himself with common symbols from everyday life: light, water, bread, a vine, a shepherd, a gate. Yet these everyday items are used to explain the most profound and unfathomable mystery of all: how God became a human being to bring eternal life to all who believe. Paradoxically, new believers love John because even a child can understand it, while the most brilliant scholars struggle to probe its theological depths.

John writes to call his readers to faith in Jesus Christ, the Son of God. John 20:30–31 provides a clear statement of purpose: "Jesus did many other miraculous signs in the presence of his disciples, which are not recorded in this book. But these are written that you may believe that Jesus is the Christ, the Son of God, and that by believing you may have life in his name." The phrase "that you may believe" also could be translated "that you may continue to believe." John likely writes both to confirm the faith of believers and to provoke faith in unbelievers.

The gospel has seven "I am" statements, which help to explain Jesus' identity: the bread of life (6:35); the light of the world (8:12; 9:5); the gate (10:7); the good shepherd (10:11, 14); the resurrection and the life (11:25); the way, the truth, and the life (14:6); and the true vine (15:1).

The main body of the gospel has two parts, the Book of Signs containing seven key miracles, which reveal Jesus' identity, and the Book of Glory, where Jesus' passion is repeatedly described as his "glorification." The seven "signs" are: water into wine (2:1–11); official's son healed (4:43–54); healing of the disabled man at Bethesda pool (5:1–15); feeding of the 5,000 (6:1–14); walking on water (6:16–21); healing the man born blind (9:1–12); and Lazarus raised (11:1–43). An eighth sign, the miraculous catch of fish (21:1–14), is in the epilogue.

↑This Aramaic inscription identifies the ossuary (bone box) as belonging to Caiaphas, the high priest who oversaw Jesus' Jewish trial.



↓THE JERUSALEM OF JESUS' DAY

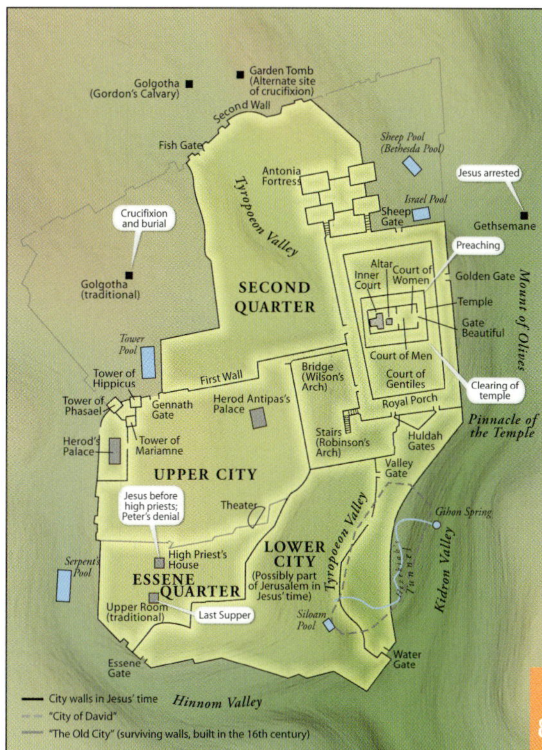


## Author

John, the brother of James and son of Zebedee, identified only as "the disciple whom Jesus loved" (21:20).

## Recipients

The gospel was likely written to believers and unbelievers in the region of Ephesus, where John is thought to have been ministering. He writes to assure believers of the truth of the gospel and to call unbelievers to faith in Jesus (20:30–31).

# Acts

## Summary Overview

Acts is the exciting sequel to the gospel of Luke (known together as Luke–Acts), telling the story of how Jesus' followers were empowered and guided by the Holy Spirit to take Jesus' message of salvation from Jerusalem to the ends of the earth.

← *Harbor of Attalia near Perga on the Mediterranean Sea. Paul, Barnabas, and Mark sailed to the port of Attalia and Perga on their first missionary journey (Acts 13:13).*



## Key Themes

***Jesus' Commission to His Disciples.*** "You will receive power when the Holy Spirit comes on you; and you will be my witnesses in Jerusalem, and in all Judea and Samaria, and to the ends of the earth" (1:8).

***The Coming of the Holy Spirit.*** The pouring out of the Spirit on the day of Pentecost marks the dawn of the new age of salvation, empowering and guiding believers.

***God's Purpose and Plan.*** God ordained not only the death and resurrection of Jesus but also that salvation would now go to the ends of the earth.

***The Unstoppable Gospel.*** The message of salvation advances despite strong opposition and apparent setbacks.

The ***geographic movement*** of the gospel from Jerusalem to Rome.

The ***ethnic movement*** of the gospel from Jews to Samaritans to Gentiles.

***The Divine Legitimacy of the Mission to the Gentiles.*** The mission to the Gentiles is not a departure from God's purpose for Israel but its fulfillment.

***Paul, God's Apostle to the Gentiles.*** Paul is not unfaithful to his Jewish roots but is fulfilling God's purpose for Israel: to be a light of revelation to the Gentiles (Isa. 49:6).

## Author

Luke, a physician and part-time missionary companion of the apostle Paul. Luke probably was a Gentile.

## Recipients

Like the gospel of Luke, Acts is addressed to Theophilus, who was probably the patron who financially supported its writing. Yet Luke surely writes to a larger Christian audience, predominantly Gentile churches needing assurance of their identity as the true people of God.

## Acts—The Gospel to the Ends of the Earth

| The Gospel to Jerusalem, Judea, Samaria, and Syria<br>Chs. 1–12 | The Gospel to the Ends of the Earth (The Gentile Mission)<br>Chs. 13–28 |
|---|---|

# Purpose

While the gospel of Luke records what Jesus *began to do* (Acts 1:1) through his life, death, and resurrection, Acts records what he *continues to do* as the risen and exalted head of the church through the Holy Spirit whom he has poured out (2:33). Central to Luke's purpose in Acts is to show that the Christian movement now spreading rapidly throughout the Mediterranean region is indeed the work of God, the climax of his plan of salvation for the world. To show this, Luke demonstrates:

- that despite his crucifixion, Jesus is indeed the Jewish Messiah, now reigning at the right hand of God;
- that the salvation of the Gentiles was ordained by God and was all along part of his purpose and plan; and
- that the apostle Paul is not a renegade Jew but is God's chosen apostle to bring salvation to the Gentiles.

How did Jesus deliver his urgent life-saving message to everyone in the world? The answer is "one sandal-shod footstep at a time," village by village, person to person. The book of Acts tells the remarkable story of how, in a few short decades, the good news of Jesus Christ spread like a wildfire from the tiny backwater province of Palestine across the Roman Empire, reaching the very heart of the civilized world—Rome itself. The message of Acts is that this amazing task could not have been accomplished by any human effort. It was indeed the work of God, accomplished through men and women empowered and guided by the Holy Spirit.

The book progresses outward geographically, from Jerusalem to Judea, to Samaria, and to the ends of the earth. It climaxes in Rome, the center of the Roman world, with Paul freely proclaiming the gospel message to Jews and Gentiles alike (28:30–31). The book also progresses ethnically, as first Jews, then Samaritans, and finally Gentiles received the message.

© Dr. James C. Martin

↑ *Paul was kept under guard at Herod's palace (bottom left in photo) in Caesarea until Paul's accusers could arrive. Paul remained in Caesarea for two years. Porcius Festus then succeeded Felix and took charge over Paul's trial (Acts 23–25).*

← *THE GOSPEL MESSAGE SPREADS.*

# Romans

© Dr. James C. Martin

## Summary Overview

The central theme of the letter is the righteousness of God (1:16–17). All people, whether Jew or Gentile, are sinful and stand condemned before a righteous and perfect God. It is only through the sacrificial death of Christ on the cross that people can be made right with God. On the basis of Christ's payment for sin, God "justifies," or declares righteous, those who have faith in him.

← *The Appian Way was the first paved road system leading out of Rome, reminding us of Paul's desire to visit the believers in Rome (Romans 1:10–15).*

## Key Theme

***The Righteousness of God***. People are made right with God ("justified") by faith alone apart from human effort, a salvation available to all regardless of ethnic identity.

## Interesting Facts about Romans

- Paul's plan to visit Rome on his way to Spain was changed by his arrest in Jerusalem (Acts 21–28). As a prisoner, though, he eventually got to Rome and preached the gospel there (Acts 28:30–31). Paul may have gone to Spain after his release, but this is uncertain since Acts ends with Paul still in prison.
- The letter was evidently carried by Phoebe, a woman and deacon (or "servant") from the church at Cenchrea (16:1).
- The letter was dictated by Paul to a secretary (or, *amanuensis*) named Tertius, who identifies himself in 16:22.

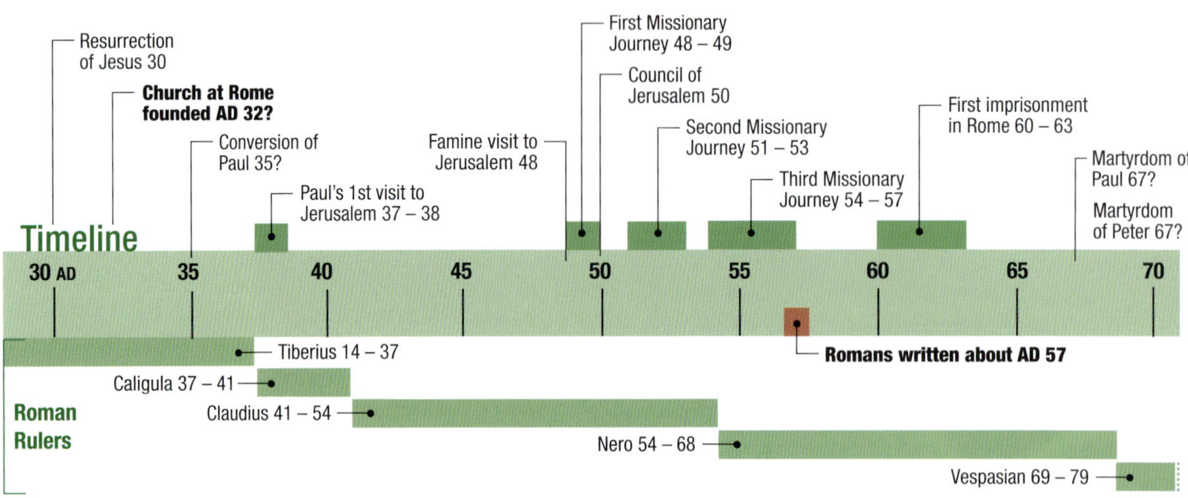

↑ *Imperial Forum and Palatine Hill, seat of the Roman government and palace of the Roman emperors.*

## Purpose

*Magnum opus*—Latin for "great work"—is a phrase used to describe the finest writing produced by an author. If Paul has a magnum opus, it is Romans, his articulate and systematic presentation of the gospel. The letter to the Romans has had a profound effect on human history, influencing such Christian luminaries as St. Augustine, Martin Luther, William Tyndale, John Wesley, and John Bunyan. Luther's study of the book sparked the Protestant Reformation, changing the course of Christianity and the history of the world. In his *Preface to the Book of Romans*, Luther called it "the most important part of the New Testament and the very purest Gospel . . . It can never be read or meditated on too much or too well, and the more it is handled the more delightful it becomes, and the better it tastes."

When Paul wrote this letter he had not yet visited the church in Rome. It is not known how or when the church began, but it may have been started by Roman Jews visiting Jerusalem on the day of Pentecost (Acts 2:10–11). Some of these may have responded to Peter's powerful sermon about the resurrection of Jesus and returned to establish the church at Rome. By the time Paul wrote, the Roman church was well established and had a good reputation among other churches throughout the Roman world (Rom. 1:8).

At the beginning of Romans, Paul states his desire to visit the church in Rome in order to preach the gospel to them, to share his spiritual gifts with them, and to be encouraged by them (1:11–15). He gives the church a summary of his gospel to show them they share a common faith. Later he mentions he wants to gain their support for a missionary outreach into Spain (15:24). Paul was always looking westward, seeking to preach the gospel where it had not yet been heard. Paul may be writing for other reasons as well: to explain the relationship of Jews and Gentiles in God's plan of salvation, to encourage Jews and Gentiles in the church to unity in Christ, and to defend the gospel of grace against legalistic tendencies.

### Author

The apostle Paul, whose Jewish name was Saul, written from Corinth about AD 57.

### Recipients

The church at Rome.

↓ *PAUL'S ARREST AND IMPRISONMENT EVENTUALLY BROUGHT HIM TO ROME.*

# 1 Corinthians

## Summary Overview

The church at Corinth had been established for several years, but the Christians there were acting like spiritual children. In this practical letter, Paul addresses many of these problems—divisions, immorality, pride, and selfishness—and tells the church it is time to grow up.

← *A view of the ancient site of Corinth (bottom right of photo) shows the Corinthian Gulf in the background.*



## Key Theme

***Divisions in the Church***. Paul appeals to the Corinthians to agree among themselves and to end their divisions so that they may be "united in mind and thought" (1:10).

## Interesting Facts about 1 Corinthians

- **First Corinthians contains the great love chapter (ch. 13), perhaps the most beautiful expression of self-sacrificial love ever penned.**
- **First Corinthians also contains the most systematic defense of the resurrection in the New Testament (ch. 15).**

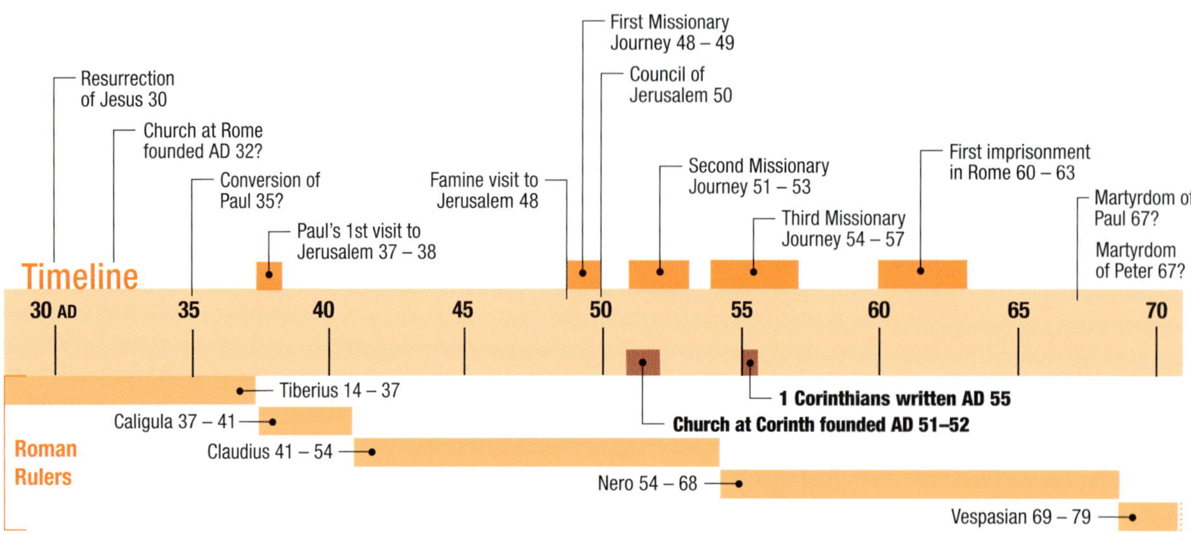

## Purpose

After founding the church at Corinth on his second missionary journey, Paul returned to his home base at Antioch in Syria. On his third missionary journey, he spent three years in Ephesus, a key city of Asia Minor across the Aegean Sea from Corinth (Acts 18:23–19:41).

While in Ephesus, Paul began to hear of troubles in the Corinthian church. He seems to have written a short letter to correct some of these issues (1 Cor. 5:9). Yet reports of problems persisted. Members of the household of a woman named Chloe told Paul of divisions in the church (1:11). A three-man delegation (Stephanas, Fortunatus, and Achaicus) came with a financial gift from the church (16:17) and may have brought a list of questions from the church (1 Cor. 7:1). In response to these problems and questions, Paul wrote the letter we call 1 Corinthians.

Paul writes to the Corinthians to correct a number of problems in the church and to answer questions the church has for him. The problems of the church include disunity, immorality, and lawsuits (chs. 1-6). The questions from the church relate to marriage, food sacrificed to idols, orderly worship, spiritual gifts, the nature of the resurrection, and a collection of money for the poor church in Jerusalem (chs. 7-16). Paul also seems to be responding to a growing challenge to his authority in the church. The believers at Corinth were recent converts from the lowest and most degraded paganism. As with many believers from difficult family or societal backgrounds, they were struggling in a variety of areas. Paul not only encourages and rebukes the church, he also sets forth general principles of conduct by which to judge all areas of life. For this reason the letter is extremely practical and relevant for today.

## Author

The apostle Paul, written from Ephesus during Paul's third missionary journey, about AD 55.

↑ CORINTH

## Who Was Paul?

Paul was one of the most remarkable men in human history. His Jewish name was Saul and he was born in Tarsus, in the region of Cilicia (modern southeast Turkey). Though born outside of Israel and well acquainted with Greek ways, Paul was trained in Jerusalem under the tutelage of Gamaliel, one of the leading Jewish rabbis of his day.

As a young man, Paul was so zealous for his faith that he began persecuting the new Christian church, viewing it as a distortion of Judaism and promoting a false messiah. But while headed for Damascus to persecute Christians, the resurrected Jesus appeared to Paul and called him into his service. Paul "the persecutor" was suddenly transformed into Paul "the apostle" (*apostle* means "one sent out with a commission"). As a missionary, evangelist, church planter, and creative theologian, Paul became one of the leading proponents of Christianity.

It was Paul more than any other who set out the theological implications of the coming of Jesus. For Paul, Jesus' sacrificial death on the cross paid for the sins of the world and reversed the results of Adam's fall. Jesus' resurrection meant that the new age of salvation—the kingdom of God—had dawned. Salvation was now to be proclaimed by his church to the whole world.

## Recipients

The church at Corinth.

## The Church at Corinth

Paul established the church at Corinth on his second missionary journey (Acts 15:36–18:22). After founding churches in Philippi, Thessalonica, and Berea (in Macedonia, northern Greece), Paul went south to Athens where he preached his famous Mars Hill address. He then moved on to Corinth, where he found lodging and work (tentmaking) with Aquila and Priscilla, a Jewish-Christian couple. Paul remained for eighteen months in the city, developing and nurturing the church.

# 2 Corinthians

## Summary Overview

When the church at Corinth rejected Paul's authority as an apostle, he felt betrayed by a church he had poured his heart and soul into. Yet he didn't turn his back on them. Instead, he worked hard to restore his relationship with the church. This emotional and heartfelt letter is the result of that reconciliation.

← *In Corinth on his second missionary journey, Paul was brought before this platform known as "the judgment seat" to be tried by the proconsul, Gallio (Acts 18:12–17). The temple prostitutes of the city lived on the Acro-Corinth, seen in the background.*



## Key Theme

***Reconciliation***. Paul writes to reconcile with the church and to defend his authority as an apostle.

## Author

Paul the apostle, written in Macedonia, AD 55–56.

## Recipients

The church at Corinth.

## The City of Corinth

Corinth was a key crossroads for commerce and communication, strategically located on the narrow isthmus between the Saronic Gulf on the south and the Ionian Sea to the north. The city had a natural defense in the Acro-Corinth, a mountain which towered 1,500 feet above the city. Originally a Greek city, Corinth was destroyed by Rome in 146 BC and rebuilt by Julius Caesar in 44 BC. Under the Romans, Corinth thrived and became one of the wealthiest and most powerful cities of Greece. The city also excelled culturally, with many theaters, gymnasia, and other public facilities. Pagan temples and altars were scattered throughout the city. As with similar commercial and urban centers, Corinth also had a well-known reputation for immorality and vice. It is not surprising that a church trying to survive there would have many difficulties.

## Timeline

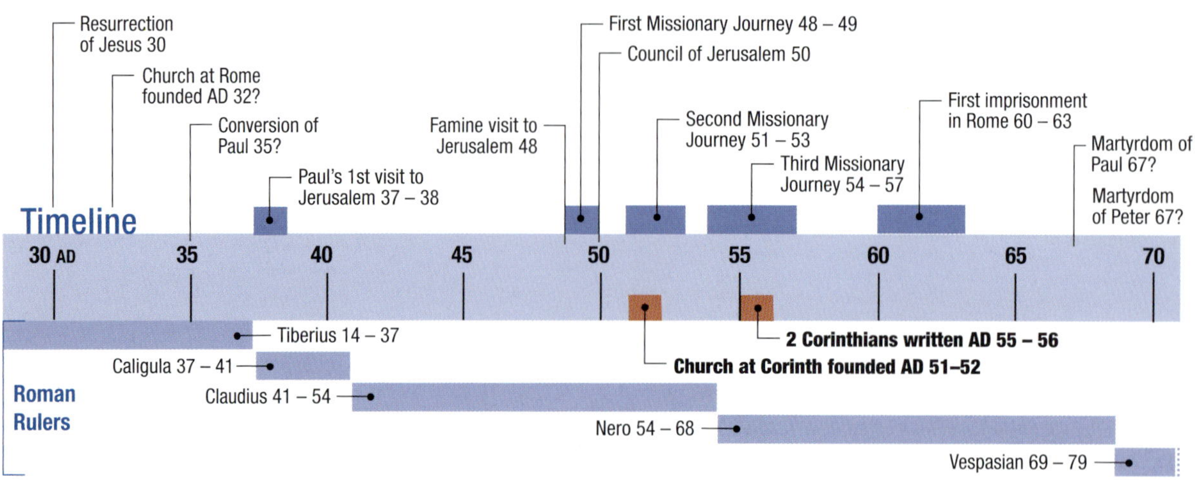

## Purpose

After writing 1 Corinthians, Paul heard reports that his letter had not resolved some of the problems in the church. Because of a growing challenge to his authority in the church, Paul decided to visit Corinth. His visit ended in disaster when he was publicly humiliated and rejected (2 Cor. 2:1; 12:14, 21; 13:1–2). False apostles attacked his authority.

Paul did not return to Corinth as he had promised (2:1). This change of plans gave his opponents more ammunition. They accused him of saying one thing and doing another (1:15–17). Paul then wrote a severe letter (2:3–4; 7:8) and sent it to the church with Titus. He was so anxious to hear the response, he headed north to Troas, then crossed over to Macedonia (2:12–13; 7:5), where he finally met Titus, who brought the good news that the majority of the church had finally repented of their rebelliousness against Paul (7:5–9).

In Macedonia Paul wrote this letter to express joy at the warm response the church had now given him (chs. 1–7) and to remind the church of their commitment to financial support for Christians in Judea (chs. 8–9). In the next four chapters Paul defends his authority as an apostle (chs. 10–13). He followed this letter with a personal visit to Corinth (Acts 20:1–4).

The key descriptive word for 2 Corinthians is "ministry." Paul gives a brilliant and stirring description and defense of the Christian ministry—what it means to be a servant and ambassador of Jesus Christ.

The book also gives us a unique look into the heart and soul of Paul. The church at Corinth had been stirred up by false teachers, who attacked Paul's teachings and authority. From Paul's response we can determine some of their charges. They claimed he was fickle (1:17–18, 23), proud and boastful (3:1; 5:12), worldly (10:2), unimpressive in appearance and speech (10:10; 11:6), unstable in thought (5:13; 11:16–19), not a true apostle (11:5; 12:11–12), and dishonest (12:16–19). Even after the Corinthians repented of their error, Paul felt the need to defend his actions and authority among them. It has been said that while Romans shows the mind of the apostle (with its logical and systematic description of the gospel), 2 Corinthians shows his heart. The words seem to spill out as Paul writes from indignation, tears, relief, and joy. It is the most personal of Paul's letters.

## Interesting Facts about 2 Corinthians

- **Paul wrote at least four, and perhaps five, letters to the Corinthians. All but two (1 and 2 Corinthians) have been lost.**
- **Second Corinthians 8–9 contains the most important passage in the New Testament on the responsibilities and joys of giving to support the Lord's work.**
- **Paul's famous "thorn in the flesh" passage describes a mysterious ailment or demonic attack which plagued him throughout his ministry (12:7). Scholars speculate on what this "thorn" was.**
- **Paul's "resume" is a listing of the great suffering he underwent for the gospel (11:21–33).**
- **Some people believe that 2 Corinthians 10–13 is actually the severe and sorrowful letter of 2 Corinthians 2:4; 7:8, attached later by an editor. Others think it is a fifth letter which Paul wrote to the church after he sent 2 Corinthians. More likely, it is an original part of 2 Corinthians.**

### PAUL'S CONTACTS AND CORRESPONDENCE WITH THE CORINTHIAN CHURCH

***First visit:*** Paul establishes the church; stays 18 months, *c.* AD 51–52

Corinthians A:
A short letter written from Ephesus to respond to immorality in the church (1 Cor. 5:9), *c.* AD 54–55

Corinthians B:
***1 Corinthians***: *Correction for an Immature Church*; written from Ephesus, *c.* AD 55

***Second visit:*** Journey from Ephesus; painful visit, *c.* AD 55

Corinthians C:
Severe and sorrowful letter (2 Cor. 2:4; 7:8)

Corinthians D:
***2 Corinthians***: *Defense of Paul's Apostolic Ministry*; written from Macedonia, *c.* AD 55–56

***Third visit:*** Church repents; Paul comes and stays 3 months; writes ***Romans***, *c.* AD 56

Corinthians E?:
2 Corinthians 10–13?, hypothetical fifth letter, comprising the last four chapters of 2 Corinthians, *c.* AD 56

# Galatians

© Dr. James C. Martin

## Summary Overview

Paul writes to combat "Judaizers," who are telling the believers in Galatia that they must be circumcised and keep the law of Moses to be saved.

← *General geographical area of the Roman province of Galatia where Paul addressed his letter to the Galatians.*

## Key Theme

***Salvation***. Paul defends the gospel, emphasizing that salvation is a gift from God that comes through faith in Jesus Christ, not from human works. He writes: "Neither circumcision nor uncircumcision means anything; what counts is a new creation" (6:15).

## Author

Paul the apostle, probably written from Antioch, Syria, around AD 49 (although some argue for the mid-50s).

## Recipients

The churches in Galatia.

## The Churches in Galatia

The region of Galatia (part of modern Turkey) was named after the Gauls (or Celts) who had come down from the north to settle the area of north-central Asia Minor. The Romans later established a province named Galatia which comprised a much larger area, including land to the south of the original Galatian kingdom. There is some debate as to whether Paul is writing to churches in the northern or southern areas. According to Luke, Paul started churches in four towns in the south on his first missionary journey: Pisidian Antioch, Iconium, Lystra, and Derbe (Acts 13–14).

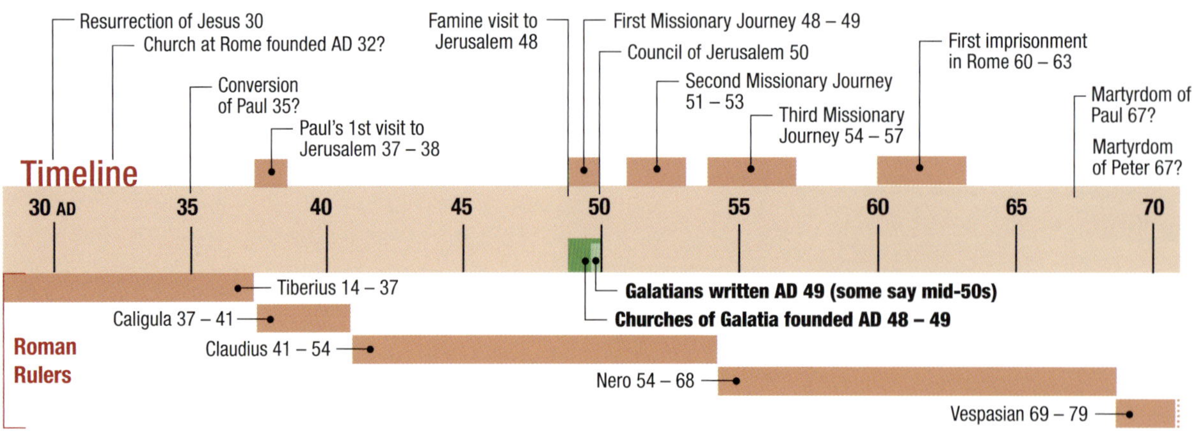

## Purpose

We have an expression in English that comes from times of war: "What hill are you willing to die on?" By this we mean what are the nonnegotiables in your life—those things you would sacrifice everything for. Protection of family? Faith in God? Love for country? The apostle Paul was a man of great flexibility who could adapt his message to a variety of cultural contexts and settings. Yet the essence of the gospel message—salvation by faith alone in Jesus Christ—was a nonnegotiable for Paul, a hill he would die defending. For this great truth Paul would never compromise.

Sometime after establishing these churches in Galatia, Paul heard reports that the Galatian believers were being influenced by "Judaizers," Jewish Christians who claimed that Gentiles needed to be circumcised and keep the law of Moses in order to be saved. Paul saw this teaching as a serious threat to the authentic gospel message that salvation is a free gift from God which comes through faith alone in Jesus, not through any human works.

Paul is hopping mad and ready for a fight. He fires off this passionate plea to the Galatians not to give up their precious freedom in Christ by returning to slavery to sin and legalism. After his greeting, Paul skips his customary thanksgivings for the church and jumps right into the problem: desertion from the faith by turning to a false gospel. He first defends the authenticity of the true gospel from his own life, showing that he did not receive this message from any human agent, but directly from God. He then turns to theological arguments, demonstrating that salvation by works inevitably fails. The law only condemns, it cannot save. Finally Paul sets out the practical argument, showing that true freedom comes from living by the power of the Spirit.

↑ *Remnants of Antioch's ancient first-century synagogue lay beneath the ruins of this Byzantine church.*

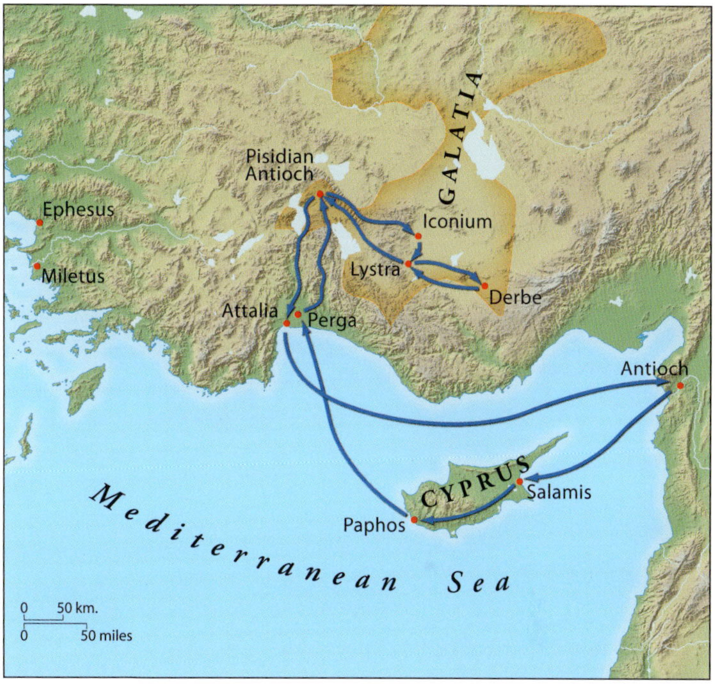


↑ *PAUL'S FIRST MISSIONARY JOURNEY, WHEN HE ESTABLISHED CHURCHES IN GALATIA*

## Interesting Facts about Galatians

- Galatians may have been Paul's earliest letter, written shortly after his first missionary journey (about AD 49). Others place the letter later, in the mid to late 50s.
- Galatians contains the great passage on the "fruit of the Spirit," the evidence of the Holy Spirit in a believer's life: love, joy, peace, patience, kindness, goodness, faithfulness, gentleness, and self-control (5:22).
- Galatians has been called Paul's "mad" letter, because he so passionately defends the gospel message. Some of Paul's strongest and most emotional language appears in Galatians. After his greeting, the first words out of his mouth are "I am astonished!" (1:6). He says that anyone who preaches a different gospel ought to be "eternally condemned!" (1:8–9). He mocks those calling for Gentile circumcision and says they should go all the way and castrate themselves (5:12). Paul clearly had strong feelings on this issue!

# Ephesians

## Summary Overview

If you could write one letter to your children or grandchildren, passing on your most cherished beliefs, what would you say? The letter to the Ephesians has sometimes been called the "quintessential Paul," concisely summarizing the essence of Paul's faith and theology.

← *Aerial view of Ephesus, including the theater and central street of the city (i.e., Cardo).*



## Key Theme

***God's Purpose in Christ***. The central theme is the divine purpose and plan of God in bringing redemption to his people and the practical outworking of that purpose in the life of the believer.

## Author

The apostle Paul, probably written from prison in Rome, about AD 60–62.

## Recipients

The church in Ephesus or as an "encyclical" to be circulated among various churches in Asia Minor.

## The Church at Ephesus

Ephesus was the most important commercial center in the Roman province of Asia, a major port city at the mouth of the river Cayster leading to the Aegean Sea. Paul established the church there on his third missionary journey and stayed for about three years, longer than any other single church. He preached first in the synagogue, and when opposition arose moved to the lecture hall of a man named Tyrannus. Luke relates that from this base the whole province of Asia heard the gospel (Acts 19:8–10).

## Timeline

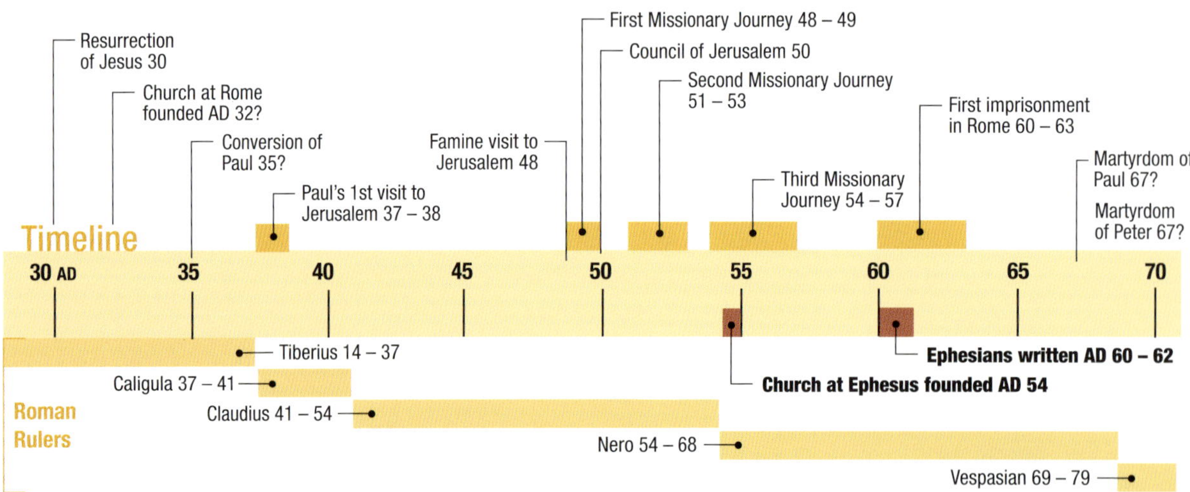

## Purpose

The letter covers a vast amount of doctrine and practice in a very short space. It is one of four "prison letters" (Ephesians, Philippians, Colossians, Philemon) probably written during Paul's first Roman imprisonment, around AD 60 (Acts 28). It was evidently carried by Tychicus (6:21), who also accompanied the letter to the Colossians (Col. 4:7).

Ephesians shares many common themes and similar language with Colossians and was probably written about the same time. Its purpose seems to be to provide the church with a concise summary of God's plan of salvation and to encourage Jews and Gentiles to unity in the faith.

Ephesians may be divided into two parts. In the first three chapters Paul speaks doctrinally concerning God's divine purpose in Christ and the believers' position in Christ. In the final three chapters, he speaks practically concerning how believers ought to live in light of their position in Christ.

↑ *A statue of Artemis, who was venerated at Ephesus as a goddess of fertility (Acts 19:24–41).*

## Interesting Facts about Ephesians

- **The first chapter of Ephesians is perhaps the greatest passage in the Bible on God's sovereign choice and purpose in the believer's life.**
- **Ephesians says a great deal about the unity believers share in Christ: one body, one Spirit, one hope, one Lord, one faith, one baptism, one God and Father of all (4:4–6).**
- **Ephesians contains an extended section on how Christian relationships should be maintained within the Greco-Roman household, including husbands and wives, parents and children, and slaves and masters (5:21–6:9).**
- **Ephesians contains the famous passage on the "armor of God," where Paul uses the metaphor of a Roman soldier's armor to describe the weapons with which believers fight their spiritual war (6:10–20).**

← *EPHESUS LIES ON THE COAST OF WESTERN ASIA MINOR.*

# Philippians

© Dr. James C. Martin

## Summary Overview

Paul's letter thanks the Philippians for their support of his ministry and encourages them to greater unity, joy, and contentment in Christ.

← *The apostle Paul walked down this part of the Egnatian Way on his journey from Kavala to Philippi.*

## Key Theme

***Knowing Christ***. The most pervasive theme is the great joy of knowing Christ, summed up in Paul's command, "Rejoice in the Lord always. I will say it again: Rejoice!" (4:4).

## Author

The apostle Paul, probably written from prison in Rome, about AD 60–62.

## Recipients

The church in Philippi.

## The Church at Philippi

The church at Philippi was started by Paul on his second missionary journey and was the first church established in Europe. In Troas on his second journey, Paul received a vision to cross from Asia to Macedonia. There was no synagogue in Philippi, so Paul and Silas went to a place of prayer by the river where they met Lydia, a businesswoman. She became the first convert in the city and welcomed them into her home. In the days that followed, Paul ministered in the city. He cast a demon out of a fortune-telling slave girl who had been harassing them. The girl's owners were furious at the loss of revenue and had Paul and Silas arrested, beaten, and imprisoned. That night in prison, an earthquake struck and their chains fell off. Through these events, the jailer and his household responded to the gospel. The church at Philippi had been launched (Acts 16:11–40).

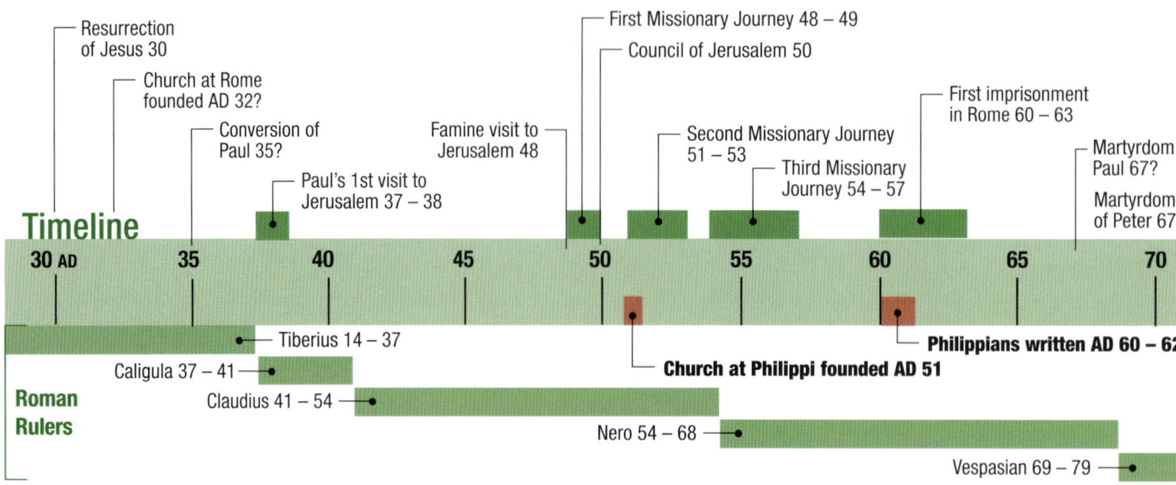

## Purpose

While all of Paul's epistles are real letters written to real people, Philippians is perhaps the most "newsy" of them all, much like a letter one would write to dear friends. It is full of encouraging words, news of Paul's situation, and thanksgiving for the support he has received from his Christian brothers and sisters at Philippi.

Paul's relationship to the church at Philippi was warm and close. The church was a giving one, and at least twice before had helped him financially (4:16). They were truly partners in ministry (1:5). Shortly before this letter was written, the church had sent another gift with Epaphroditus, who stayed in Rome to minister to Paul's needs. Epaphroditus had subsequently become ill and almost died, causing great concern both for Paul and for the church (2:25–30; 4:14–18).

Paul wrote to tell the Philippians he was sending Epaphraditus back with commendations for his faithful service (2:25–30). He thanks the church for their financial support and partnership (4:10–19). He informs the church of his circumstances (1:12–30), of his plan to send Timothy shortly (2:23), and of his own desire to visit them (2:24). He calls the church to greater unity and service to others in the face of some conflicts and disunity in the church (2:2–4; 4:2–3). He also warns the Philippians of the threat of Judaizers, Jewish Christians preaching a legalistic salvation by works (3:2–11).

Paul's entire passion in life is "to know Christ" (3:10). He has learned to be content in any and every circumstance, since all his strength comes from Christ (4:13). Paul writes about how he rejoices in his present circumstances because the gospel continues to be proclaimed despite his imprisonment (1:12–14). He can rejoice even when others preach from wrong motives, for "whether from false motives or true, Christ is preached" (1:15–18). He can rejoice whatever the outcome of his trial (1:18–26), because release will bring joy to the Philippians at their reunion, but death would bring even greater joy in the presence of Jesus (1:21).

↑ *Agora (marketplace) at Philippi.*

← *PHILIPPI, THE FIRST CHURCH IN EUROPE*

## Interesting Facts about Philippians

- **Philippi was a small city, but because it was a Roman colony, the city housed a Roman military outpost and its citizens enjoyed special privileges from Rome. Paul alludes to this idea of "citizenship" in 3:20.**
- **Philippians contains a great hymn to Christ (2:5–11), the clearest statement in the New Testament of the incarnation, Christ's willingness to "empty himself" (the *kenosis*) of his position of glory in heaven to become a human being and to suffer a humiliating death on the cross as payment for our sins.**

# Colossians

## Summary Overview

Paul writes to combat a growing heresy in the church at Colosse. This false teaching, by stressing human speculation and legalistic works for salvation, devalued the person and work of Christ. In response, Paul affirms that Jesus is the "image" of the invisible God; the fullness of deity dwells in him. He is head of his body, the church. Through his death and resurrection, he brought reconciliation between God and humanity. Any human wisdom or philosophy pales in comparison to Christ's divine glory.

← *The ancient site of Colosse.*

## Key Theme

***Supremacy and Sufficiency of Christ***. Paul opposes the false teaching in the church at Colosse, emphasizing that Christ is the creator and sustainer of all things and the one mediator between God and human beings.

## Author

The apostle Paul, written from prison in Rome, about AD 60–62.

## Recipients

The church in Colosse.

## The Church at Colosse

The city of Colosse was located in the region of Phrygia (south central Turkey), on the banks of the river Lycus, about 100 miles east of Ephesus. Though Paul had never personally visited the church (2:1), it probably was started during his third missionary journey, when he spent three years in Ephesus. Acts 19:8–10 reports that during this time the gospel spread throughout the province of Asia. The Colossian church appears to have been established by Epaphras, a native of Colosse and one of Paul's companions (1:7; 4:12; Philemon 23).

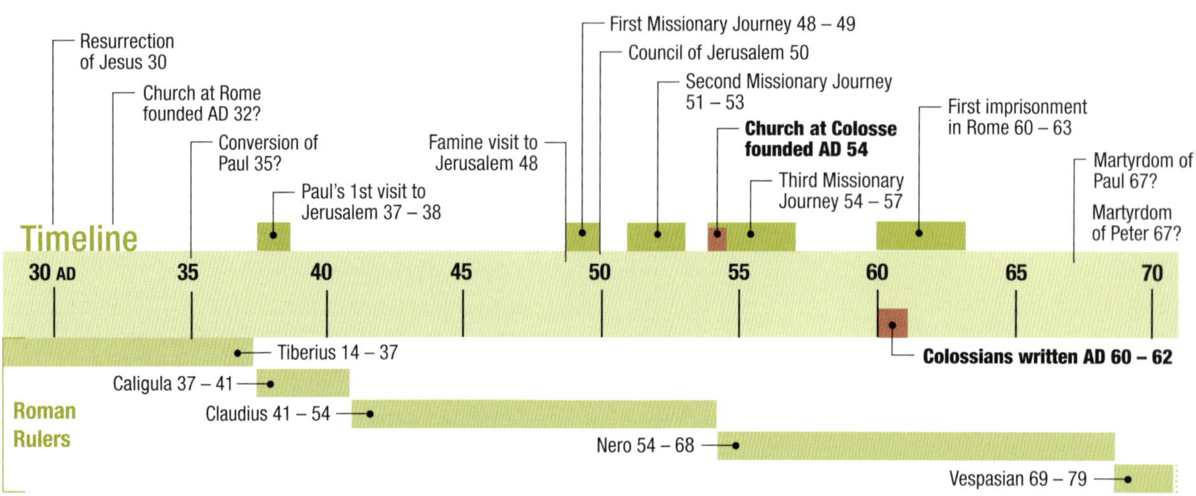

## Purpose

Religious counterfeits are all around us—people claiming to have found a new way to God or to have achieved true spiritual enlightenment. In this letter Paul confronts a spiritual counterfeit that is threatening the church at Colosse.

Scholars have debated the nature of this "Colossian heresy." If it was a single teaching (rather than a variety of problems), it seems to have involved a syncretism (combining) of Jewish asceticism and mysticism with an early form of Gnosticism. Gnostics considered the material world to be evil and salvation to be achieved by attaining special "knowledge" (*gnosis*) of spiritual realities.

This growing heresy, which may have been reported to Paul by Epaphras, devalued the person and work of Jesus and exalted certain human works and special spiritual knowledge as the means of salvation. From what we can piece together, the heresy included empty philosophical speculation based on human traditions (2:8), dietary and Sabbath observances (2:16), false humility (2:18), worship of angels and other visionary experiences (2:18), the practice of asceticism and self abasement (2:20–23), and legalism: "Do not handle! Do not taste! Do not touch!" (2:21).

Paul exercises his authority as an apostle to call the church back to the truth of the gospel: salvation through Christ alone. He stresses the supremacy of Christ—in creation (1:15–18) and in redemption (1:19–23). In chapter 2, Paul contrasts the weak and insufficient heresy with the all-sufficient, all-powerful Christ. Finally, in chapters 3 and 4, Paul addresses the practical side of these doctrinal truths. The believer's union with Christ in his death, resurrection, and exaltation is the foundation upon which the Christian life must be built.

At the time of writing, Epaphras is in Rome with Paul (4:12), and Paul refers to him as a "fellow prisoner" (Philem. 23). Whether Epaphras was actually imprisoned or was providing support for Paul is uncertain. In any case, Tychicus brings the letter and the news about Paul and Epaphras to the Colossians (4:7–8; Eph. 6:21). Tychicus is traveling with Onesimus, Philemon's runaway slave now returning home (4:9), which means this letter was sent together with the letter to Philemon (Philem. 10).

↑ *Paul's letter to the Colossians was sent to Colosse in the valley of the Lycus River.*

## Interesting Facts about Colossians

- **Gnosticism, an early form of which Paul seems to be opposing in Colossians, would become the greatest religious threat to Christianity in the second century.**
- **Colossians was sent with the letter to Philemon, and perhaps also with Ephesians.**
- **Ephesians is closely related to Colossians in theme and style. While Colossians stresses Christ as the head of the church, Ephesians emphasizes the church as the body of Christ.**

↓ *COLOSSE*

# 1 Thessalonians

© Dr. James C. Martin

## Summary Overview

Paul praises the young church at Thessalonica for standing firm and remaining faithful in the face of severe persecution. He encourages them to love one another even more, to grow in righteousness and purity, and to continue to focus on their ultimate hope for the glorious return of their Lord and Savior Jesus Christ.

← *View of the harbor of Thessalonica with Mount Olympus in the background. Paul reminds the church of the Thessalonians that his visit to them was not a failure (1 Thessalonians 2:1).*

## Key Themes

***Encouragement to Persevere.*** The church at Thessalonica was suffering serious persecution. Throughout the letter Paul praises the church for its patient endurance and urges them to continue in faith, hope, and love (1:2–3).

***Hope for the Return of Christ.*** In times of crisis, the believer's ultimate hope is the return of Christ, who will deliver God's people and will judge the wicked. Over and over again Paul returns to this theme (1:3, 10; 2:19; 3:13; 4:13–18; 5:1–11).

***Love for Fellow Believers.*** Paul praises the Thessalonian believers for their love for one another but encourages them to greater and greater love (1:3; 3:12; 4:9–10; 5:13).

## Author

The apostle Paul, written about AD 51, from Corinth.

## Recipients

The church at Thessalonica, established by Paul on his second missionary journey.

## The City of Thessalonica

Thessalonica was a prominent seaport and the capital of the Roman province of Macedonia. It was located on the Via Egnatia, the main road from Rome to the East. The city had a large Jewish population, and this Judaism had attracted many God-fearers—Gentiles who worshiped the true God of Israel.

## Timeline

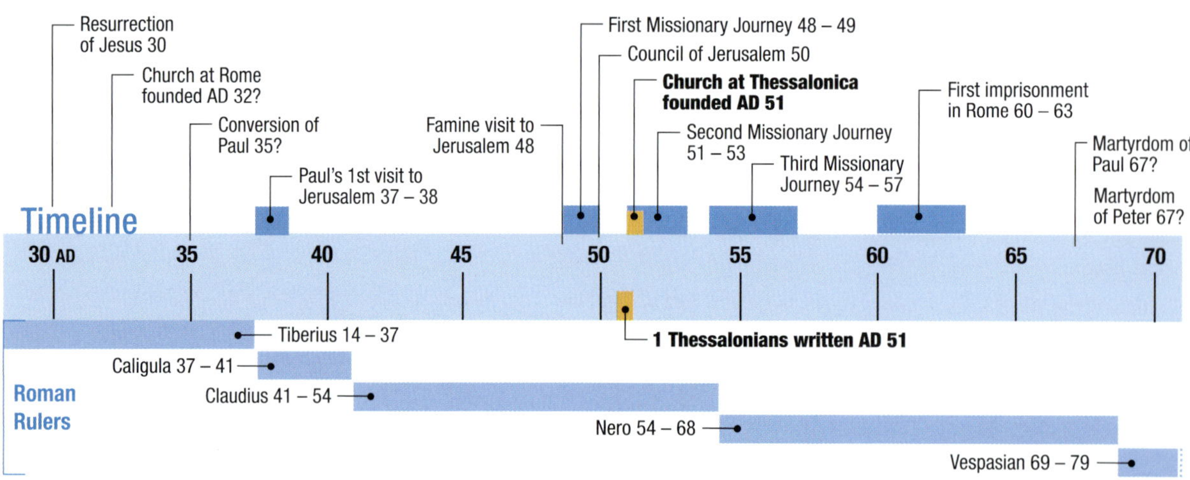

## Purpose

According to the book of Acts, Paul established the church at Thessalonica on his second missionary journey. Traveling with his missionary companions Silas and Timothy, Paul came to the city around AD 51 after establishing the church at Philippi. As was his custom, he began preaching in the Jewish synagogue, winning some Jews and a large number of God-fearing Gentiles to Christ (Acts 17:1–4).

Paul's successful ministry in Thessalonica stirred jealousy among unbelieving Jews, who provoked a riot against him and his companions. After about a month of ministry, they were forced to leave, fleeing south to Berea. When Paul's Jewish opponents pursued him there, he went on to Athens (Acts 17:5–15).

All along the way, Paul was deeply concerned about his new spiritual children at Thessalonica. Could such young believers hold up under severe persecution? Anxious, Paul sent Timothy back to Thessalonica to see how the church was doing (2:17–3:5), while he moved on to Corinth, where Timothy eventually joined him. Timothy's report was encouraging and exciting. The Thessalonians were standing firm in their faith (3:6–7). Full of joy, Paul wrote this letter of encouragement and praise to the Thessalonian church.

The first half of the letter (chs. 1–3) deals with Paul's relationship with the Thessalonians and the nature of his ministry while among them. The second half (chs. 4–5) provides instructions on godly living and on the return of Christ.

*← Paul crossed through the Cilician Gates in what is now southern Turkey on his second missionary journey. The Taurus mountains in the background range from 10,000 to 12,000 feet.*



### Interesting Facts about 1 Thessalonians

- **First Thessalonians contains the most famous biblical passage on the rapture of the church (4:13–18).**
- **The important theme of the return of Christ occurs in each of the letter's five chapters.**
- **It was the first or second letter written by Paul. (Galatians might have been earlier.)**

*↓ THE CHURCH IN THESSALONICA WAS ESTABLISHED DURING PAUL'S SECOND MISSIONARY JOURNEY.*

# 2 Thessalonians

## Summary Overview

Paul had heard that the church at Thessalonica was getting sidetracked from its fundamental mission because of inaccurate reports about the arrival of the day of the Lord. He writes to calm the church and to correct the false teaching they have received. He also deals with the idleness of those who refused to work and the busybodies who were causing problems.

← *Excavation remains of the Roman Cardo in Thessalonica. Paul encourages the church of the Thessalonians to stand firm in the midst of their persecution (2 Thessalonians 2:15).*



## Key Themes

***Encouragement for Maturity***. Paul thanks God for the Thessalonians' faith and encourages them to continued endurance in the face of persecution (1:3–12; 2:13–3:5).

***Correction of Misconceptions***. Paul seeks to comfort and correct the Thessalonians about their misconceptions concerning the day of the Lord (2:1–17).

***Accountability***. Paul calls into account those who refuse to work and act like busybodies (3:6–15).

## Author

The apostle Paul, written from Corinth, about AD 51.

## Recipients

The church at Thessalonica.

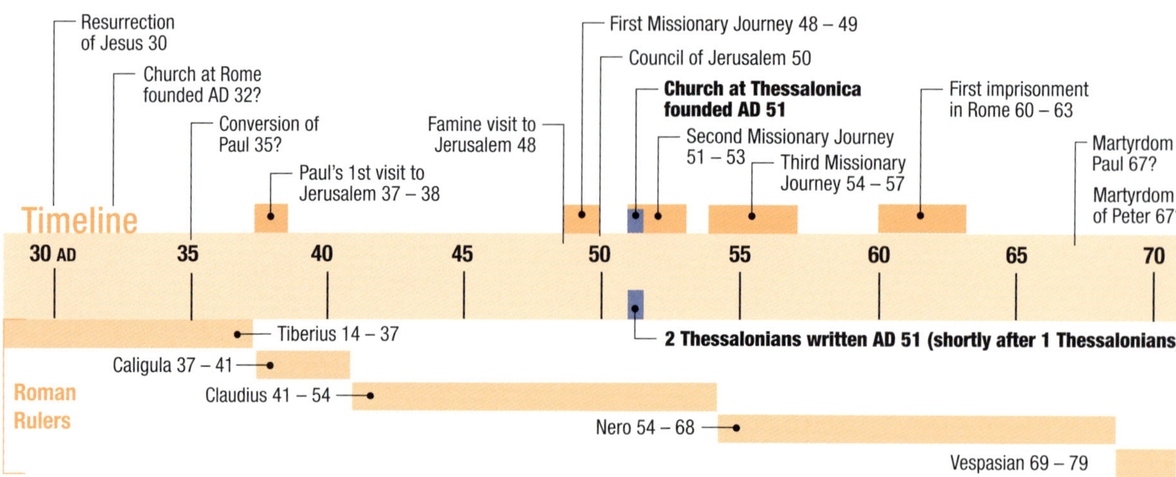

## Purpose

After sending his first letter to the Thessalonians, word reached Paul about a new problem in the church. Some Thessalonians had come to believe that the day of the Lord—the time of God's final judgment—had already begun (2:1–2). Perhaps some wondered whether the persecution they were experiencing was the beginning of the end-time persecution Jesus had predicted. Paul is not sure of the origin of the rumor, but refers to a prophecy, a message, or a forged letter supposedly from him (2:2).

Another problem is idleness, busybodies who refuse to work. Some Thessalonians may have quit their jobs because they thought the end of the world was about to arrive. Paul's answer is basically: "Calm down and get back to work, the day of the Lord has not yet arrived." He offers two reasons: the great "rebellion" (or apostasy) has not begun and "the man of lawlessness" has not yet been revealed (2:3).

For their length, the two Thessalonian letters contain more teaching about "eschatology" (the study of the end times and the return of Christ) than any other part of the New Testament. Paul uses a number of terms and phrases in 2 Thessalonians which often puzzle the modern reader. Here are a few:

↑ *A seventeenth-century painting by Claude Vignon depicts the apostle Paul writing a letter to one of the New Testament churches.*



- *The "coming of our Lord"* (2:1): The Greek term *parousia*, here translated "coming," is often used for the return of Christ.
- *The day of the Lord* (2:2): A term referring to the time when God will judge the nations and restore his people. While the term can refer to any cataclysmic judgment in human history (such as the destruction of Babylon), the Bible also refers to a great and final day when God will bring human history to its culmination.
- *The great rebellion* (2:3): Paul describes a great revolt against God which will prepare the way for the man of lawlessness.
- *The man of lawlessness* (2:3–12): An evil figure who will set himself up as divine in opposition to God and will persecute the people of God. The man of lawlessness is probably the same as the "antichrist" of 1 John 2:18 and the "beast" of Revelation 11:7; 13:1–18.
- *The restrainer* (2:5–7): Paul refers to something that is "holding back" the man of lawlessness. Scholars debate whether this "restrainer" is the Holy Spirit, the Roman Empire, the rule of government, Paul himself, or something else.

# 1 Timothy

## Summary Overview

Paul writes to encourage and instruct his disciple Timothy on the issues of opposing false teachers and doctrine (1:3–20, 4:1–16, 6:3–5), properly conducting worship in the church (2:9–15), appointing leaders (3:1–16), relationships within the church (widows, 5:3–16; elders, 5:17–25; masters and slaves, 6:1–2), and the danger of materialism (6:6–10). He charges Timothy to "fight the good fight of the faith" and "to guard what has been entrusted to your care" (6:12, 20).

← *Timothy, Paul's young assistant, was instructed to remain in Ephesus in order to supervise the church and refute false teachings. Here he walked the streets of Ephesus lined with monuments and temples dedicated to Roman emperors, idols, and city leaders.*



## Key Themes

***False Teachers.*** Paul instructs Timothy to command certain men not to teach false doctrines (1:3–11).
***Worship Instructions.*** Instructions on proper worship in the church (2:8–15).
***Church Leader Qualifications.*** Paul gives a list of attributes for church leaders (3:1–16).

## Interesting Facts about 1 Timothy

- **The authenticity of the Pastoral Epistles (1–2 Timothy, Titus) has been questioned by some scholars due to differences in style and theology with other letters of Paul. Yet there is not enough firm evidence to overthrow Pauline authorship. Differences in theology can be accounted for by the different circumstances addressed. Stylistic differences may have been produced by Paul's use of a scribe to write the letter, a common practice in the ancient world (and one which Paul used elsewhere, Rom. 16:22).**
- **In both 1 Timothy 3:1–13 and Titus 1:6–9 Paul provides his disciples with lists of qualifications for church leaders (elders, overseers, and deacons). These lists are often used for choosing church leaders today.**
- **First Timothy 2:11–15 is the most controversial passage concerning the role of women in the church. The debate centers on whether Paul's statements here are intended only for the first-century church at Ephesus or for all Christians everywhere.**

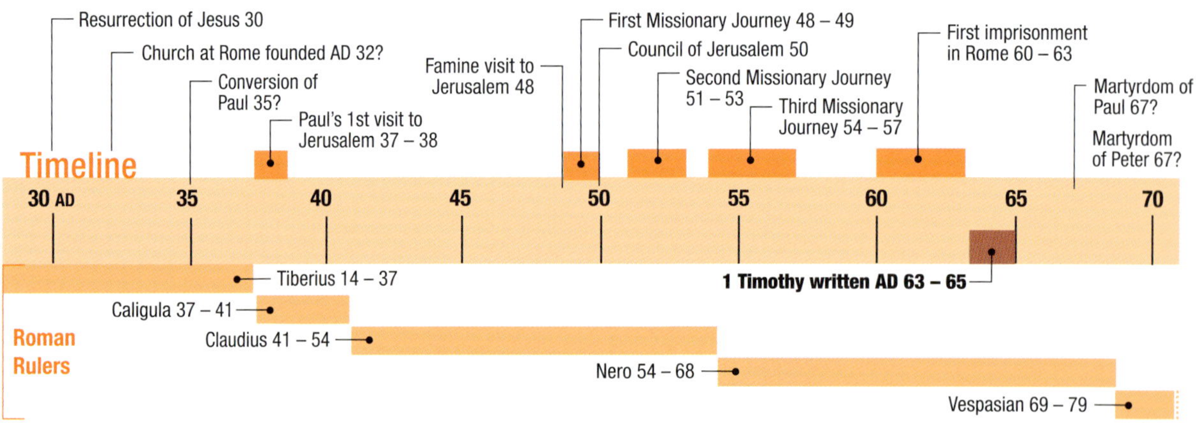

## Purpose

First and 2 Timothy and Titus are called the Pastoral Epistles because they contain principles for the pastoral care of churches and qualifications for leaders. Paul sent these letters to two of his young disciples to encourage and support them in their ministry. An obvious distinction between these and other Pauline letters (except Philemon) is that they are addressed to individuals rather than churches. It seems likely, however, that they were also meant to be read to the whole congregation.

The situations addressed in the Pastoral Epistles do not fit Paul's travels as we know them from the book of Acts, and it is likely that these three letters were written after Paul's release from his first imprisonment. Although Acts ends with Paul in custody in Rome, his accusers from Jerusalem probably never made the long trip to Rome to press charges against him (Acts 24:1). Paul's freedom while under house arrest in Acts 28:30–31 and his comments in Philippians 1:25–26 also suggest he was released and continued his ministry.

During Paul's subsequent travels, he learned that false teaching was beginning to take hold in the church at Ephesus, and he became concerned about the church's leadership and oversight. He therefore appointed Timothy to supervise leadership training and to combat the false teaching. Yet Paul was concerned about the pressures on his younger assistant, so he wrote this letter—probably from Macedonia (1:3)—to encourage and instruct him. The purpose of the letter is stated in 3:14–15: "Although I hope to come to you soon, I am writing you these instructions so that, if I am delayed, you will know how people ought to conduct themselves in God's household, which is the church of the living God, the pillar and foundation of the truth."

Finally Paul was arrested again and taken to Rome. There he wrote his last letter, 2 Timothy.

### Author

The apostle Paul, written about AD 63, probably from Macedonia.

### Recipient

Paul's disciple Timothy.

### Who Was Timothy?

Timothy was a native of Lystra in the province of Galatia, the offspring of a mixed marriage between a Greek father and a Jewish mother (Acts 16:1). While growing up, Timothy was taught the Scriptures by his mother and grandmother (2 Tim. 1:5). Paul may have led Timothy to Christ on his first missionary journey. When Paul passed through Lystra on his second journey, he was so impressed with Timothy that he took him along. Paul circumcised him so as not to offend the Jews in that area (Acts 16:2–3). Timothy was Paul's missionary companion for much of the rest of his ministry: in Macedonia and Asia Minor on Paul's second journey (Acts 17:14–15; 18:5), in Ephesus on his third journey (Acts 19:22), to Corinth and back to Troas at the end of the third journey (Acts 20:4). Whether Timothy went with Paul to Jerusalem where Paul was arrested is uncertain, but he was with Paul during his first Roman imprisonment (Phil. 1:1; Col. 1:1; Philem. 1). Paul names Timothy as a coauthor at the beginning of six of his letters (2 Corinthians, Philippians, Colossians, 1 and 2 Thessalonians, Philemon).

Timothy may have been somewhat timid by nature (2 Tim. 1:6–7), and Paul repeatedly spurs him to greater authority and action (1 Tim. 1:3; 4:11–12; 5:7; 6:2; 2 Tim. 3:14; 4:2, 5). Paul considers Timothy to be his closest disciple, praising him for his deep and unselfish concern for others (Phil. 2:19–23). Near the end of his life, Paul urges Timothy to come to him in prison (2 Tim. 4:9, 21).

# 2 Timothy

## Summary Overview

As Paul writes this last letter to Timothy, he is well aware that his time on earth is nearly over. He commissions Timothy to faithfully carry on the ministry that the Lord has given him. The letter is full of military and athletic metaphors: Paul has fought the good fight; he has finished the course; he has kept the faith. Now he exhorts Timothy as a good soldier of Jesus Christ to do the same, to use the spiritual weapon of the Word of God to overcome all obstacles to the spread of the gospel.

← *"This is my gospel, for which I am suffering even to the point of being chained like a criminal" (2 Timothy 2:8–9). According to tradition Paul was imprisoned here at the Marmertine prison in Rome.*

## Key Theme

***Guard the Gospel*.** To encourage and give instructions to Timothy to carry on after Paul's departure.

## Timeline

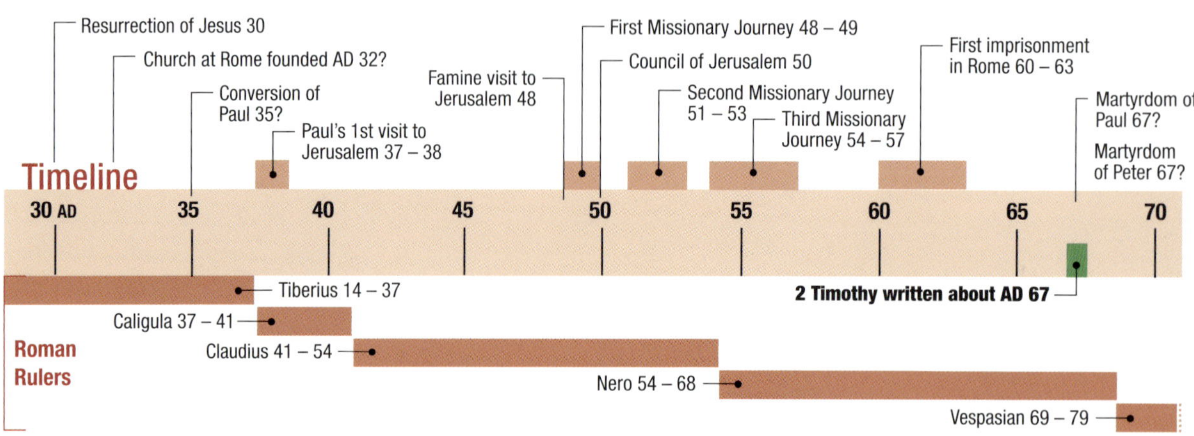

## Purpose

After ministering freely for several years, Paul was again arrested (probably in Troas, 4:13) and sent to Rome. This arrest was perhaps the result of the persecution of the Christians begun by the Roman emperor Nero. This time the situation was far more serious than during his first imprisonment, when he was under house arrest and expected to be released (Acts 28:30–31; Phil. 1:25–26). Now Paul is chained as a common criminal in a dungeon and assumes his trial will end in execution (1:16; 2:9; 4:6–8, 18).

This second letter to his disciple Timothy, his "dear son" in the faith (1:2), has been called Paul's swan song or his last will and testament. When a person's death draws near, his or her perspective on what is truly important comes into sharper focus. Paul is acutely aware of the importance of guarding the purity of the gospel which he has labored his whole life to advance. You can feel his heart speaking when he says to Timothy to "guard the good deposit that was entrusted to you" (1:14). Paul writes to encourage and instruct Timothy in his ministry, especially in light of false teaching in the church, and to "pass the torch," exhorting Timothy to faithfully carry on the ministry Paul has begun. Paul also asks Timothy to come visit him in prison. In his lonely prison cell, Paul longs for the fellowship of his close brother. He speaks emotionally of the fact that everyone deserted him (1:15; 4:10, 16) and that "only Luke is with me" (4:11).

### Author

The apostle Paul, written about AD 67, from prison in Rome, a short time before his execution.

### Recipient

Timothy.

← *The martyrdom of Paul in Rome, as imagined by a sixteenth-century Italian artist.*



## Interesting Facts about 2 Timothy

- **Paul probably was arrested in Troas, because he asks Timothy to bring the cloak and scrolls he left there (4:13).**
- **Paul refers to many of his most trusted companions: Luke, Titus, Mark, Priscilla, Aquila, and others.**
- **This was Paul's last letter. Soon after he was beheaded on the Ostian Way, west of Rome.**

# Titus

© Dr. Barry J. Beitzel

## Summary Overview

This letter encourages and gives instructions to Titus in his leadership role on the island of Crete. It shares many characteristics with 1 Timothy, since both relate to combating heresy, teaching sound doctrine, appointing leaders, and relationships within the church.

← *Basilica of Titus on Crete.*

## Key Themes

***Sound Doctrine***. Paul stresses the teaching of sound doctrine and warns against those who would distort the truth.

***Good Deeds***. This letter puts a major emphasis on good deeds and the conduct of various groups within the church.

## Author

The apostle Paul, written about AD 63–65, probably from Nicopolis, Macedonia, or Achaia.

## Recipient

Titus, Paul's disciple.

## Who Was Titus?

Titus was most likely a convert of Paul's, because Paul refers to him as "my true son" (1:4). He was a Gentile. In Galatians 2:3 Paul uses Titus as an illustration to demonstrate that Gentiles are saved by faith. He says that the Jerusalem apostles accepted Titus as a true believer even though Titus was not circumcised. He must have been quite mature and a very trusted companion. Paul sent Titus to represent him in Corinth during Paul's worst troubles with the church in that city (2 Cor. 2:13; 7:6–7, 13–15). His maturity is further seen in the fact that Paul left him in charge at Crete, a very difficult area of ministry. According to 2 Timothy 4:10, Titus had been with Paul during his second Roman imprisonment, but had left to work in Dalmatia (modern Bosnia, Serbia, and Croatia).

## Timeline

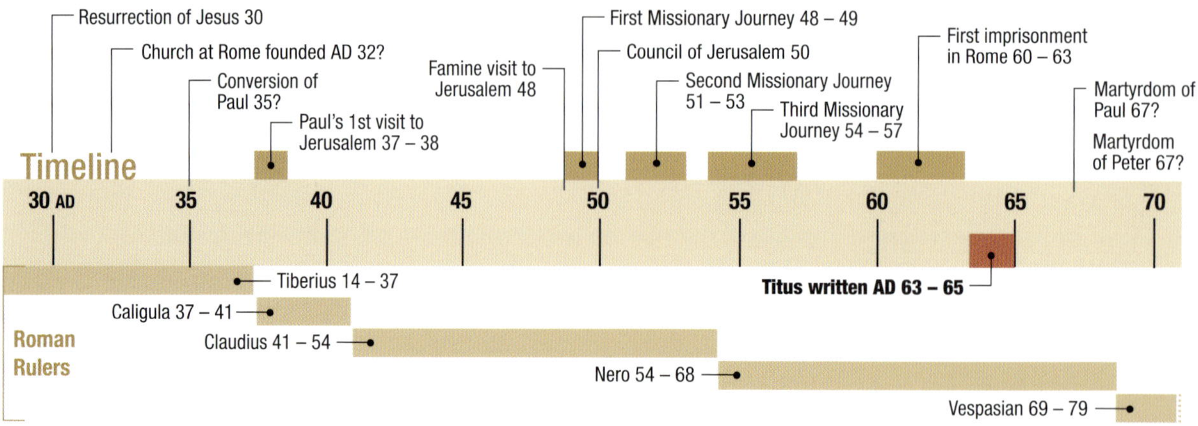

## Purpose

After his release from his first Roman imprisonment, Paul visited the island of Crete, then left his missionary companion Titus there to supervise the churches, to "straighten out what was left unfinished and appoint elders in every town" (1:5). Soon afterward, Paul wrote a letter of encouragement and instruction to his young assistant.

Though Crete was a great civilization of the past, the people of Crete had a reputation for low moral character. "To Cretanize" came to mean "to be a liar." Paul picks up on this ethnic stereotype in Titus 1:12, where he quotes the sixth-century BC Cretan philosopher Epimenides who said, "Cretans are always liars, evil brutes, lazy gluttons." Titus clearly had his work cut out for him in such a challenging environment.

Paul wrote instructions for appointing elders (1:5–9), warnings about false teachers (1:10–16), and instructions on teaching different groups in the church (ch. 2) and for Christian living (ch. 3).

↑ *TITUS RECEIVED THIS LETTER WHILE ON CRETE.*

← *This silver coin from Crete represents the Roman Emperor Caligula (AD 37–41) as the Cretan idol Dictaean Zeus. The entrenched pagan culture of Crete caused the apostle Paul to instruct Titus to appoint elders who will "hold firmly to the trustworthy message as it has been taught, so that he can encourage others by sound doctrine and refute those who oppose it" (Titus 1:9).*



### Interesting Facts about Titus

- **In both 1 Timothy 3:1–13 and Titus 1:6–9 Paul provides his disciples with lists of qualifications for church leaders (elders, overseers, and deacons). These lists are often used for choosing church leaders today.**
- **Paul's quoting of a pagan philosopher in Titus 1:12 is unusual for a New Testament writer, but not unheard of. In Acts 17:28 Paul again quotes Epimenides ("For in him we live and move and have our being") together with the Cilician poet Aratus (315–240 BC): "We are his offspring." In 1 Corinthians 15:33 he quotes the Greek playwright Menander (342–291 BC): "Bad company corrupts good character."**

# Philemon

© Dr. James C. Martin

## Summary Overview

Paul appeals to Philemon to accept back his runaway slave Onesimus, not as a slave but as a brother in Christ, even as Philemon would welcome the apostle himself (vv. 16–17). The letter is a classic example of a heartfelt appeal from one brother to another.

← *Paul writes to Philemon on behalf of Onesimus and sends greetings to the church that meets in his home at Colosse (Philemon 2). Small farming homes now occupy the ancient site of Colosse where Philemon once lived.*

## Purpose

Of the four Prison Epistles (Ephesians, Philippians, Colossians, Philemon), this is the only one written to an individual. Paul is writing to Philemon, a leader in the church at Colosse in whose home the church meets. Paul is writing concerning one of Philemon's slaves named Onesimus who has run away.

Onesimus left Colosse, perhaps after stealing some of his master's money (vv. 18–19), and eventually ended up in Rome. There Onesimus met Paul, who evidently led him to Christ (Paul says Onesimus became "my son" while in prison, v. 10). Realizing that he must right his wrong, Onesimus decides to return to Philemon and submit himself to his authority. Paul wrote this letter of intercession for Onesimus. Paul urges Philemon, his "dear friend and fellow worker" (v. 2), to forgive his runaway slave and receive him as a new brother in Christ.

This letter is closely related to Colossians and was likely carried together with it. The same individuals, Tychicus and Onesimus, are accompanying the two letters. Archippus (probably Philemon's son, v. 1) is sent a special message in Colossians 4:17, and Paul sends greetings from his same companions (Aristarchus, Mark, Epaphras, Luke, and Demas, Col. 4:7–14; Philem. 23–24).

Notice the ways Paul appeals to Philemon: as a dear friend in Christ (v. 1), in obedience to Paul's authority (vv. 8, 21), for the sake of Christian love (v. 9), for Paul's own sake, as an old man and a prisoner (vv. 9, 13), for the sake of Onesimus, Paul's "son," and a brother in Christ (vv. 10, 16–17), as a benefit to Paul's ministry (vv. 11, 13), as a partner in ministry (v. 17), with an offer to pay for Philemon's financial losses (vv. 18–19), in exchange for the spiritual "life" Paul gave Philemon (v. 19), and as an opportunity to refresh and encourage another brother (v. 20).

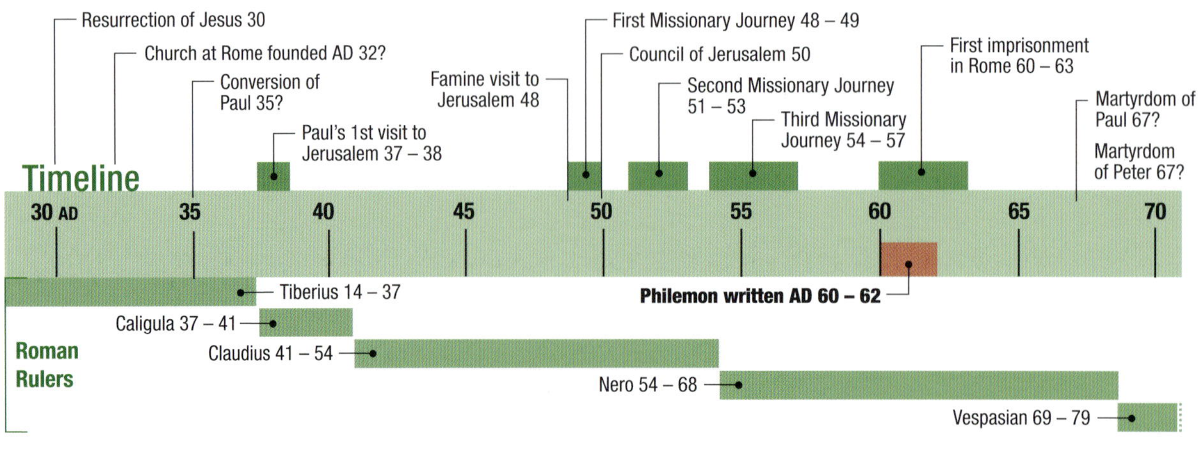

## Slavery in the New Testament

The fact that New Testament writers do not outright condemn slavery has been an embarrassment to the church and at times has tragically been used to condone this unjust institution. Yet a closer reading of the New Testament reveals the implicit message that slavery is an evil which must be abolished:

- In 1 Corinthians 7:22, Paul encourages slaves to win their freedom if possible. He also says a slave is the Lord's "freedman," showing that in Christ's kingdom there is no slavery.
- Galatians 3:28 refers to the full equality of all believers in Christ, Jews and Gentiles, men and women, slaves and masters.
- Ephesians 6:5–9 encourages slaves to live in peace and obedience to their masters for the sake of the gospel, but verse 9 makes it clear that there is no favoritism with God, who is the Lord of slave and master alike.
- Colossians 3:22–24 says slaves will receive their reward from the Lord, showing they have the same essential value and dignity as their masters.
- In Philemon 16–17 Paul hints that he expects Philemon to set Onesimus free, since he is a brother in Christ.

But why does Paul not condemn slavery outright? A few thoughts:

- First, we must realize that slavery in the Roman Empire was a very different institution than in the American South. Slaves could own property, have homes and families, and rise to almost any social position. They sometimes functioned as managers of large and wealthy households.
- More importantly, Paul was called by God to take the gospel to the Gentiles, and he could not be sidetracked by other concerns, even so noble a cause as freedom for slaves. The Roman Empire depended heavily on slave labor, and to call for manumission would have resulted in Paul's immediate arrest and execution, and the end to his apostolic ministry. Paul believed the time was short, and he had a task to fulfill for God. For him the eternal significance of the gospel message outweighed the temporal injustice of slavery.
- Christians would eventually lead the emancipation movement to end slavery. The tragedy is that it took so long for many Christians to realize that the gospel's message of freedom from sin and death was fundamentally incompatible with the institution of human slavery.

↑ *Limestone relief of a Roman slave.*

### Author

The apostle Paul, written about AD 60–62, from prison in Rome.

### Recipients

Philemon and the church which met in his home.

↓ *PHILEMON WAS A LEADER IN THE CHURCH AT COLOSSE.*

# Hebrews

## Summary Overview

A letter/sermon calling a group of Jewish Christians to stand firm in their faith and not to return to their old way of life.

← *Ancient mosaic from a synagogue floor reveals Jewish symbols including the seven-branch candlestick and curtain of the temple. Hebrews states Jesus went beyond this temple curtain before us, and has entered on our behalf (Hebrews 6:19).*



## Key Themes

***Christ's Superiority and Sacrifice.*** The author frequently uses the word *better* to describe the person and work of Christ. He is better than angels, Moses, and Joshua. He has brought a better revelation, a better priesthood, a better covenant, a better sanctuary, and a better sacrifice.

***New Covenant.*** The message is that the new covenant has fulfilled and now supersedes the old covenant.

***Christ's Humanity.*** Hebrews stresses the true humanity of Jesus Christ. He became fully human—like his brothers and sisters—in order to make atonement for their sins (2:5–18; 4:14–5:10).

## Author

Author unknown, though the recipients knew who he was. The letter was written around AD 67–70. From the letter we learn the author knew Timothy (13:23); was a skilled Hellenistic (Greek-speaker) writing in a very fine and polished Greek style; was well acquainted with the Old Testament; and always quoted from the Greek Septuagint. He had a pastor's heart, caring deeply for the spiritual welfare of these believers. He was a creative theologian who had thought deeply about the relationship between Judaism and Christianity.

## Recipients

A congregation of Jewish Christians, probably in Rome or Jerusalem.

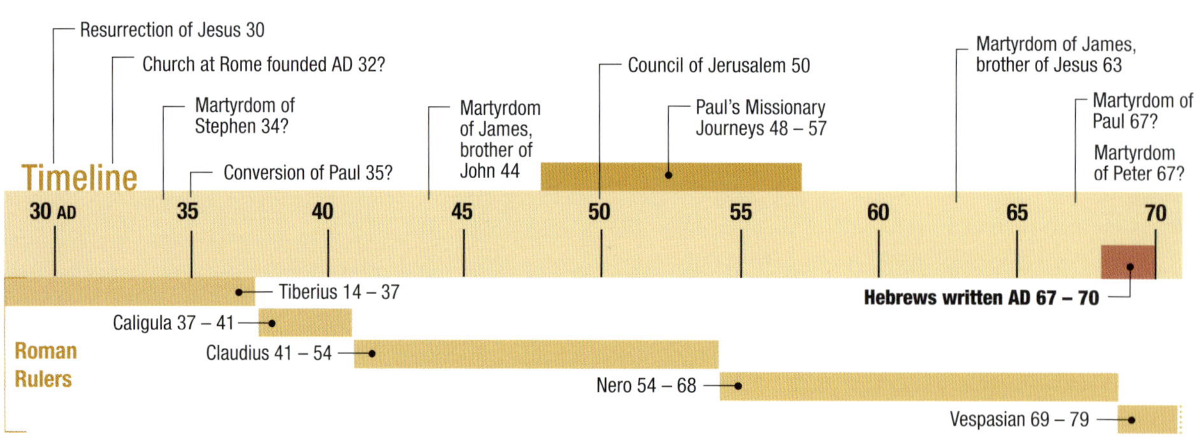

## Purpose

Hebrews is one of the most powerful presentations of the gospel ever written, a bridge between the Old Testament world of promise—with its covenants, priests, and sacrifices—and the New Testament world of fulfillment, where Christ functions as the high priest of a new and greater covenant with God. Hebrews reminds us that Jesus is our one mediator, whose once-and-for-all sacrifice paid for sins, completed our humanity, and opened the way to God.

The readers appear to be Jewish Christians ("Hebrews"), who because of persecution and other pressures were in danger of drifting away from the faith and reverting back to Judaism. They are second-generation Christians, a well-established community that in the past has experienced persecution but not yet martyrdom (2:3; 10:32–34; 12:4; 13:7). By this stage they ought to be teachers, but they are still immature in many ways (5:11–6:3). There have apparently been recent defections from the community (10:25), and there is a danger that others will leave, returning to the security they found in Judaism. The author calls the readers to stand firm in their faith. The new covenant they have received is far superior to the old, providing true forgiveness of sins and a restored relationship with God. Jesus is the complete revelation from God, the only way of salvation. To turn back and follow the old would bring spiritual disaster.

The progress of the argument moves back and forth between two literary forms: theological rhetoric (or argumentation) and practical exhortation (or parenesis). In the theological sections, the author builds a systematic defense for the superiority and completeness of Christ and the new covenant over the preparatory nature and incompleteness of the old. The old covenant's purpose was to prepare the way for the new, which supersedes and replaces it.

In the practical sections, the author encourages the readers to faithfulness and warns those who were beginning to fall away about the eternal dangers of rejecting Christ. The author introduces five warning passages cautioning of the severe consequences of falling away. As the letter progresses these passages grow more and more severe as readers are warned not to stray from the faith.

*→Replica of a Roman original (Figure of Marsyas). This bas-relief of the theater at Hierapolis (Pamukkale, Turkey) portrays the Roman punishment of hanging. "Others were tortured and refused to be released, so that they might gain a better resurrection" (Hebrews 11:35).*



## Interesting Facts about Hebrews

- **Though Hebrews is a letter written to a particular audience, its fine literary style and careful structure make it read much more like an essay or a sermon than a letter. The author himself calls it a "word of exhortation" (13:22).**
- **Hebrews 11 contains the great "hall of fame" of faith, famous believers who persevered in the face of trials and suffering.**

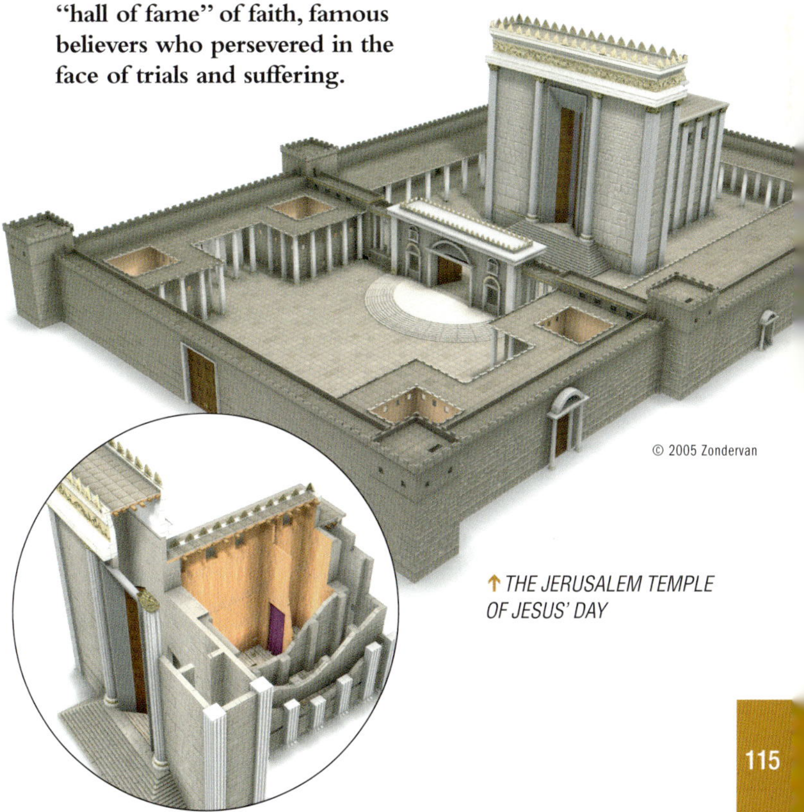



*↑ THE JERUSALEM TEMPLE OF JESUS' DAY*

# James

© The House of Anchors

## Summary Overview

Written to encourage Jewish Christians to a vibrant faith that proves itself through concrete action. The book deals with practical matters of how a Christian ought to live.

← *Rough waves on the Sea of Galilee are a reminder from James not to doubt "because he who doubts is like a wave of the sea, blown and tossed by the wind" (James 1:6).*

## Key Themes

***Faith and Works****.* This is the key theme in James. Mere profession of faith is worthless without the evidence of a changed life. To say "I have faith" means nothing if it is not backed up with actions (1:19–27; 2:14–26).

***The Christian and Trials****.* James begins by calling his readers to experience joy—the peace which comes from trusting in God—when they face the daily trials of life. Many of James's readers were evidently suffering persecution for their faith (1:1–18).

***Showing Partiality****.* Evidently a major problem among James's readers was divisions between rich and poor. James affirms that God shows no partiality and commands his readers to treat one another with the respect due those created in the image of God (2:1–13).

***The Deadly Tongue****.* Like a wildfire, words of gossip and slander can do great damage. James warns believers to be careful what they say, since the tongue can be a deadly weapon (1:19, 26; 3:1–12; 4:1–12).

***Riches and Poverty****.* James warns against the danger of riches and of treating the poor and oppressed with contempt. God will exalt the humble and will bring down the proud (1:9–11; 5:1–12).

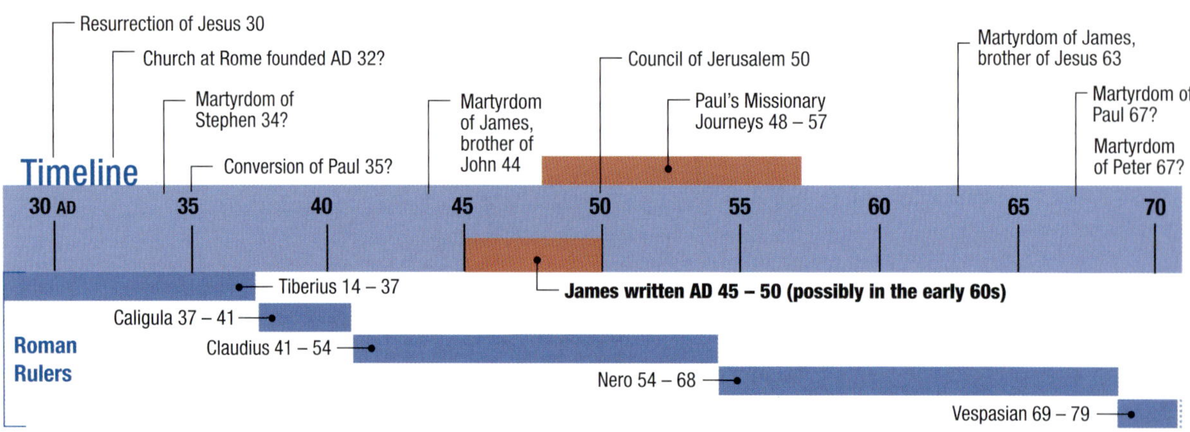

## Purpose

In this practical letter, the first of the so-called General Epistles (James through Jude) James calls on believers to demonstrate their authentic faith through their actions. He addresses his letter to "the twelve tribes scattered among the nations" (1:1). This is probably a term for Jewish Christians living outside of Israel, though some think it could mean the whole church as the "true Israel." A more specific audience and occasion may perhaps be identified with reference to the scattering of Jerusalem Christians following the stoning of Stephen (Acts 8:1). Upon hearing of various problems in these dispersed congregations, James writes as a pastor and leader, authoritatively calling them to authentic Christian living.

The book is concerned primarily with practical matters related to the believer's walk. How ought Christians to live out the faith they declare? "Faith without works is dead," James says. There is no such thing as true faith that does not show itself in a life of godliness.

Some date James in the 60s of the first century. Others think it is much earlier, perhaps the first New Testament book to be written (around AD 45–50). Church leaders are called by Jewish terms, teachers and elders, rather than by (somewhat) later terms like overseers and deacons, and the word for "synagogue" is still used for the meeting place of Christians (2:2). Also, because James seems to address only Jewish Christians (1:1), this may suggest the mission to the Gentiles is just getting started.

*↑ First-century marble statue from Rome representing a prince from the Julio-Claudian Dynasty on horseback. "If anyone considers himself religious and yet does not keep a tight rein on his tongue, he deceives himself and his religion is worthless" (James 1:26).*

## Interesting Facts about James

- James is perhaps the most Jewish book in the New Testament. Only the references to the "Lord Jesus Christ" in 1:1 and 2:1 confirm its distinctly Christian character.
- James is a book of practical wisdom for daily life and has sometimes been called the "Proverbs of the New Testament."
- James also has been called the "Amos of the New Testament" because, like this Old Testament prophet, he emphasizes the social responsibilities of the believer.
- James delights in vivid images from the natural world, speaking of waves on the sea (1:6), the sun's withering of grass and flowers (1:10–11), bits in horses' mouths (3:3), ships on the sea (3:4), forest fires (3:5), wild animals (3:7), trees and fountains of water (3:11–12), and sowing and harvesting (3:18).
- James appears to have been strongly influenced by the teaching of Jesus and includes many allusions to his teaching, especially the Sermon on the Mount. For example: on joy in trials (compare 1:2 and Matt. 5:11–12); on doing, not just hearing (1:22 and Matt. 7:24); on blessings for the poor (2:5 and Luke 6:20); on producing fruit (3:10–12 and Matt. 7:16–19); on peacemaking (3:18 and Matt. 5:9); and on swearing oaths (5:12 and Matt. 5:34–36).

### Author

James, the half-brother of Jesus, written probably from Jerusalem as early as AD 45–50, but possibly in the 60s.

### Recipients

Jewish Christians dispersed throughout the Roman Empire.

### Who Was James?

While several men in the New Testament are named James (Greek for "Jacob"), this is almost certainly the half-brother of Jesus and leader in the Jerusalem church. Joseph and Mary had other children after Jesus was born, four sons—James, Joseph, Simon, and Judas—and at least two daughters (Mark 6:3; Matt. 13:55). James, like his other brothers, did not believe in Jesus until after the resurrection, when Jesus appeared to him (John 7:5; 1 Cor. 15:7). He is listed with the believers who gathered together after the resurrection, and he quickly became a prominent leader in the Jerusalem church (Acts 1:14; 12:17). Paul met with James and Peter on his first trip to Jerusalem after his conversion (Gal. 1:18–19), and it was James who gave the decision at the Jerusalem Council that Gentile converts did not need to be circumcised to be saved (Acts 15:12–21). James was still a key leader at Paul's last visit to Jerusalem around AD 57 (Acts 21:18). The Jewish historian Josephus describes how James was stoned to death in Jerusalem by opponents of the church around AD 63.

# 1 Peter

## Summary Overview

How can believers find the strength to face suffering and trials in their lives? Peter writes to remind Christians that in this life they are strangers and aliens in a foreign land. Their true identity is as God's children and their true home is in his presence. This certainty can enable believers to face any adversity with faith, hope, and perseverance.

← *Peter addressed his letters to believers in regions of modern Turkey including Cappadocia, with its unique geography and villages consisting of cave homes (1 Peter 1:1).*



## Key Themes

***Stand Firm through Suffering.*** Written to encourage Christians to stand firm through suffering in expectation of their eternal inheritance.

***The Believer's Identity.*** Believers suffer because of their unique identity as God's people, strangers in this world. The identity of the believer is a major theme in 1 Peter, with many terms and images drawn from the Old Testament people of God. Believers are God's chosen people, a royal priesthood, a holy nation, a people belonging to God (2:9). They are living stones, being built into a spiritual house (2:5), a community of the redeemed, purchased by the precious blood of Jesus (1:18–19).

***A Life of Holiness.*** In light of their status as God's special people, believers are to live holy and pure lives. In this way the world will see their righteous deeds and glorify God (2:12).

***A Life of Submission.*** Holiness manifests itself especially in an attitude of submission to the God-ordained authorities in life: citizens to their government, slaves to masters, wives to husbands (2:13–3:7). The goal of this submission is not to reinforce a class society but to bring glory to God by reflecting the same servant attitude and self-sacrificial love which Jesus showed to us.

## Interesting Facts about 1 Peter

- Peter evidently used Silvanus (probably another name for Silas) as his secretary to transcribe the letter (5:12).
- First Peter is written in a very fine Greek style and some wonder how a common fisherman from Galilee could write so well. But recent research has demonstrated that Greek was widely spoken throughout Palestine in Jesus' day. Silas's editing may also account in part for the polished Greek.
- First Peter 3:15 is a classic text on the need for "apologetics"—the defense of the Christian faith through convincing (yet gentle) answers.
- Church tradition tells us Peter was martyred in Rome during the persecutions of the emperor Nero by being crucified upside down.

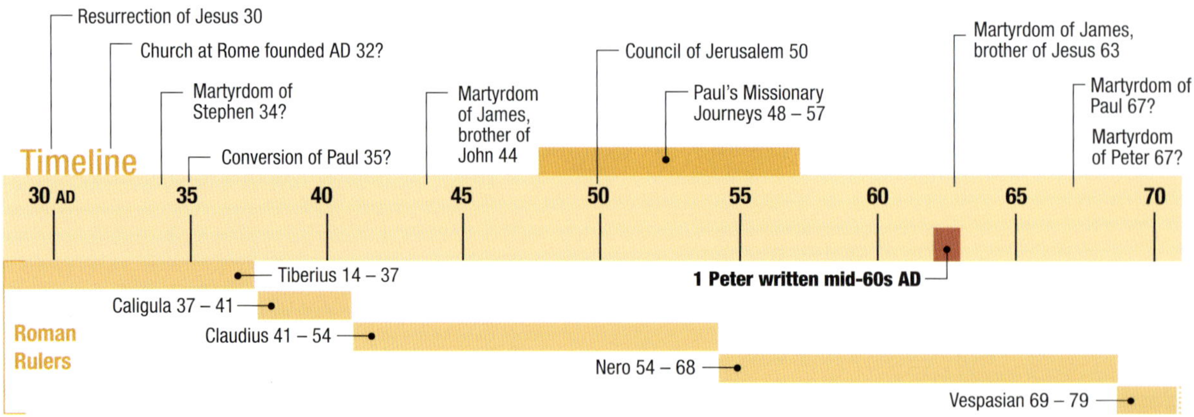

## Purpose

Peter is writing to encourage believers, who are experiencing a great deal of opposition and persecution because of their faith (1:6; 3:13–17; 4:12–19), to stand firm in the true grace of God. Peter addresses the letter to "strangers" (1:1) in a world that was growing increasingly hostile to Christians. By standing firm in the grace of God, they would be able to endure their "painful trial" (4:12), knowing their true inheritance was protected in heaven for them.

Though many themes are woven throughout the letter, the author repeatedly returns to the theme of standing firm in the face of suffering and persecution. Every chapter has references to suffering and perseverance: 1:6–9; 2:19–25; 3:8–22; 4:1–2, 12–19; 5:6–10. Believers suffer because they are set apart to God, his chosen people, aliens and strangers in the present evil world (1:1, 17; 2:9, 11). While in this world, they are to reveal their true identify through faithfulness, holiness, and obedience, following the example of Jesus who remained faithful to God through suffering and even death. "To this you were called, because Christ suffered for you, leaving you an example, that you should follow in his steps" (2:21).

Peter is probably writing in the mid-60s of the first century, and from Rome, symbolically called "Babylon" (5:13). This place of origin is likely for several reasons:

- Babylon appears as a symbolic title for Rome in Revelation 17:3–6, 9, 18 and in extrabiblical writings. Babylon was an appropriate code name for Rome since both cities were viewed as symbols of the pagan world system in opposition to God and his people.
- Church tradition tells us Peter eventually went to Rome and was martyred there.
- John Mark is with Peter when he writes (5:13), and Mark's gospel is traditionally associated with Peter and with Rome. Mark is also mentioned in connection with Rome during Paul's first and second imprisonments (Col. 4:10; 2 Tim. 4:11).

### Author

The apostle Peter, probably written from Rome in the early 60s.

### Recipients

Christians throughout Asia Minor.

### Who Was Peter?

Simon and his brother Andrew were fishermen from Galilee who were called by Jesus to be his disciples (Mark 1:16–18). Jesus nicknamed Simon "Peter" (Greek = *Petros*; Aramaic = *Cephas*), meaning "a rock" (John 1:35–42). Peter became the most prominent of Jesus' disciples and always appears first in lists of the twelve disciples. He was passionate and devoted, but also rash and impetuous. He confessed Jesus to be the Messiah (Mark 8:29) and declared his allegiance even to death (14:29). Yet he repeatedly wavered in faith, eventually denying Jesus three times (14:66–72). But Jesus saw in Peter great potential and entrusted to him the authoritative "keys of the kingdom" (Matt. 16:19), restoring him after the resurrection (John 21:15–17). In the early church Peter assumed the leadership role that Jesus had predicted. He proclaimed the gospel to the Jews of Jerusalem on the day of Pentecost (Acts 2:14–41) and eventually to the Samaritans (8:14–25) and the Gentiles (10:1–48). He demonstrated boldness and courage in the face of persecution, telling the Sanhedrin that the disciples must obey God rather than any human authority (4:19; 5:29).

Peter stayed in Palestine for the early years of the church and was active in the Jerusalem Council's decision concerning the salvation of the Gentiles (Acts 15:7–11). Though Peter is not mentioned in Acts after the Council of Jerusalem, from his own writings and from Paul's letters it is clear he went on missionary travels (sometimes with his wife, 1 Cor. 9:5) to Asia Minor, Greece, and eventually to Rome (1 Cor. 1:12; 1 Peter 1:1; 5:13).

# 2 Peter

## Summary Overview

The problem of false teachers within the church is Peter's main focus in this letter. Now near the end of his life, Peter sees dangerous new teachings beginning to infiltrate the church, and so writes to combat them. He points out that the best opposition to false teaching is a solid understanding of the truth. Believers can identify and avoid spiritual counterfeits by being grounded in the faithful and true Word of God.

← *Second letter of Peter on papyrus (facsimile shown here) dated to about AD 200. Peter writes his letter reminding his readers that he was an eyewitness of the majesty of Jesus (2 Peter 1:16).*



## Key Themes

***True Christian Faith***. Peter writes about the Christian's calling (1:3–4) and the manner of life that should characterize that calling (1:5–11). Believers can resist false teachings by holding fast to the message of Jesus passed down by the eyewitnesses and confirmed by the prophets (1:12–21) and by putting it into practice through godly living.

***Warnings against False Teachers***. Peter points out that false teachers introduce destructive heresies that deny Christ. They are immoral, arrogant, deceptive, and greedy, exploiting weak and unstable people for their own gain.

***The Promise of the Lord's Coming***. In response to false teachers who were denying that Christ would return, Peter says God's Word will prove as reliable in the future as it has been in the past. Peter urges believers to lead lives of faithfulness and godliness in preparation for the Lord's return.

## Interesting Facts about 2 Peter

- **Second Peter is closely related to the letter of Jude, with the two sharing similar themes and common language. Both were written to combat false teaching.**
- **Peter makes an interesting comment about the difficulty of understanding Paul's letters, and how some people distort their meaning (2 Peter 3:16). This is the only place in the New Testament where one inspired author refers to another's writings.**
- **Second Peter 1:20–21 is a key statement in Scripture on the nature of divine inspiration.**

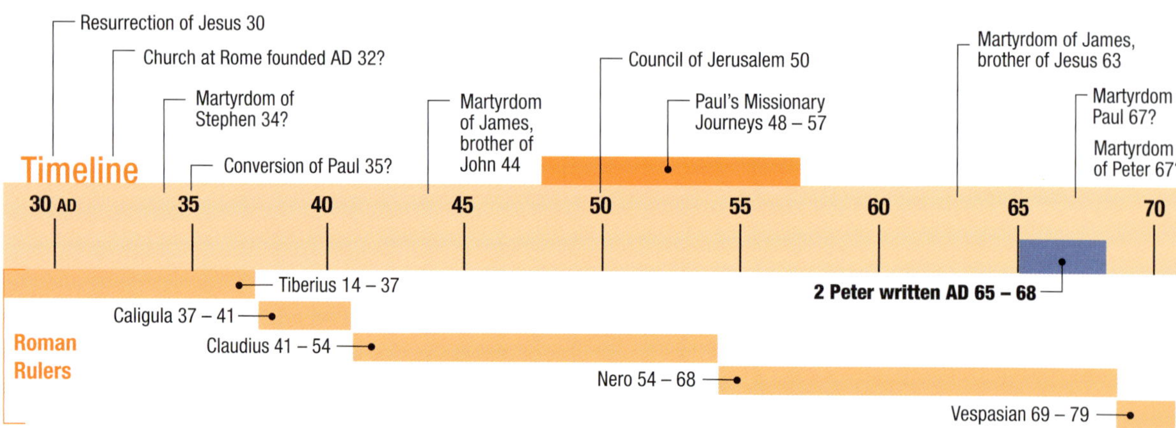

## Purpose

It is said that the best way to identify counterfeit money is to get to know the real stuff very well. This is Peter's message in 2 Peter. False teachers have begun to infiltrate the churches to whom Peter is writing. The antidote, Peter says, is a thorough grounding in the Word of God—the authentic gospel of Jesus Christ.

If 1 Peter was written to encourage believers who were experiencing the *external* problem of persecution, 2 Peter focuses on the *internal* problem of false teachers in the church. Peter writes to combat the dangerous new teachings that are beginning to infiltrate the church. The best defense is a good offense. By having a thorough knowledge of the Word of God, believers can recognize and avoid spiritual counterfeits.

Second Peter was not widely known or quoted in the early church, and there are significant differences in style and content with 1 Peter. Many scholars therefore doubt that Peter wrote it (which is ironic, given the book's theme). Some claim the letter was originally a "testament" to Peter, written by one of his disciples to honor him after his death. However, the evidence for pseudepigraphy (false authorship) is inconclusive at best. There are both differences and similarities with 1 Peter and statistical conclusions about style are unreliable for such a short letter. The differences in content may have resulted from the different situation addressed, and the unique style may be attributed to Peter's use of Silas as his secretary in 1 Peter (5:12). Together with the early church, it seems best to accept the letter as authentic, written by the apostle Peter shortly before his execution in Rome, sometime between AD 65 and 68.

### Author

The apostle Peter, written in the mid to late 60s, probably from Rome.

### Recipients

Written to Christians throughout Asia Minor.

↓ *PETER'S LETTERS WERE WRITTEN TO THE CHURCHES OF PONTUS, GALATIA, CAPPADOCIA, ASIA, AND BITHYNIA.*

# 1 John

## Summary Overview

In this letter John's spiritual children are under spiritual attack from false teachers. Like a good father, John responds with comfort and assurance. For those who are trying to deceive them he has stern and angry words.

← *According to tradition, John was buried on the hill near the ancient ruins of Ephesus. John encouraged his readers to be assured of eternal life in the name of the Son of God (1 John 5:13).*



## Key Themes

***Fellowship with God.*** Assuring believers of their true fellowship with God.
***Reject False Teachers.*** John refutes the claims of the false teachers and urges his readers to hold firm to the truth he has taught them.

## Interesting Facts about 1 John

- Some early church writers identify John's opponent in Ephesus more specifically with a Gnostic named Cerinthus. Cerinthus distinguished between two separate individuals, the man Jesus (who was merely human) and the Christ–Spirit, who came upon Jesus at his baptism, but then abandoned him on the cross—since it was inconceivable for a spirit to die. For Cerinthus the cross of Christ had no saving significance, and salvation came only through secret knowledge imparted by the Christ–Spirit.
- Church tradition says John was the youngest of the twelve apostles and was the last to die, sometime near the end of the first century.

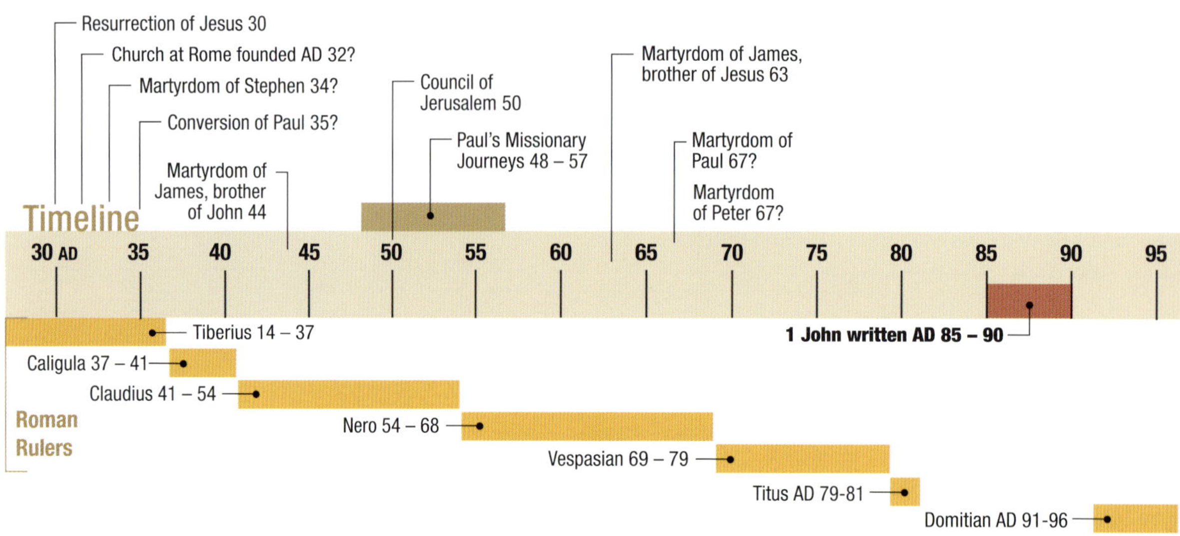

## Purpose

False teachers had arisen in the Christian communities to which John was ministering. They opposed fundamental teachings of the church, including the identity of Jesus Christ and his sacrificial death on the cross. These heretics had now departed, taking some members of the congregation with them. The remaining believers were shaken in their faith, wondering whether they were missing out on the truth. John identifies these false teachers as "antichrists" and links their arrival to the end-time apostasy from the faith (2:18–19).

John writes to assure church members of the certainty of their faith and to refute the claims of the false teachers. Assurance ultimately comes through the "anointing" believers have received—the internal testimony of the Holy Spirit who brings assurance and knowledge of the truth (2:20, 27).

The central theme is true fellowship with God (1:3). Through their teaching and their departure, the heretics had provoked doubts in some, and John writes to assure them of their abiding relationship with God (2:28; 5:13). He also refutes the claims of false teachers that they have the true knowledge of God (2:4).

John gives three main "tests of life," evidence of authentic fellowship with God. These run as repeated themes throughout the letter:

- Love for fellow believers (2:7–10; 3:10–24; 4:7–5:3)
- Obedience to God's commands (1:5–2:6; 2:29–3:10; 3:23–24; 5:4–21)
- Belief that Jesus is the Christ, the Son of God (2:18–28; 3:23–4:6; 4:14–15; 5:1, 5)

John alludes to the teaching of the heretics with statements like "If we claim . . ." or "The one who says. . . ." The false teachers failed each of these tests: they showed hate toward fellow Christians (2:9, 11); they claimed to be sinless while living in disobedience to God's commands (1:6, 8, 10; 2:4); and they denied that Jesus was the Christ, the Son of God, and rejected his atoning death on the cross (2:22–23). For John, to believe that "Jesus is the Christ" (2:22; 4:2) means that he is both fully human and fully divine and that his death is "the atoning sacrifice for our sins" (2:2).

## Who Were the False Teachers?

The beliefs alluded to in the letter suggest that the false teachers were promoting a form of incipient Gnosticism (incipient means "in its early developmental stage"). Although Gnosticism didn't develop fully into a religious system until the second century, its general features are already evident in the later books of the New Testament, especially 1 John, 2 Peter, and Jude.

*Gnosis* means "knowledge," and Gnostics believed they were saved not by faith in Jesus Christ but by special knowledge available only to those initiated in the cult. Gnosticism was syncretistic, borrowing from a variety of religious traditions, including Judaism, Christianity, and pagan religions. Gnostics taught that the material world is evil, only spirit is good. This dualism often led to immoral behavior, since some Gnostics claimed what they did with their bodies did not affect their spiritual state. Rejection of the material world also led to a denial that God could take on true human form and a denial that his death paid the penalty for our sins. Many Gnostics were also Docetists, claiming that Christ only *appeared* to be human.

## Author

The apostle John, written between AD 85 and 95, probably from Ephesus.

## Recipients

A Christian community shaken by false teachers, probably in the province of Asia.

## Who Was John?

John was a fisherman from Galilee, the brother of James and the son of Zebedee (Mark 1:19–20). Jesus nicknamed James and John "Sons of Thunder" (Mark 3:17), perhaps because of their fiery personalities (Luke 9:49, 54; Mark 10:35–39). Peter, James, and John are often identified as the "inner circle" of Jesus' disciples (Mark 5:37; 9:2; 14:33). In the early chapters of Acts, John appears with Peter as one of the key leaders of the Jerusalem church (Acts 3:1–5, 11; 4:1–23; 8:14, 17, 25). Church tradition says that John left Jerusalem before its destruction in AD 70 and ministered for some time in and around Ephesus. The seven churches mentioned in Revelation 2–3 probably were part of John's ministry.

# 2–3 John

## Summary Overview

Both 2 and 3 John address the issue of traveling teachers and encourage the readers to be discerning, supporting those teachers who preach the truth and avoiding those who promote heresy or preach from ulterior motives.

← *Large homes in Ephesus reveal the financial prosperity of the city. John desired his friend Gaius to prosper in every way and use that prosperity for the benefit of God's people (3 John 1:2).*



## Key Themes

***Staying Faithful to the Truth.*** John exhorts the readers to a life of love and obedience toward God.

***Discernment concerning Traveling Teachers***. John warns believers to discern truth from error and to give hospitality only to traveling teachers who proclaim the true teaching of Christ.

## Interesting Facts about 2–3 John

- It was common in the early church for itinerant evangelists and teachers to move from community to community, finding support and hospitality from local Christians.
- The personification of a church as a woman (2 John 1) also occurs in 1 Peter 5:13, where Peter refers to "she who is in Babylon," probably a reference to the church in Rome.
- The false teachers of 2 John, like those in 1 John, appear to be promoting an early form of Gnosticism, since the Gnostics denied that Jesus Christ "had come in the flesh" (v. 7).

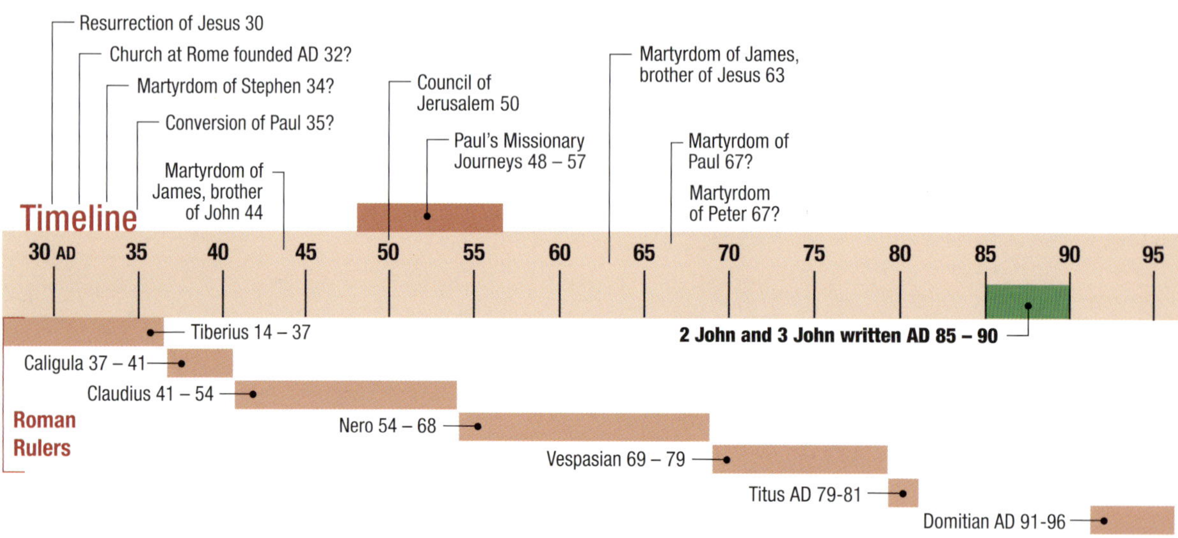

## Purpose

In 2 John, the apostle expresses joy that the church is remaining faithful to the apostolic teaching which the readers had "heard from the beginning" (vv. 4, 6). He encourages them to love one another (v. 5), to live in obedience to God's commandment (v. 6), and to avoid traveling teachers who do not proclaim the truth. These false teachers were deceivers who denied that Jesus Christ was both truly human and truly divine (v. 7).

Third John also deals with problems related to traveling teachers and evangelists. Evidently, some of these teachers had been mistreated by a certain Diotrephes. Gaius, on the other hand, to whom the letter is addressed, had given them hospitality. John uses his apostolic authority to rebuke Diotrephes and to praise Gaius for his good work. John also commends to Gaius a man named Demetrius who is probably delivering the letter. Demetrius may also have been a traveling teacher.

↑ *John warns against philosophies that led to participation into the "mystery religions" such as the cult of Mithra (2 John 7–11).*

## Author

The author identifies himself as "the elder" and is assumed to be the apostle John, for the language and style are similar to 1 John and to the gospel of John. Both letters were probably written from Ephesus about AD 85–90.

## Recipients

2 John: "The chosen lady and her children"—most likely a reference to a church, probably in the province of Asia.

3 John: Gaius, a church leader, probably also in Asia, who had lent support to traveling teachers.

↓ *TRADITION SUGGESTS THAT THE LETTERS OF JOHN WERE WRITTEN FROM EPHESUS.*

# Jude

© Dr. James C. Martin, The Cairo Museum

## Summary Overview

Jude warns against false teachers in the church.

← *Egyptian chariot. Jude uses the illustration of the Lord's delivery of the Israelites from the Egyptians (Jude 1:5).*

## Key Themes

***Discerning Truth from Error.*** The false teachers Jude writes about were promoting an immoral lifestyle and a false view of Jesus Christ.

***Living a Life of Holiness.*** The antidote to false teaching is to "build yourself up in your most holy faith and pray in the Holy Spirit" (v. 20).

## Interesting Facts about Jude

- In his short letter Jude cites two extrabiblical Jewish writings. Verse 14 quotes from the Jewish apocalyptic work known as Enoch, and verse 9 appears to allude to an intertestamental work known as the Assumption of Moses.
- Angels are seldom identified by name in Scripture, but Jude refers to Michael the archangel, who also appears in Daniel (10:13, 21; 12:1) and in Revelation (12:7). The only other named angel in Scripture is Gabriel (Daniel 8:16; 9:21; Luke 1:19, 26).
- Jude was probably either the third or fourth son born to Joseph and Mary after Jesus. Matthew lists him fourth among the brothers of Jesus (Matt. 13:55), while Mark lists him third (Mark 6:3).

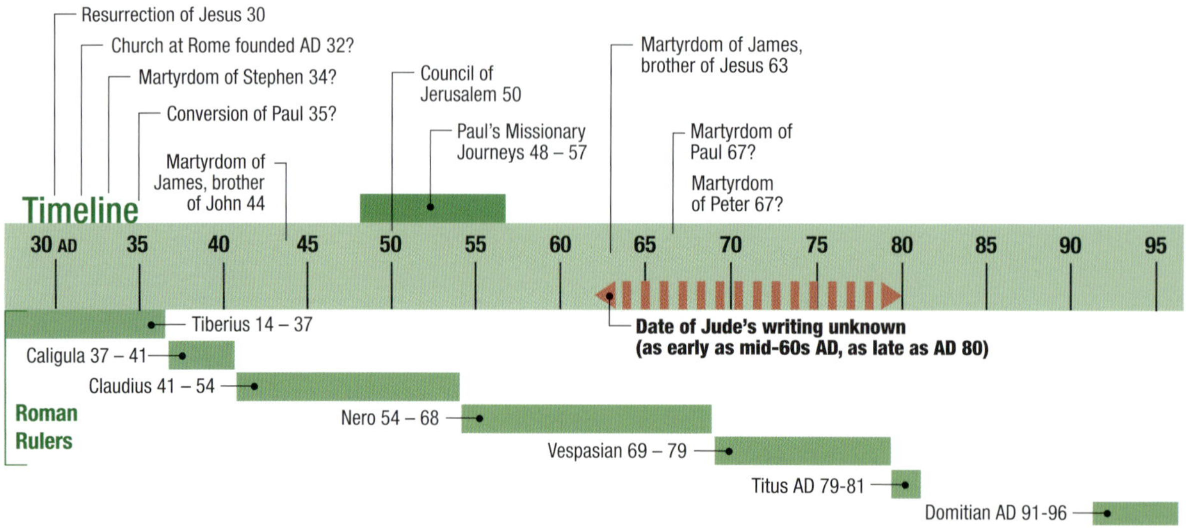

## Purpose

Jude says that his original purpose was to write on the topic of salvation (1:3), but because of false teaching creeping into the church, he felt the need to respond to this threat. The letter, like 2 Peter, was written to defend against a growing heresy.

As in 2 Peter, the exact nature of the heresy is uncertain, but seems to have been an early form of antinomian ("anti-law") Gnosticism. Gnosticism was a second-century heresy which considered the material world to be evil and salvation to come through a kind of spiritual "knowledge" (*gnosis*) gained through special rituals. Some Gnostics used their antimaterialistic worldview as an excuse to live immoral lives. Jude says that they "change the grace of our God into a license for immorality and deny Jesus Christ our only Sovereign and Lord" (v. 4).

Second Peter 2:1–3:4 is very close in content to Jude 4–18, and the relationship between these two has been a matter of much debate. Some think Peter is borrowing from Jude, while others think the opposite. If Peter borrowed from Jude, then a date in the mid-60s is likely (since Peter was martyred about AD 67). If Jude is using Peter, then the book could be as late as AD 80.

↑ *Burn layer at tell Numeira, possible location of Gomorrah. Jude instructs his readers to avoid falling into the perversions of Sodom and Gomorrah.*

↓ *MANY SCHOLARS BELIEVE THE BIBLICAL CITIES OF SODOM AND GOMORRAH WERE LOCATED AT THE SOUTHERN END OF THE DEAD SEA.*

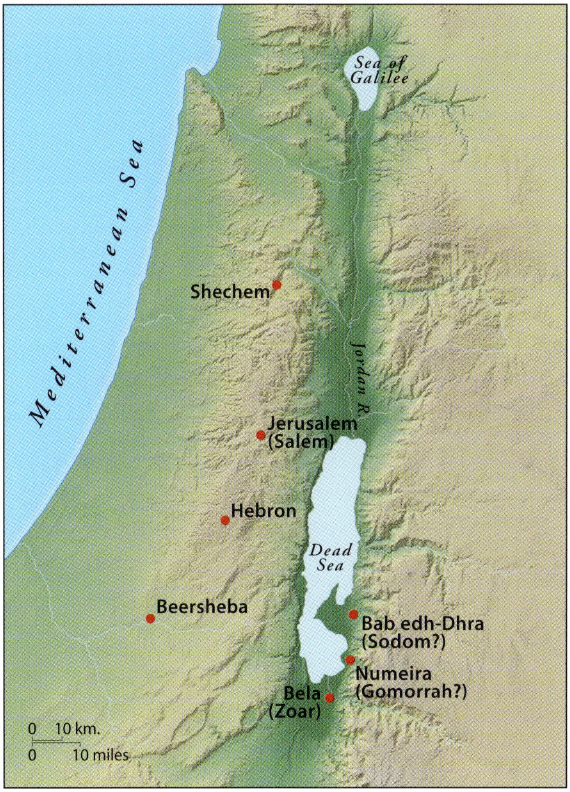


## Author

Jude, a brother of James and half-brother of Jesus, possibly written in the mid to late 60s of the first century.

## Recipients

Christian believers, locality unknown.

## Who Was Jude?

The author of the book identifies himself as "a brother of James," probably a reference to James the half-brother of Jesus, author of the letter of James, and leader in the church at Jerusalem. This would make Jude another half-brother of Jesus, mentioned in Matthew 13:55 and Mark 6:3.

We know very little about Jude. Like James, he did not believe in Jesus during Jesus' ministry (John 7:3–8). He probably believed after seeing the resurrected Lord, since Jesus' brothers are present with other believers in Jerusalem following the resurrection (Acts 1:14). He seems to have had an itinerant preaching ministry within the early church (1 Cor. 9:5).

# Revelation

## Summary Overview

Revelation provides a vision of God's ultimate purpose for humanity. The central message is God's sovereignty over human history. Cataclysmic disaster is predicted for the world, yet through it all God is in control. Through Jesus Christ, the glorious Lamb who was slain, he will conquer Satan and evil, deliver his people, and create a new heaven and a new earth where his people will dwell with him for all eternity.

← *"Then they gathered the kings together to the place that in Hebrew is called Armageddon" (Revelation 16:16). Looking north over Megiddo (Armageddon) into the Jezreel Valley.*



## Key Principles for Interpreting Revelation

***Recognize the Symbolic Nature of Apocalyptic Imagery.*** The apocalyptic genre of Revelation uses symbolic imagery to communicate both historical realities and spiritual truths. Locusts from the pit, for example, symbolize destructive evil and should not be interpreted as literal descriptions of modern warfare (such as attack helicopters, as some have claimed). The original readers would never have recognized such a meaning.

***Focus on General Rather than Specific Meaning.*** Throughout history the identification of scenes in Revelation with specific persons or events has always proven to be mistaken, discrediting Christians and dishonoring God. This is why it is important to focus on the general meanings of these symbols: the need for perseverance and faithfulness through trials, God's judgment against sin, and the ultimate victory of God over evil.

***The Old Testament Is the "Code Book" for the Symbols of Revelation.*** The book of Revelation has more allusions to the Old Testament than any other New Testament book, and it is this background which illuminates the meaning of its symbols. Too often readers try to interpret the book by reading today's newspapers instead of within its own historical and literary context.

***Recognize that the Context Is the First Century.*** While Revelation certainly describes the consummation of all things at the end of time, it was written to seven historical churches and must be understood within the world in which these Christians lived. Whatever future events the book concerns, these must be understood first and foremost from the perspective of the church's first-century conflict with paganism and an increasingly hostile Roman Empire.

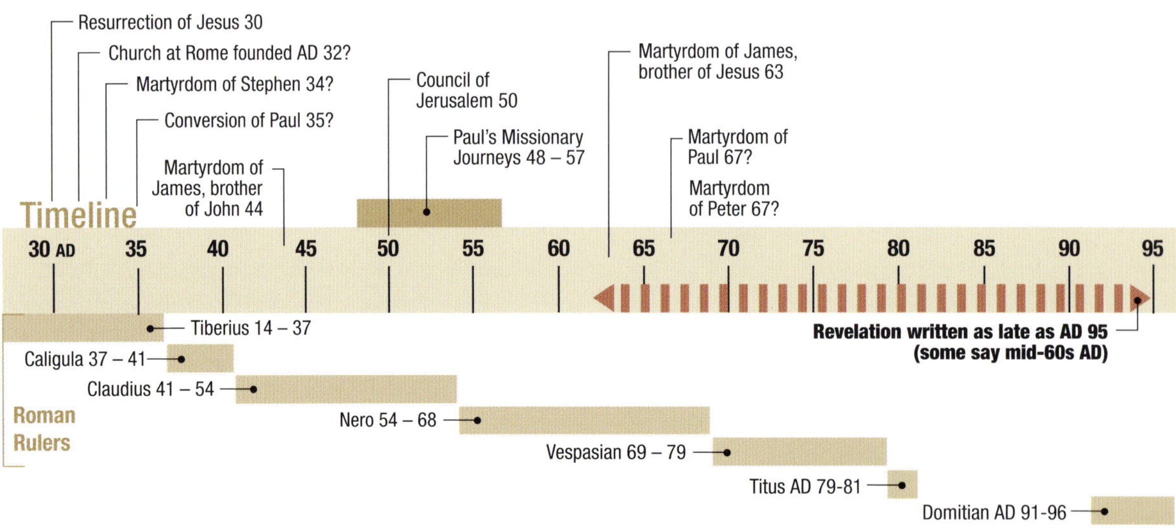

## Purpose

Revelation is without a doubt the most difficult book in the New Testament. Its apocalyptic imagery and puzzling symbols have baffled readers throughout the centuries. Yet while interpreters have drawn wildly differing conclusions concerning the timetable the book sets forth and the meaning of specific symbols, its fundamental message is clear. It can be summed up in two words: "God wins!" No matter how bad things get or how much the world seems to be spinning out of control, God is the sovereign Lord of all things. Through the victory achieved by Jesus Christ—the victorious Lamb who was slain—he will deliver his people from every adversity and bring them safely into his eternal kingdom. Forever he will be their God and they will be his people.

The book contains seven letters addressed to the churches at Ephesus, Smyrna, Pergamum, Thyatira, Sardis, Philadelphia, and Laodicea. References in these letters indicate that at least some were experiencing persecution (2:10, 13). Their greatest danger, however, is complacency and compromise with the evil world system. They are called to wake up and put their spiritual house in order, since Jesus is coming soon to save and to judge.

The occasion of the book is described in Revelation 1:9. Because of his teaching and testimony concerning Jesus, John has been exiled to Patmos, a small island in the Aegean Sea, southwest of Ephesus. John is "in the Spirit" on the Lord's day (Sunday) when a vision is given to him.

John is commanded to write in a book "what you have seen, what is now and what will take place later." He is first given a message to seven churches, then an extended vision concerning "what will take place later," coming judgments against the world and the consummation of all things.

↑ *Statuette of the Roman emperor Nero (AD 54–68), who was thought by some to be the antichrist described in Revelation.*

The revelation itself begins with a scene of the glorious throne room of God. A sealed scroll is presented which no one is worthy to open. No one, that is, except Jesus Christ, the Lamb who was slain to redeem people from every tribe, language, and nation (ch. 5). When the Lamb opens the seals, the cataclysmic judgments of God are poured out through a series of seven seals, seven trumpets, and seven bowls (chs. 6–16). These judgments are periodically interrupted with interludes—144,000 servants sealed, the two witnesses, the allegory of the woman and the dragon, the two beasts—which interpret and expand upon God's purpose and plan.

The sevenfold judgments are followed by a description of the rise and fall of Babylon—a symbol of Rome and the evil world system. Babylon is portrayed as a great prostitute who rules the earth and persecutes the people of God (chs. 17–18). As the book climaxes, Babylon is destroyed in judgment and Christ returns, riding a white horse and coming with the armies of heaven (ch. 19). The dragon (Satan) is seized and sealed in the Abyss, and Christ reigns for a thousand years (the "millennium"). Satan is subsequently released and leads a final rebellion against God. He is defeated and cast into the lake of fire (ch. 20). God creates a new heaven and a new earth, and a glorious new Jerusalem descends from heaven, the eternal dwelling place of God's people (chs. 21–22). The book ends with an encouragement to persevere, for Jesus is coming soon!

More about

# Revelation

© Cameraphoto Arte, Venice/Art Resource, NY

↑ An Italian painter's portrayal of the four horsemen of the Apocalypse, as described in Revelation 6.

## Genre (Literary Form)

Revelation is a combination of three distinct literary forms:

***Epistle***. The book contains a greeting typical of other letters, identifying the author and the recipients. After an introductory vision, John is given seven letters to seven churches.

***Prophecy***. The book explicitly identifies itself as prophecy (Rev. 1:3; 22:7, 10, 18–19) and contains many elements common to prophetic literature: messages from God to his people, warnings against unbelief, oracles of judgment and deliverance.

***Apocalypse***. Most importantly, the book is apocalyptic, a type of literature which flourished in Israel from the second century BC onward. Apocalypses were generally written during periods of political instability and foreign oppression, when God's people were severely tested. They use highly symbolic language to look toward the intervention of God in human history to deliver the righteous, judge sinners, and establish his kingdom.

## Interpreting Revelation

There are four different approaches, or presuppositional grids, through which the book of Revelation has been viewed.

The ***historicist*** interpretation views the Revelation as a symbolic description of the progress of church history from the time of John to the second coming and the new creation. Symbols in the books are identified with specific events throughout history. Because of its extreme subjectivity, this view is generally rejected today. Each generation has tended to interpret the events differently and to view itself as the last generation.

The ***preterist*** interpretation claims the book deals entirely with events of the first-century conflict between the church and its opponents, especially imperial Rome. The book predicts the church's victory and deliverance at the soon return of Christ. Some claim the author was mistaken and the events failed to take place. Other more conservative preterists say the events were fulfilled spiritually in the destruction of Jerusalem in AD 70 and/or in the fall of Rome.

The ***idealist*** interpretation claims the book is a symbolic description of the age-long struggle between God and Satan as well as the eventual triumph of Christianity over paganism. In this view, the book is equally applicable to any period of church history.

The ***futurist*** interpretation argues that the book is prophetic and describes events which will occur immediately before the second coming of Christ. Most of the book concerns the time known as "the tribulation," which is followed by the second coming of Christ, the final judgment, and the new creation.

## Interesting Facts about Revelation

- **Scholars debate whether the title of the book, "The revelation of Jesus Christ" (1:1), means "the revelation *about* Jesus Christ" or "the revelation given *by* Jesus Christ." In fact, both are true. The book reveals who Jesus is, the Lamb who provides salvation and victory to God's people. Yet the Revelation is also made by Jesus, who alone is worthy to open the seals that unfold the purpose and plan of God (5:9).**
- **There are various symbolic numbers in the book—12, 666, and 144,000—but the most common is 7. There are seven churches, spirits before God's throne, golden lampstands, stars, horns and eyes on the Lamb, seals, trumpets, bowls, thunders, heads and crowns on the dragon, angels, last plagues, heads on the beast, hills on the city (Rome), and kings of the earth. The number seven in Scripture often indicates completeness.**
- **The number of the beast, 666, may be a code word for the emperor Nero (Rev. 13:18). Letters were often used for numbers in the ancient world (A = 1; B = 2, etc), and so names could be represented cryptically with a series of numbers, a practice known as "gematria." The Hebrew letters which spell out the name "Caesar Nero" add up to 666.**

## Author

The author identifies himself as "John" the servant of Jesus Christ (1:1, 4, 9), traditionally thought to be the apostle John. Some, however, think this might be another John "the elder," referred to by the early church historian Eusebius. Most scholars date the book to the late first century, about AD 95 during the persecution of the church by the Roman emperor Domitian. Some, however, claim it is much earlier, during the persecutions of the emperor Nero in the mid-60s.

## Recipients

Seven churches in the province of Asia.

↑ *THE SEVEN CHURCHES OF ASIA (REVELATION 1–3)*

# Names Glossary

## A

**Aaron**–Brother of Moses called to be the first high priest of Israel.

**Abednego**–One of three friends who along with Daniel served in the king's court in Babylon.

**Abel**–Second son of Adam and Eve who was killed by his brother, Cain.

**Abigail**–First the wife of the foolish Nabal and later the wife of King David.

**Abihu**–Aaron's son who (along with his brother Nadab) died for offering "strange fire" to the Lord.

**Abimelech**–Philistine ruler who took Sarah into his harem without knowing that she was Abraham's wife.

**Abiram**–One of the two sons of Eliab who rose up against Moses and Aaron during Korah's rebellion.

**Abishai**–King David's nephew, his two brothers were Joab and Asahel.

**Abner**–A relative of King Saul's who served as commander and chief of his army.

**Abraham**–God made a covenant with him, promising that through him all nations would be blessed; he is the father of the Jewish nation.

**Absalom**–King David's third son, he rebelled against his father and was murdered by Joab.

**Achan**–A Judahite who stole some of the spoils from Jericho, he and his family were stoned for his disobedience.

**Adam**–The first human being God created; he and his wife Eve disobeyed God and caused sin to enter the human race.

**Ahab**–Son of Omri who reigned in the northern kingdom of Israel, he and his pagan wife Jezebel worshiped Baal.

**Ahasueras (Xerxes)**–Son of Darius the Great and the Persian king in the book of Esther.

**Ahaz**–One of the evil kings of Judah who was the father of the great king Hezekiah.

**Ahijah**–Prophet from Shiloh during the days of Solomon, he predicted that the kingdom would divide.

**Amaziah**–The ninth king of Judah, he was successor to his father Joash at age 25.

**Amnon**–King David's first son, whose downfall was the rape of his half-sister Tamar.

**Amos**–A small-town sheepherder called by God to prophesy to the northern kingdom of Israel.

**Ananias and Sapphira**–A married couple who were members of the church in Jerusalem; they were both struck dead when they lied to Peter regarding the amount of money they gave to the church.

**Andrew**–Brother of Simon Peter, he was a fisherman by trade and one of the twelve apostles.

**Anna**–A widow and prophetess who praised God when the infant Jesus was presented at the temple; she declared to others that he would be significant in the redemption of Jerusalem.

**Annas**–Jewish high priest from AD 7–15 who remained influential during Jesus' public ministry.

**Antiochus Epiphanes**–Greek-Syrian ruler who desecrated the temple and is often associated with the book of Daniel.

**Aquila and Priscilla**–A married couple who worked alongside the apostle Paul in ministry in Corinth and Ephesus; they led Apollos to a deeper understanding of Jesus.

**Archelaus**–Son of Herod the Great who ruled Samaria, Judea, and Idumea until he was deposed by Rome in AD 6.

**Artaxerxes**–King of the Persian Empire during the days of Ezra and Nehemiah.

**Asa**–Ahijah's son and successor, the third king of the southern kingdom of Judah after the kingdom divided.

**Asaph**–One of the Levites who David appointed over the service of music in the tabernacle.

**Ashurbanipal**–Assyrian ruler noted for the large library he built in his capital, Nineveh.

**Azariah (Uzziah)**–Son of Amaziah who reigned over the southern kingdom of Judah for 52 years.

## B

**Balaam**–Prophet hired by Balak to bring a message of cursing to Israel but who brought them a message of blessing instead.

**Balak**–King of Moab who hired Balaam to speak a message of cursing upon the Israelites in the wilderness.

**Barak**–He, along with the prophetess Deborah, led Israel's victory over the Canaanites during the period of the judges.

**Barnabas (Joseph)**–Called the "son of encouragement," he was influential in the spread of the gospel and accompanied Paul on his first missionary journey.

**Baruch**–Served as the associate and scribe of the prophet Jeremiah.

**Bathsheba**–Uriah's wife with whom King David committed adultery and later married.

**Beelzebub**–The prince of demons, another name for Satan.

**Belshazzar**–Babylonian king who called for Daniel to interpret the mysterious handwriting on the wall.

**Bildad**–One of Job's friends who made the false claim that Job's sin had caused his affliction.

**Boaz**–He took Ruth, a Moabitess, to be his wife; their son Obed was the grandfather of King David.

## C

**Caesar Augustus (Octavian)**–First true "emperor" of Rome; ruler of the Roman Empire at the time of Jesus' birth; he ruled 30 BC–AD 14.

**Caiaphas**–Jewish high priest during Jesus' public ministry.

**Cain**–First son of Adam and Eve who killed his brother, Abel.

**Caleb**–One of two spies who filed a positive report among the twelve Moses sent to Canaan.

**Cornelius**–A God-fearing Roman centurion whose conversion as a response to Simon Peter's preaching marked the beginning of the Gentile mission.

**Cyrus**–Persian king who enabled the Jews to rebuild the temple in Jerusalem.

## D

**Daniel**–A Jewish statesman who served in the Babylonian court, noted for his ability to interpret dreams.

**Darius the Mede**–King of Persia who became the king of Babylon after the death of Belshazzar.

**Dathan**–One of the two sons of Eliab who rose up against Moses and Aaron during Korah's rebellion.

**David**–Son of Jesse and Israel's greatest king, from whose lineage Christ descended.

**Deborah**–Prophetess and judge in the book of Judges.

**Delilah**–Temptress who seduced Samson into revealing the secret of his strength.

**Demas**–A man who initially supported the apostle Paul but later deserted him because of his love for the present world.

**Domitian**–Roman emperor from AD 91–96; the apostle John was likely exiled to the island of Patmos during his persecution.

## E

**Ebed-Melech**–Ethiopian eunuch who saved the prophet Jeremiah's life.

**Ehud**–One of the judges who delivered Israel from the hands of the Moabites.

**Eli**–Priest at Shiloh who trained the boy Samuel but failed to train his own rebellious sons.

**Elihu**–Last of Job's friends to speak, like the others he claimed that suffering could be a form of discipline.

**Elijah**–A prophet to Israel during the reigns of Ahab and Ahaziah, he spent much energy trying to demonstrate the impotence of the false god Baal.

**Eliphaz**–One of Job's friends who made the false claim that Job's sin had caused his affliction.

**Elisha**–Successor to Elijah as a prophet to Israel and suppressor of Baal worship.

**Elizabeth and Zechariah**–The devout couple, both from priestly descent, who became the parents of John the Baptist after many years of barrenness.

**Elymas**–A sorcerer and false prophet who stood in opposition to Paul and Barnabas's gospel message to Sergius Paulus and was cursed with blindness.

**Epaphroditus**–Sent by the church at Philippi to deliver gifts to Paul and to assist him when he was imprisoned in Rome.

**Epaphras**–A native of Colosse and one of Paul's companions, he appears to have been the founder of the Colossian church.

**Esarhaddon**–King of Assyria in the seventh century BC; son of Sennacherib.

**Esau**–Firstborn of Isaac's twin sons, he sold his birthright to his younger brother Jacob.

**Esther**–Jewish queen of Persia who protected her people from an annihilation plot.

**Ethan**–One of the chief musicians appointed by King David to serve in the tabernacle.

**Ethiopian eunuch**–Court official of the queen of Ethiopia who was led to faith in Christ by Philip and insisted on being baptized on the spot.

**Eutychus**–A young man whose life was restored by Paul after falling out of a third-story windowsill while the apostle was preaching in Troas.

**Eve**–The first woman God created; she and her husband Adam disobeyed God and caused sin to enter the human race.

**Ezra**–Priest and scribe after the return from the exile who played a vital role in reestablishing the law among the Jews.

## F–G

**Felix**–Roman governor of the province of Judea whom Paul was brought before in Caesarea; he ruled from AD 52–60.

**Festus**–Successor of Felix as the Roman governor of Judea, he granted Paul's request to appeal to Caesar.

**Gabriel**–Angel who announced the births of John the Baptist and Jesus Christ; he also helped Daniel interpret two visions.

**Gallio**–Roman proconsul of Achaia from AD 51–53, the Jews brought an accusation against Paul before him that proved unsuccessful.

**Gideon**–Judge of Israel known for testing God with a fleece, he delivered Israel from the hands of the Midianites.

**Goliath**–Philistine giant killed by the young David in a one-on-one challenge.

**Gomer**–Prostitute whom Hosea married in obedience to God's command.

## H–I

**Haggai**–Post-exile prophet who exhorted his people to get up and rebuild the temple.

**Haman**–Persian official in the book of Esther who plotted to kill all the Jews living in Persia.

**Hananiah**–False prophet whose death was predicted by Jeremiah.

**Hannah**–Mother of Samuel, who dedicated him to the Lord from birth.

**Heman**–One of the chief musicians appointed by King David to serve in the tabernacle.

**Herod Agrippa I**–Son of Aristobulus who gained rule over Judea and Samaria from AD 41–44; he executed James the son of Zebedee and arrested Peter.

**Herod Agrippa II**–Son of Agrippa I, he and his sister Bernice heard Paul's defense in Caesarea at the request of Festus; he ruled from AD 50–100.

**Herod Antipas**–Son of Herod the Great and tetrarch of Galilee and Perea during the period of Jesus' ministry.

**Herod the Great**–The Idumean (Edomite) ruler who gained the throne of Israel after the Roman conquest of Palestine and ruled from 37–4 BC.

**Hezekiah**–Son of Ahaz, and one of the greatest kings of the southern kingdom of Judah.

**Hiram**–King of Tyre, associated with his friendliness and generosity toward David and Solomon, especially related to the building of the temple.

**Hosea**–Prophet to the northern kingdom of Israel during Jeroboam II's reign.

**Isaac**–The first descendant of God's promise to Abraham, the father of Esau and Jacob.

**Ishbosheth**–He was proclaimed king of Israel upon his father Saul's death.

**Ishmael**–Abraham's first son born to him by Hagar, Sarah's maidservant.

## J–K

**Jacob**–Isaac's youngest twin son, his twelve sons became the twelve tribes of Israel.

**Jael**–Wife of Heber who murdered Sisera, the commander of the Canaanite army.

**Jairus**–Synagogue ruler whose twelve-year-old daughter Jesus brought back from the dead.

**James, half-brother of Jesus**–Leader in the Jerusalem church and key figure at the Jerusalem Council, he is the author of the epistle of James.

**James, son of Zebedee**–One of the twelve apostles; Jesus nicknamed him and his brother John "sons of thunder"; he was the first apostle to die as a martyr.

**Jehoiachin**–Son of Jehoiakim who reigned over Judah for three months before he was taken into captivity by Nebuchadnezzar.

**Jehoiada**–High priest of the temple, he helped the boy-king Joash rule Judah in his early years.

**Jehoiakim**–Josiah's son, he succeeded Jehoahaz as king of Judah but was a vassal of Babylon.

**Jehoshaphat**–King of Judah who faithfully taught the law but made a foolish alliance with Ahab.

**Jehu**–King of Israel who killed Ahab's descendants and priests of Baal; brought an end to the dynasty of Omri and Ahab.

**Jephthah**–Judge who delivered Israel from the Ammonites but made a foolish vow and had to sacrifice his daughter upon victory.

**Jeremiah**–Prophet to the southern kingdom of Judah during the period leading up to Babylon's final siege of Jerusalem.

**Jeroboam**–First king of Israel after the kingdom divided, he corrupted worship there by setting up golden calves.

**Jeroboam II**–Son of Joash, king of Israel, and an outstanding political leader in the eighth century BC.

**Jeshua**–High priest who led in the rebuilding of the temple after the exile.

**Jethro**–Midianite priest and Moses' father-in-law.

**Jezebel**–King Ahab's Phoenician wife, noted for her wickedness and worship of Baal.

**Joab**–Military commander throughout the majority of David's reign.

**Joash**–Declared king of Judah at age seven when Queen Athaliah was overthrown.

**Job**–A blameless man who endured terrible suffering; the champion of the book that bears his name.

**John Mark**–Cousin of Barnabas and author of the gospel of Mark, he was a companion of both the apostle Paul and the apostle Peter.

**John the Baptist**–Forerunner of Jesus Christ who preached a baptism of repentance and was beheaded by Herod Antipas during the time of Jesus' ministry.

**John, son of Zebedee**–One of the twelve apostles, he is also known as "the beloved disciple"; he is credited with the authorship of the fourth gospel, three epistles, and possibly Revelation.

**Jonah**–Reluctant prophet who preached to Nineveh, the capital of Assyria.

**Jonathan**–The oldest son of King Saul and close friend of David.

**Joseph (OT)**–Jacob's favorite son who was sold into slavery by his brothers, he became an important administrator of Egypt.

**Joseph (NT)**–A descendant of King David who was the husband of Mary, the mother of Jesus.

**Joseph of Arimathea**–The member of the Jewish Sanhedrin whom all four gospels identify as the one who buried Jesus' body in his own tomb.

**Joshua**–He was commissioned by Moses to lead the conquest of Canaan.

**Josiah**–Son of Amon and king of Judah known for his extensive religious reforms.

**Judah**–The fourth of Jacob's twelve sons and founder of the tribe of Judah, from whom David was descended.

**Judas Iscariot**–Jesus' disciple who betrayed him to the chief priests for 30 pieces of silver.

**Jude, brother of James**–Half-brother of Jesus who seems to have been an itinerant preacher in the early church, he is the author of the epistle bearing his name.

**Korah**–Levite who led a rebellion against Moses and Aaron in challenge of their authority.

## L–M

**Laban**–Rebekah's brother who tricked his trickster nephew Jacob on more than one occasion.

**Lazarus**–Brother of Mary and Martha whom Jesus raised from the dead after he had been in the grave for four days.

**Leah**–Laban's oldest daughter who became Jacob's first wife through her father's deception.

**Luke**–A physician and part-time missionary companion of the apostle Paul who composed both Luke and Acts.

**Lydia**–Gentile convert from Thyatira, she hosted Paul and Silas during their stay in Philippi.

**Manasseh**–Son of Hezekiah whose reign in Judah was, unlike his father's, characterized by unfaithfulness to God.

**Martha**–Sister of Mary and Lazarus noted especially for her complaint to Jesus about her sister not helping with household duties.

**Mary Magdalene**–A woman from Magdala delivered from demon possession; she was a devout follower of Jesus and the first to see him after his resurrection.

**Mary of Bethany**–Sister of Martha and Lazarus noted for her special devotion to Jesus.

**Mary**–Mother of Jesus who conceived as a virgin while pledged to be married to Joseph.

**Matthew (Levi)**–One of the twelve apostles, a tax collector by trade, identified as the author of the gospel bearing his name.

**Melchizedek**–King of Salem and priest of God Most High who blessed Abraham.

**Merodach-Baladan**–Enemy of Assyria and usurper of Babylon who sent envoys to Hezekiah.

**Meshach**–One of three friends who along with Daniel served in the king's court in Babylon.

**Michael**–Angel who acted on behalf of Israel in the book of Daniel; Jude refers to him as "the archangel"; in Revelation he leads the angels in heaven in war against Satan.

**Michal**–Daughter of King Saul and wife of King David.

**Miriam**–Sister of Moses and Aaron.

**Mordecai**–Esther's cousin who destroyed Haman's plan to exterminate the Jewish people.

**Moses**–Led the Hebrew people out of Egypt to the plains of Moab, across from Canaan.

## N–O

**Nabonidus**–Last king of Neo-Babylonian kingdom, invaded by Cyrus II of Persia.

**Nabopolassar**–He rebelled against Assyria and established a new dynasty in Babylon; father of Nebuchadnezzar.

**Nadab**–Aaron's son who (along with his brother Abihu) died for offering "strange fire" to the Lord.

**Naomi**–Mother-in-law of Ruth and Orpah whose husband and sons died in Moab.

**Nathan**–Prophet who served in the court during the reigns of David and Solomon.

**Nathanael**–A skeptical Jew who came to believe Jesus' role as Messiah after the incident under the fig tree; some identify him as one of the twelve apostles, perhaps Bartholomew.

**Nebuchadnezzar**–King of Babylon who invaded Judah and destroyed Jerusalem in 586 BC.

**Nehemiah**–Led and exhorted the Jewish people in rebuilding the walls of Jerusalem after the exile.

**Nero**–Roman emperor to whom Paul appealed following his first imprisonment; both Peter and Paul were probably martyred during his reign, which spanned AD 54–68.

**Nicodemus**–A ruler of the Jews and a Pharisee in the gospel of John whom Jesus taught the necessity and nature of the "new birth."

**Noah**–Built an ark for his family and all kinds of animals to survive the devastation of the flood.

**Og**–King of Bashan whose kingdom and territory Moses conquered.

**Orpah**–Ruth's sister and Naomi's daughter-in-law who returned to Moab after the death of her husband.

**Othniel**–Judge who delivered Israel from the oppression of the Mesopotamians.

## P–Q

**Paul (Saul)**–A Pharisee and once-persecutor of Christians who was converted on the road to Damascus; he preached the gospel to the Gentiles and wrote many New Testament books.

**Philemon**–A man from Colosse to whom Paul wrote an epistle concerning his runaway slave Onesimus.

**Philip the disciple**–One of the twelve apostles, he proclaimed to Nathanael that Jesus was Israel's Messiah.

**Philip the evangelist**–One of the seven chosen to look after the Hellenistic Jews in the Jerusalem church; he preached the gospel in Samaria and to the Ethiopian eunuch.

**Philippian jailer**–The guard during Paul and Silas' imprisonment in Philippi who was converted and baptized after the earthquake struck and their chains fell off.

**Phillip**–Son of Herod the Great and tetrarch of Iturea and Trachonitis who ruled from 4 BC–AD 33.

**Phinehas**–Grandson of Aaron who succeeded his father Eleazar as high priest of Israel.

**Phoebe**–A minister (or deacon) of the church at Cenchrea whom Paul commended for her invaluable service.

**Pontius Pilate**–Roman prefect, or governor, of the province of Judea during the time of Jesus' ministry.

**Queen of Sheba**–Queen who traveled to observe the wisdom and riches of Solomon.

## R–S

**Rachel**–The favorite wife of Jacob and the mother of Joseph and Benjamin.

**Rahab**–Prostitute whose life was spared for protecting two of Joshua's spies in Jericho; according to Matthew's geneaology she was the mother of Boaz, thus an ancestor of Jesus.

**Rebekah**–Wife of Isaac and mother of Jacob and Esau; she favored her younger son Jacob.

**Rehoboam**–The son and successor of Solomon's single kingdom of Israel who became the first king of Judah after the kingdom divided.

**Ruth**–A Moabitess who became the wife of Boaz; their son Obed was the grandfather of King David.

**Samson**–Judge of Israel who failed to deliver himself from the hands of Delilah but managed to deliver Israel from the hands of the Philistines.

**Samuel**–Hannah's son, who was the last judge of Israel as well as a prophet and priest who anointed both Saul and David as king.

**Sanballat**–Governor of Samaria who resisted Nehemiah's effort to rebuild the walls of Jerusalem.

**Sarah**–Wife of Abraham and mother of the Jewish nation, she gave birth to Isaac at age 90.

**Satan/the Devil**–The rebel angel and chief adversary of God and humanity.

**Saul**–First king of Israel's monarchy whose direct acts of disobedience led God to later reject his kingship.

**Sennacherib**–King of Assyria who invaded Judah during the reign of Hezekiah.

**Sergius Paulus**–Proconsul of Cyprus who converted to Christianity after witnessing Elymas's sudden blindness during Paul and Barnabas's first missionary journey.

**Shadrach**–One of three friends who along with Daniel served in the king's court in Babylon.

**Shishak**–Pharoah of Egypt who invaded Jerusalem during Rehoboam's reign and took temple and palace treasures.

**Sihon**–King of the Amorites whose kingdom and territory Moses conquered.

**Silas (Silvanus)**–Paul's companion during his second missionary journey; he and Paul boldly praised God during their imprisonment in Philippi.

**Simeon**–A Jew who blessed and prophesied over the infant Jesus when he was presented at the temple in Jerusalem.

**Simon Peter (Cephas)**–Arguably the most prominent apostle of Jesus Christ and one of the most important figures associated with the birth and growth of the early church.

**Simon the sorcerer**–A prominent magician in Samaria who, although converted, was rebuked by Peter for offering money in exchange for the Holy Spirit.

**Simon the zealot**–One of the twelve apostles who may have been a member of a religious or political party known as the "Zealots" (or "Cananaeans").

**Sisera**–Commander of Canaanite army whom Israel defeated under Barak and Deborah.

**Solomon**–Son and successor of David, king of Israel known for his wisdom, wealth, and many wives.

**Sons of Korah**–Important singers in the temple whose music contributed to many of the Psalms.

**Stephen**–One of seven chosen to look after the Hellenistic Jews in the Jerusalem church; stoned for his radical defense against the Sanhedrin, he was the first Christian martyr.

## T–V

**Theophilus**–Person to whom the two volumes of Luke–Acts were addressed.

**Thomas**–One of the twelve apostles, also called Didymus (the "twin"), he is noted for his refusal to believe without proof that Jesus Christ had risen.

**Tiberius Caesar**–Roman emperor during the period of Jesus' public ministry; he ruled from AD 14–37.

**Timothy**–A native of Lystra, Paul's spiritual son and missionary companion appointed to oversee the church in Ephesus. The letters of 1–2 Timothy were written to him.

**Titus**–A Gentile traveling companion of Paul appointed to oversee the church in Crete. The letter of Titus was written to him.

**Tobiah**–Ammonite official who opposed Nehemiah's effort to rebuild the walls of Jerusalem.

**Vashti**–Queen of Persia deposed in the book of Esther.

## Z

**Zacchaeus**–A rich tax collector, small in stature, who climbed up a tree in order to see Jesus.

**Zechariah**–Post-exilic prophet who encouraged the Jews to finish rebuilding the temple.

**Zedekiah**–The last king of Judah, whose political rebellion led to the fall of Jerusalem.

**Zerubbabel**–Led Jewish exiles from Babylon to Jerusalem and helped rebuild the temple.

**Zipporah**–Daughter of a Midianite priest and the wife of Moses.

**Zophar**–The harshest of Job's friends who falsely claimed Job's sin had caused his affliction.

# Terms Glossary

## A

**Adversary**–In the book of Job, the Hebrew word *satan* is a role, not a name, so it is best to translate it as "the adversary."

**Alpha and Omega**–First and last letters of the Greek alphabet; the phrase means "the first and the last."

**Apostle**–A term meaning "someone sent with a commission," it is often used with reference to Jesus' twelve disciples, but also of early followers like Paul who were commissioned by Jesus to take the gospel to all nations.

**Ark of the Covenant**–A chest made of wood overlaid with gold that contained some of the important signs of God's favor. It was the most sacred object of Israel as it represented the footstool of the invisible throne of the invisible God. The cherubim adorning the top were guardians flanking the throne of God.

**Ascension**–The event when Jesus ascended to heaven and the right hand of God 40 days after his resurrection.

## B

**Baal Worship**–"Baal" was the Canaanite god Hadad, the storm god associated with fertility. Since Israel was a predominantly agrarian society, they often turned to Baal with hopes of procuring good harvests.

**Baptism**–Jesus' baptism by John the Baptist indicated his affirmation of John's mission and the inauguration of Jesus' own preaching ministry. After his resurrection, Jesus commanded all of his disciples to be baptized in the name of the Father, the Son, and the Holy Spirit.

**Beatitudes**–The sayings that begin with "blessed are" and serve as the introduction to Jesus' Sermon on the Mount in the gospel of Matthew.

**Birthright**–The material inheritance given to children on the death of the father. It usually went to sons with the firstborn receiving twice what the other sons received.

**Book of the Twelve**–Another term for the 12 minor prophets.

**Branch**–An Old Testament term describing the future, ideal king from David's line.

**Burning Bush**–The place where God revealed himself to Moses and explained his plan and Moses' role in it.

## C

**Chief Priests**–Former high priests along with those from prominent priestly families.

**Circumcision**–The sign of a family's membership in the covenant.

**Classical Prophets**–Prophets who address the people as a whole and begin to declare national judgment for sin.

**Conquest**–The wars through which God gave the Israelites possession of the land.

**Cosmic Tree**–In the ancient world they often imagined a tree at the center of the world that had its top branches in the heavens and its roots in the netherworld. It was the source of provision and protection for the creatures of the world. This is probably the tree described in Nebuchadnezzar's dream in Daniel.

**Council of Jerusalem**–A meeting in Jerusalem where it was declared that Gentile converts to Christianity would not be required to obey Jewish laws, including circumcision.

**Covenant**–God's agreement with Abraham and his descendants by which he purposed to bring blessing to the world.

**Crucifixion**–A Roman method of execution whereby the victim was nailed or tied to a cross or stake and allowed to die a slow and excruciating death caused by exhaustion and exposure; Jesus was crucified by the Romans at the instigation of the Jewish leaders in Jerusalem.

**Cycles of the Judges**–The cycle of unfaithfulness, subjugation, supplication to God for help, and deliverance through a judge. There are six such cycles described in the book of Judges, connected with Othniel, Ehud, Deborah, Gideon, Jephthah, and Samson.

## D

**Day of Pentecost**–The pouring out of the Holy Spirit on the day of Pentecost marked the dawn of the new age of salvation and the birth of the Christian church.

**Day of the Lord**–A time when the current state of affairs will be replaced with the Lord's intended order—a time of justice and covenant fulfillment. This will result in judgment on those opposing God and blessing for God's people. Though many nations experience a "day of the Lord" (for example, Babylon, when it was judged), there will be a final "Day of the Lord" when a permanent world order of God's choosing will be established.

**Deacons**–A leadership office or role in the early church (Greek: *diakonos*); the term could also be translated "servant" or "minister"; qualifications for deacons are given in 1 Timothy 3.

**Decalogue**–Another name for the Ten Commandments—the central laws that God gave to Moses on stone tablets.

**Devoted to the Lord**–Sometimes called the "ban," this refers to the instruction that the Israelites were given during the conquest of Canaan to destroy a city entirely, including all residents—no quarter, no captives, no plunder, except that precious metals taken belonged to the sanctuary.

**Disaster from the North**–Jeremiah's way of referring to an invader who would bring widespread destruction. This designation is quite ambiguous because anyone coming from the east (the Mesopotamian nations of Assyria or Babylonia) would go northwest along the Euphrates river before turning and coming south into Israel.

**Disciple**–A term meaning "follower," sometimes used of all who followed Jesus, sometimes of his twelve special followers.

**Divided Monarchy**–After the reign of Solomon, the kingdom was divided in two. The south—Judah—was comprised of two tribes and was ruled by David's line, with its capital in Jerusalem. The north—Israel—was ruled by a series of dynasties and eventually established its capital in Samaria.

**Divination**–Ancient kings' advisors aided the king through a process called divination in which signs were sought or investigated as a means to understand the gods and to decide on a course of action. Part of divination was the interpretation of dreams.

## E–F

**Elders**–A leadership office in the early church (Greek: *presbyteros*), probably adopted from the term used of leaders in the Jewish synagogue; qualifications for elders are given in Titus 1.

**Election**–God's choice of individuals or groups to serve as his people in relationship with him.

**Essenes**–A Jewish sect which rigorously kept the law and often lived in monastic communities; the Dead Sea Scrolls were probably an Essene library.

**Exile**–Refers to when the Israelites were taken away from their land after being defeated by conquering armies. The north (Israel) was exiled by the Assyrians after the destruction of Samaria in 722 BC; the south (Judah) was exiled by the Babylonians after the destruction of Jerusalem and the temple in 586 BC. Most technically, the exile refers to the time that the people of Judah were in Babylon (586–539 BC).

**Exodus**–When God delivered Israel from Egypt and slavery to bring them to the land he promised them.

**Fall**–The result of the disobedience of Adam and Eve that brought sin into the world and alienated God from humankind.

**Feasts**–Days given special meaning because of God's work among his people. These were considered sacred times and were also highly regulated.

**Flood**–God's judgment on the world brought about by the lawlessness and violence of humanity. Only Noah and his family were spared.

**Fool**–One who shows a lack of good judgment and an inability to live in consistent, integrated ways. The fool chooses to act in ways that suggest he does not believe God will act.

## G–H

**Genealogy**–A table or list which shows the line of descent from an earlier ancestor(s). Genealogies are often meant to show someone's legitimacy for a particular role or status.

**Gentiles**–All nations other than the Jews; a Gentile is a non-Jew.

**Golden Calves**–During the divided monarchy two of these were set up at shrines in Bethel (Israel's southern border) and Dan (its northern border). Because bull-calves were often thought of as pedestals on whose backs the deity stood, these were probably intended to be substitutes for the ark.

**Great Commission**–Jesus' final command to his followers after his resurrection, commissioning them to make disciples of all nations.

**Herodians**–Political party that supported the political ambitions of the family of Herod and viewed Jesus' activities with suspicion.

**High Priest**–The highest religious office in Judaism; the high priest oversaw temple worship and the religious life of the Jews.

**Holiness**–The result of the sum total of godly traits.

**Holy of Holies**–The central area of the sanctuary where the ark was kept and where God's presence dwelt. The only access to this area was by the high priest once a year.

**Holy War**–In the ancient world all warfare was understood as being commanded by deity, fought by deity, and serving deity's purposes. The important distinction in the wars of Israel was that all the spoils belonged to God rather than the people.

## I–J–K

**I AM**–The name God gives himself at the burning bush. It is from the same verb ("to be") as the name "Yahweh" and identifies him not only as the one who IS, but probably also as the one who "causes to be."

**Imprecatory Psalm**–A psalm or section of a psalm in which the psalmist calls down specific curses on his enemy, indicating how his enemy would have to be treated for justice to be done.

**Inclusio**–A literary device that uses a word or phrase to frame a discussion. In Ecclesiastes the inclusio is the phrase "Meaningless, meaningless, everything is meaningless," which occurs in 1:2 and 12:8.

**Jews**–Originally referring to members of the tribe of Judah, the term came to be used of all Israelites; it can refer to nationality or to religious practice (adherents of Judaism).

**Judge**–A political/military leader who brought justice to the people of Israel by defeating foreign oppressors.

**Kingdom of God**–The central theme of Jesus' preaching, referring especially to God's sovereign reign and authority, but also to the consummation of the reign in an end-time (eschatological) kingdom. Matthew usually uses the term "kingdom of heaven."

**Kingship Covenant (Davidic Covenant)**–To reveal himself to Israel and the world, God elected human kings (David and his line) to serve as the instruments of his kingship.

**Kinsman Redeemer**–In Israelite society responsibility for the well-being of the members of the clan and protection of the property of the clan lay with the clan. A kinsman redeemer was one who arranged for the freedom of those who had been reduced to debt slaves or for the reclamation of land belonging to the clan. It was a way of providing for those who had become disenfranchised or destitute.

## L

**Lament Psalm**–A psalm that expresses a problem that the author would like God to address. Focuses on a petition and often includes a vow of praise in the expectation that God will answer.

**Land of Milk and Honey**–A phrase used to describe the natural resources of Israel. This term did not indicate that the land was fertile farm country or rich in minerals, but that it was good for herding (milk byproduct) and for fruit (the honey of the date palm).

**Law**–Sometimes called the Torah, this refers to God's revelation of guidelines that would allow his people to stay in relationship with him (the covenant), to preserve his presence among them, and to imitate his holiness.

**Levirate Marriage**–The propagation of the family line was very important, so if a man died before his wife could bear him a child, it was the duty of his brother to bear a child for the dead man by the widow.

**Levites**–Descendants of Jacob's son Levi who were dedicated as a tribe to serve Yahweh and the temple.

**Lord's Supper**–The ordinance which Jesus established while he was eating the Passover meal with his disciples the night before his crucifixion.

**Love Poetry**–This type of literature existed throughout the ancient world. In the Song of Songs, it is erotic, often subtly so, whereas in the larger ancient world it is at times more graphic, even bawdy. Love poetry was sometimes used in the context of fertility festivals and would generally evoke feelings of passion whatever one's sociological situation might be.

## M–N–O

**Magi**–Probably Persian or Arabian astrologers who charted the stars and attached religious significance to their movements.

**Messiah**–From the Hebrew meaning "Anointed One," this term did not achieve its full theological significance until the end of the Old Testament period. It refers to God's anointed king—specifically a king from David's line, and eventually an ideal king from David's line. Translated into Greek as "Christ" (*Christos*).

**Minor Judges**–Those deliverers mentioned in the book of Judges not connected to cycles.

**Nazirite**–A person who engaged in a designated period of dedication to God.

**New Covenant**–A new stage of God's agreement with his people whereby he is revealed through the law written on their hearts. Mediated by Jesus Christ, it fulfills the Old Testament covenants and provides true forgiveness of sins and a restored relationship with God.

**Olivet Discourse**–Jesus' message to the disciples given on the Mount of Olives concerning the destruction of the temple and the end of the age.

**Oracle**–A message given from God to a prophet to declare to a particular audience.

**Oracles Against the Nations**–All of the major prophets and a few of the minor prophets feature oracles of judgment against a number of nations, small and great. These were not generally proclaimed to or in the nation itself, but were declared to Israel to give them a sense of hope and of God's sovereignty.

**Overseers**–A leadership office in the early church (Greek: *episkopos*), sometimes translated "bishops"; qualifications for overseers are given in 1 Timothy 3 and Titus 1.

## P–Q

**Parable**–A short story or analogy illustrating a moral or spiritual truth.

**Passover**–The commemoration of the tenth plague, when God spared the Israelites but punished the Egyptians with the death of their firstborn sons.

**Patriarchs**–The founding ancestors of the nation Israel—Abraham, Isaac, and Jacob.

**Peter's Confession**–A key transitional passage in the first three gospels, as Peter acknowledged that Jesus is the Messiah, and Jesus began speaking about his upcoming death.

**Pharaoh**–The title of the supreme ruler of Egypt.

**Pharisees**–A religious and political party in first-century Judaism which adhered strictly to the written law of Moses and to a large body of oral traditions which arose over time.

**Plagues**–Ten acts of judgment against Egypt to persuade Pharaoh to let the Israelites leave.

**Post-exilic Period**–The people of Israel who had been living in exile in Babylon were given permission to return to their land in 538 BC. Their return initiated the post-exilic period.

**Praise Psalm**–A psalm that expresses praise for who God is and what he has done. Typically does not include petitions.

**Pre-classical Prophets**–Prophets serving before the mid-eighth century BC who addressed mainly the king and whose oracles were not collected into books.

**Priests**–Levites from the family of Aaron, who offered sacrifices in the temple.

**Promised Land**–The land of Canaan to which God brought Abraham. Conquered under Joshua, it became the kingdom of Israel under David and Solomon. The gift of the land was one of God's covenant promises.

**Prophecy**–God's proclamation of his plan, whether past, present, or future.

**Purim**–The feast celebrating the deliverance of the Jews in the time of Esther.

**Qoheleth**–The Hebrew title used for the one whose wisdom is represented in the book of Ecclesiastes. The basic translation of the word suggests "one who gathers." It is uncertain what is being gathered (e.g., disciples, wisdom sayings, perspectives, experiences).

## R

**Reformer Kings**–Rulers who instituted reform and tried to restore true worship during the divided kingdom.

These included Asa, Jehoshaphat, Joash, Hezekiah, and Josiah.

**Remnant**–Used in various ways throughout the Old Testament—sometimes those who survive a catastrophic invasion, sometimes those who are left in the land after many are deported, sometimes those who are deported and in exile.

**Restoration**–The prophets had proclaimed that after a time in exile the people of God would return to their land, rebuild the temple, and be ruled by an ideal king from David's line. This would be a time of the rise in political and spiritual advance.

**Resurrection**–The renewal of body, soul, and spirit into a glorified and eternal state of existence. Jesus' resurrection was the vindication of his person and message and the "firstfruits" of the resurrection of all believers.

**Retribution**–The idea that God would bless his people with covenant blessings when they were faithful, but punish them with covenant curses when they were not.

**Retribution Principle**–The belief that those who were righteous would prosper and those who were wicked would suffer. The converse was often believed as well, as expressed in the book of Job: that those who were prospering must be righteous, and those who were suffering must be wicked.

**Royal Psalm**–A psalm that focuses on how God works through his anointed king.

## S

**Sabbath**–The seventh day set aside each week to acknowledge God's control and provision by relinquishing for that day one's own attempts to control and provide for oneself.

**Sacred Space**–An area established by God's presence which required strict rules for both behavior and access. If the sanctity of the space was not preserved, the people risked losing the benefit of God's presence. Several zones of increasing sanctity surrounded the Holy of Holies in the tabernacle and temple.

**Sacrifice**–Giving something of value to God (usually an animal or grain). Some sacrifices involved a blood rite that was intended to eliminate the effects of sin.

**Sadducees**–A religious and political party in first-century Judaism made up mostly of the priestly leadership and aristocracy.

**Samaritans**–Inhabitants of the region (Samaria) between Galilee and Judea; Samaritans were despised by the Jews of Jesus' day because of their mixed ancestry and because their religion was viewed as a distortion of true Judaism.

**Sanhedrin (Council)**–The Jewish high court.

**Scribes/Teachers of the Law**–Experts in the law of Moses.

**Sermon on the Mount**–Jesus' inaugural sermon recorded in Matthew, which set out the radical values of the kingdom of God.

**Servant of the Lord**–A term from Isaiah 41–53, sometimes it seems that he is Cyrus, other times a corporate group in Israel. Some have seen the characteristics of Moses, or, specifically, the prophet like Moses who is to come. Many (including New Testament authors) see the role as fulfilled in Jesus. In Isaiah, the role played by the Servant is similar to that played by the ideal Davidic king, so it is easy to conclude that the Servant is a royal figure.

**Seventy Sevens**–A term from Daniel 9, it likely refers to weeks of seven-year periods, thus seventy sevens would equal 490 years.

**Sign-acts**–A number of Ezekiel's oracles consisted of dramatic performances, some in pantomime, some using limited props, in order to act out the message.

**Solomon's Temple**–David was not allowed to build a permanent temple to serve as the sanctuary of Yahweh, but this was completed and dedicated by his son Solomon.

**Son of David**–A traditional messianic title referring to the Messiah's descent from the line of David, Israel's greatest king.

**Son of God**–A title for the Messiah indicating his unique relationship with God the Father.

**Son of Man**–Jesus' most common self-designation; the title is likely drawn from Daniel 7:13 and refers to Jesus' true humanity as well as his role as glorious redeemer.

**Spirit of the Lord**–An Old Testament term indicating God's power or authority being manifested through a person. Though these early people of God were not familiar with the idea of the Trinity, we can identify much attributed by them to the Spirit of the Lord as the work of the Holy Spirit.

**Synagogue**–Local Jewish meeting place used for worship, study, assemblies, and social events.

**Syncretism**–Mixing together of elements from different religions. When Israel brought in Canaanite Baal worship alongside their worship of Yahweh, they were guilty of syncretism. This would also be the charge if they treated Yahweh as if he were like the gods of the other nations who had needs.

## T–U–V

**Tabernacle**–The portable tent sanctuary constructed by Israel according to God's instructions.

**Temple (Herodian)**–Temple in Jerusalem built by Herod the Great, known for its architectural splendor. It was destroyed by the Romans in AD 70.

**Temptation (of Christ)**–Following his baptism, Jesus was tempted for 40 days by Satan in the wilderness. This testing was analogous to Israel's 40 years in the wilderness and to Adam and Eve's testing in the garden; while these others failed when tempted, Jesus succeeded.

**Theocracy**–The reign of God and the establishment of his kingdom.

**Theodicy**–Explaining God's justice in light of evil or suffering. In the book of Job the theodicy focused on how God's justice works in individual lives. In Habakkuk it focuses on how God works with nations.

**Tower of Babel**–Building project that offended God and prompted him to confuse the languages.

**Transfiguration**–The mountaintop revelation of Jesus' true glory to his disciples Peter, James, and John.

**Triumphal Entry**–The traditional designation for Jesus' entrance into Jerusalem on Palm Sunday, riding on a donkey and fulfilling the prophecy of Zechariah.

**Twelve Tribes**–The Israelites were organized socially and politically by tribes descended from the sons of Jacob.

**"Under the sun"**–The author of Ecclesiastes' way of referring to our temporal lives in this world—our experience in this life.

**United Monarchy**–The period of Saul, David, and Solomon (just over a century long), when all twelve tribes were united under a single king.

**Valley of Dry Bones**–A vision of Ezekiel's that symbolized the nation that is dead coming back to life.

## W–Y–Z

**Watchman**–Ezekiel's role as a prophet was described as being a watchman who watches for coming trouble and warns the people.

**Wife of Noble Character**–The description in Proverbs 31 is intended not to give an ideal profile of what every woman should be, but a composite profile of what would constitute wise behavior in various female activities.

**Wilderness**–This refers to desolate regions, not necessarily to desert. Middle Eastern wildernesses were rocky, not sandy.

**Wisdom**–That sense or insight which brings order to every aspect of life because one understands the proper place of God.

**Wisdom Psalm**–A psalm addressed to people rather than to God, offering advice or thoughts about relating to God and understanding him.

**Yahweh**–The personal name of the God of Israel.

**Zealots**–Jewish insurrectionists who engaged in revolutionary activities against the Roman authorities.

# Index

## A



## B



## C

## H



## I



## J



## K



## L

## M



## N



## O



## P



## Q



## R

## S



## T



## U



## V



## W



## X



## Y



## Z

# Photo Credits

p. 14 © Dr. James C. Martin.
p. 15 © Dr. James C. Martin. The Egyptian Ministry of Antiquities. Photographed by permission.
p. 16 © Dr. James C. Martin.
p. 17 © Dr. James C. Martin.
p. 18 © Dr. James C. Martin.
p. 19 © Dr. James C. Martin.
p. 20 © Dr. James C. Martin.
p. 21 (top) © Dr. James C. Martin; (bottom) © The Israel Museum, Jerusalem.
p. 22 © Dr. James C. Martin.
p. 23 © Dr. James C. Martin. Musée du Louvre; Autorisation de photographer et de filmer—LOUVRE. Paris, France. Photographed by permission.
p. 24 © Dr. James C. Martin.
p. 25 © Dr. James C. Martin.
p. 26 © Dr. James C. Martin.
p. 27 © Dr. James C. Martin.
p. 28 © Direct Design.
p. 29 © Dr. James C. Martin.
p. 30 © Dr. James C. Martin.
p. 31 © Dr. James C. Martin. The British Museum. Photographed by permission.
p. 32 © Dr. James C. Martin.
p. 33 © Dr. James C. Martin. The Israel Museum, Jerusalem. Photographed by permission.
p. 34 © Dr. James C. Martin.
p. 35 © Dr. James C. Martin. The Israel Museum, Jerusalem. Photographed by permission.
p. 36 © Dr. James C. Martin. The British Museum. Photographed by permission.
p. 37 © Dr. James C. Martin.
p. 38 © Dr. James C. Martin. Musée du Louvre; Autorisation de photographer et de filmer—LOUVRE. Paris, France. Photographed by permission.
p. 39 (top) © Dr. James C. Martin. Sola Scriptura. The Van Kampen Collection on display at the Holy Land Experience in Orlando, Florida. Photographed by permission.
p. 39 (bottom) © Dr. James C. Martin. Musée du Louvre; Autorisation de photographer et de filmer—LOUVRE. Paris, France. Photographed by permission.
p. 40 © Dr. James C. Martin.
p. 41 Courtesy of Preserving Bible Times, Inc.
p. 42 © Dr. James C. Martin.
p. 43 © Dr. James C. Martin.
p. 44 © Dr. James C. Martin.
p. 45 © Dr. James C. Martin. The Cairo Museum. Photographed by permission.
p. 46 © Dr. James C. Martin. The Eretz Israel Museum, Tel Aviv, Israel. Photographed by permission.
p. 47 Courtesy of Preserving Bible Times, Inc.

p. 48 © Dr. James C. Martin.
p. 49 © Dr. James C. Martin. The British Museum. Photographed by permission.
p. 50 © Dr. James C. Martin. The British Museum. Photographed by permission.
p. 51 © Dr. James C. Martin. The Israel Museum, Jerusalem. Photographed by permission.
p. 52 © Dr. James C. Martin.
p. 53 © Dr. James C. Martin. The British Museum. Photographed by permission.
p. 54 © Dr. James C. Martin. The British Museum. Photographed by permission.
p. 55 (top) © Dr. James C. Martin. The Israel Museum, Jerusalem. Photographed by permission.
p. 55 (bottom) © Erich Lessing/Art Resource, NY.
p. 56 © Dr. James C. Martin. The Egyptian Ministry of Antiquities. Photographed by permission.
p. 57 © Dr. James C. Martin.
p. 58 © Dr. James C. Martin.
p. 59 © Dr. James C. Martin. The British Museum. Photographed by permission.
p. 60 © Dr. James C. Martin.
p. 61 © Dr. James C. Martin. The British Museum. Photographed by permission.
p. 62 © Dr. James C. Martin.
p. 63 © Dr. James C. Martin. The Israel Museum, Jerusalem. Photographed by permission.
p. 64 © Dr. James C. Martin.
p. 65 © Dr. James C. Martin. The British Museum. Photographed by permission.
p. 66 © Dr. James C. Martin.
p. 67 © Dr. James C. Martin. The British Museum. Photographed by permission.
p. 68 © Dr. James C. Martin. Musée du Louvre; Autorisation de photographer et de filmer—LOUVRE. Paris, France. Photographed by permission.
p. 69 © Dr. James C. Martin. The British Museum. Photographed by permission.
p. 70 © Dr. James C. Martin.
p. 71 © Dr. James C. Martin. The British Museum. Photographed by permission.
p. 72 © Dr. James C. Martin.
p. 73 © Dr. James C. Martin.
p. 78 © Dr. James C. Martin.
p. 79 © Dr. James C. Martin.
p. 80 © Dr. James C. Martin.
p. 81 © Dr. James C. Martin.
p. 82 © Dr. James C. Martin.
p. 83 Courtesy of Preserving Bible Times, Inc.
p. 84 © Dr. James C. Martin.
p. 85 (top) © Dr. James C. Martin. Reproduction of the city of Jerusalem at the time of the second temple. Located on the grounds of the Holyland Hotel, Jerusalem. Photographed by permission.
p. 85 (bottom) © Dr. James C. Martin. The Israel Museum, Jerusalem. Photographed by permission.
p. 86 © Dr. James C. Martin.
p. 87 © Dr. James C. Martin.
p. 88 © Dr. James C. Martin.
p. 89 © Dr. James C. Martin. On license Ministero per I Beni e le Attivita Culturali—Soprintendenza Archaeologica di Roma. Rome, Italy.
p. 90 © Dr. James C. Martin.
p. 92 © Dr. James C. Martin.
p. 94 © Dr. James C. Martin.
p. 95 © Dr. James C. Martin.
p. 96 © Dr. James C. Martin.
p. 97 © Dr. James C. Martin. The Ephesus Museum. Photographed by permission.
p. 98 © Dr. James C. Martin.
p. 99 © Dr. James C. Martin.
p. 100 © Dr. James C. Martin.
p. 101 © Dr. James C. Martin.
p. 102 © Dr. James C. Martin.
p. 103 © Erich Lessing/Art Resource, NY.
p. 104 © Dr. James C. Martin.
p. 105 © Alinari/Art Resource, NY.
p. 106 © Dr. James C. Martin.
p. 108 © Dr. James C. Martin.
p. 109 © Réunion des Musées Nationaux/Art Resource, NY.
p. 110 © Dr. Barry J. Beitzel.
p. 111 © Dr. James C. Martin. The British Museum. Photographed by permission.
p. 112 © Dr. James C. Martin.
p. 113 © Dr. James C. Martin. The Ephesus Museum. Photographed by permission.
p. 114 © Dr. James C. Martin. The Israel Museum, Jerusalem. Photographed by permission.
p. 115 © Dr. James C. Martin. Musée du Louvre; Autorisation de photographer et de filmer—LOUVRE. Paris, France. Photographed by permission.
p. 116 © The House of Anchors. Kibbutz Ein Gev. Sea of Galilee, Israel.
p. 117 © Dr. James C. Martin. The British Museum. Photographed by permission.
p. 118 © Dr. James C. Martin.
p. 120 © Dr. James C. Martin.
p. 122 © Dr. James C. Martin.
p. 124 © Dr. James C. Martin. The Turkish Ministry of Antiquities. Ankara, Turkey. Photographed by permission.
p. 125 © Dr. James C. Martin. The British Museum. Photographed by permission.
p. 126 © Dr. James C. Martin. The Cairo Museum. Photographed by permission.
p. 127 © Dr. James C. Martin.
p. 128 © Dr. James C. Martin.
p. 129 © Dr. James C. Martin. The British Museum. Photographed by permission.
p. 130 © Cameraphoto Arte, Venice/Art Resource, NY.

# The Bible in 90 Days™

## An Extraordinary Experience with the Word of God

*Ted Cooper Jr. with Jack Modesett Jr., Mark L. Strauss, and John H. Walton*

"When I study the Bible, I prepare myself to talk to others. When I read the Bible, God talks to me."
*D. L. Moody*

### JUST 12 PAGES A DAY

That's all it takes to read the Bible in ninety days. It's easier than you thought! Once you break it down into bite-sized pieces, what may have seemed a formidable challenge becomes doable and enjoyable. This specially designed large-print NIV Thinline Bible will help you get the most out of your experience.

And, although you can use *The Bible in 90 Days*™ on your own, the ideal way to explore all of its benefits is through *The Bible in 90 Days* curriculum. Adaptable to groups of any size, including an entire church, this fourteen-session curriculum includes print and video components as well as everything else needed to read God's Word as a community.

Bible, hardcover with jacket
ISBN: 0-310-93351-X

Curriculum Kit (includes Bible, 3 teaching DVDs with Leader's Guide, enhanced CD-ROM with additional teaching resources and promotional materials, and Participant's Guide)
ISBN: 0-310-26688-2

Participant's Guide, softcover
ISBN: 0-310-26684-X

*Pick up a copy today at your favorite bookstore!*

ZONDERVAN®

GRAND RAPIDS, MICHIGAN 49530 USA

WWW.ZONDERVAN.COM

We want to hear from you. Please send your comments about this book to us in care of zreview@zondervan.com. Thank you.

ZONDERVAN®

GRAND RAPIDS, MICHIGAN 49530 USA

ZONDERVAN.COM/
AUTHORTRACKER